THE STORY OF GEORGE ROMNEY

Builder, Salesman, Crusader

BOOKS BY TOM MAHONEY

THE STORY OF
GEORGE ROMNEY

Builder, Salesman, Crusader

by

TOM MAHONEY

Harper & Brothers,   Publishers,   New York

THE STORY OF GEORGE ROMNEY
Copyright © 1960 by John Thomas Mahoney

Printed in the United States of America

FIRST EDITION

M-I

Lyrics from "Beep Beep" by Donald Claps and Carl Cicchetti: © 1958 Patricia Music
Publishing Corp., 1619 Broadway, New York 19, N. Y.; © assigned 1958 to Patricia Music
Publishing Corp. and H & L Music Corp. Used by permission.

Lyrics from "Stouthearted Men": Copyright 1927 by Harms, Inc. Copyright renewed.
Reprinted by permission.

Library of Congress catalog card number: 59-13284

Contents

*Eight pages of illustrations will be found
following page 116.*

Foreword

George Romney is perhaps the most interesting and important figure to emerge on the Detroit scene in a quarter of a century. He is a David competing successfully with the Goliaths of both the automobile and appliance industries. He is a rebel against bigness in cars, labor, industry and government.

Like the late Walter P. Chrysler, Romney overcame great obstacles to convert American Motors Corporation, an ill-starred merger of faltering manufacturers, into an important new company. He dropped once-hallowed automobile names and introduced competition of a sort never before seen in the business.

His successful crusade for the compact car, in which he ridiculed by name the rival "gas-guzzling dinosaurs," reversed a forty-year trend toward bigness, high power and increased chromium, to start a major revolution in American automobile design. His crusade also earned him the resentment of his big competitors and spurred them into spending millions of dollars to compete with him in the compact-car field in 1960.

But it can be argued that his crusade saved the American automobile industry. In 1958, for the first time in the twentieth century, more automobiles were made abroad than in the United States and more cars were imported than exported. In 1959, the first was reversed, and Romney's forcing of his rivals into the smaller-car field can be credited with preserving for American workers and plants a car market which otherwise would have gone to European manufacturers.

His career is proof that it is still possible for the old-fashioned virtues to succeed spectacularly in American business, that a corporation head need not be a character from *Executive Suite,* and that Leo Durocher's baseball dictum that "nice guys finish last" is not to be accepted as a universal truth.

"A dedicated churchman," says a Wayne State University citation of Romney, "he has been actively concerned with the application of the Judeo-Christian ethic to everyday life. . . . He has used every opportunity to underline the vital nature of free competition and voluntary cooperation in our society." The University of Michigan adds: "Introspective, firm in conviction, dynamically articulate, he has put principle ahead of expediency in his personal, business and public life."

The author naturally is under great obligation to the subject and all members of his family for much hitherto unpublished information. His brothers, Maurice, Miles and Charles Romney, searched their memories and their files, as did Mrs. Amy Romney, Junius Romney and Dr. Thomas Cottam Romney. Robert Blair also supplied Salt Lake City material.

American Motors executives have given freely of their time and records with Edward L. Cushman, Howard E. Hallas, William H. McGaughey, John A. Conde, Jack J. Timpy, J. L. Brown, Jr. and others supplying much vital information. Richard E. Cross, Eugene Swaim, James Bradley of the Detroit Public Library, Lee Hills of the Detroit *Free Press* and Christy Borth of the Automobile Manufacturers Association also helped importantly on Detroit material.

Among many others, the author is indebted for information to Roy Abernethy, Fred Adams, Ellsworth C. Alvord, Andrew M. Andersen, Sam Ballard, Marshall Berges, Dave Bevan, Caroline

Foreword

Bird, Sabra Blodgett, George H. Blunck, Dr. Samuel Miller Brownell, F. A. Buttler.

Mrs. Irene Caldwell, Mrs. Verde Pratt Cardon, Roy D. Chapin, Jr., Bernard A. Chapman, Chester Chope, James T. Clark, Eleanor Cooper, Bill Davidson, Dr. Norman Drachler, Pendleton Dudley, Eugene Duffield, Stanley Ferguson, Hugh Ferry, Siler Freeman, B. B. Geyer, John Gibbons, Hays Gorey, Leslie Gould, Willard Hansen, James Hanyen, Mrs. Willis Hayward, Thomas M. Hewitt, Hugh Hitchcock.

Pyke M. Johnson, Thorn Kuhl, G. Bennett Larson, Mrs. Margaret Little, Gogo Lewis, Grace Mahoney, William D. Merrifield, Clinton L. Mills, Clarence C. Neslen, Van W. Parkinson, John R. Pichurski, Martin Powers, J. D. Ratcliff, Sanford Roggenburg.

Also John St. Peter, Mrs. John Scowcroft, Cliff Sherrill, Sam Shulsky, Gerald Smith, Robert Smith, Dr. William E. Stirton, Irvin Taubkin, John W. Thatcher, Hazel Trumble, Ray Vogel, Albert L. Warner, Mrs. Leah Widtsoe, Dave Wilkie, Andy Wilson, James P. Wood, Thomas Yutzy.

TOM MAHONEY

New York City, 1959

THE STORY OF GEORGE ROMNEY

Builder, Salesman, Crusader

I

"We Want a Busy Man"

On a December day in 1956, George Wilcken Romney, president of American Motors Corporation, welcomed to his office two visitors who had asked time to discuss "a matter of great importance to the community." They were William D. Merrifield, president of the Detroit Board of Education, and Dr. Samuel Miller Brownell, a former United States Commissioner of Education who recently had become Detroit's Superintendent of Schools. They came to the Moorish-towered American Motors building on Plymouth Road to ask Romney's help in a school crisis.

A serious, intense, cheerful and, at times, even an ebullient man of forty-nine, Romney turned his steel-blue eyes on his visitors and gave them his full attention. With only an occasional shifting of his lean five foot eleven inch, 175-pound frame, he listened intently as they outlined the problem. Enrollment had increased so much that money for a five-year building program had been used up in three years. Millions of dollars were needed for new buildings. Unless voters extended a special school tax expiring in 1959, teachers' salaries might have to be cut and the school year shortened by a month.

The Board of Education had decided that the most effective way of enlisting community support was through a citizens' advisory committee which before 1959 would make an independent study

1

of the schools and advise the Board on their long-range needs. Success of the project depended upon selection of the committee members, especially the chairman. He had to be a leader of stature and ability acceptable to labor and management and all other segments of the diverse Detroit community. The Board of Education approved the project in November and after considering three thousand names the Board narrowed the choice for chairman to one man, George Romney.

His first reaction was to refuse. "You couldn't have come to me at a worse time," he said. "American Motors needs to start making some money." He feared that he would have to make another trip to England, where construction had started October 11 on a new Kelvinator appliance factory at Bromborough. He urged the school men to find somebody with more time to head the committee.

"George," said Merrifield, "we are looking for a busy man. You fit the job description in every way. You have run the Automobile Manufacturers Association. You have worked with diverse groups. Your whole career has been one of working through people effectively. We are just so sure that you are the man we need that we are not concerned with how busy you are. We want a busy man."

"You couldn't have found a busier one," said Romney.

The school men continued their arguments. Both industry and labor had been pained at times by Romney's outspoken criticism of their power but both respected him. That, Merrifield reminded him, was a priceless asset for the school job. Another was Romney's known conviction that it was his duty to speak out on public issues. People would believe him as they would believe no one else, and public confidence was essential.

"I shouldn't do it," Romney told his visitors. "It's ridiculous that I even consider it, but let me think about it for a week. Public education is important. I would put only my family and my church ahead of it. I will give it prayerful consideration."

Romney had ample reasons for hesitating. American Motors, the fourth largest automobile and appliance manufacturing company, had been formed May 1, 1954, by uniting Nash-Kelvinator Corporation and the Hudson Motor Car Company in one of the biggest mergers in the history of American business. George W. Mason, architect of the merger, died five months later and Romney succeeded him as president, chairman and general manager.

Affairs of the new company had not gone smoothly. Its "compact" Rambler cars, smaller than the most popular American models but larger than the tiny European imports, showed promise and Romney had just decided to concentrate the firm's efforts on them. But it was losing more than $2,000,000 a month and owed $69,000,000 to banks and an insurance company. Some large stockholders were urging that the company be liquidated and business columnists were making doleful predictions about it.

Besides struggling to build American Motors, Romney at the time was engaged in time-consuming family and church-building projects. He and his wife, Lenore, and their two sons and two daughters lived outside of Detroit in suburban Bloomfield Hills, where they were building on a hillside a Swiss chalet-type house complete with mortgage. Many suburbanites, of course, excuse themselves from metropolitan problems on the grounds of non-residence.

A tithing member of the Church of Jesus Christ of Latter-day Saints, Romney was president of the denomination's Detroit Stake. In this role he was the spiritual and administrative leader of 3,600 members in eastern Michigan, western Ontario and northern Ohio. "Stake" is a geographical area of the Mormon Church, from Isaiah 54:2: "Enlarge the place of thy tent, and let them stretch forth the curtains of thine habitations: spare not, lengthen thy cords, and strengthen thy stakes." The Detroit group was strengthening theirs by building the first Stake tabernacle east of the Mississippi River since the Mormon exodus in 1846 from Nauvoo, Illinois. The

$700,000 church rising on Woodward Avenue was taking a great deal of Romney's time.

"Prayerful consideration" made his duty plain. A week later, in a characteristic decision, he accepted the chairmanship of the school committee and for the next two years devoted a large part of his time and energy to the Detroit schools, presiding at breakfast and dinner meetings, studying reports, reconciling differences of many kinds, and pleading for education before all kinds of audiences.

He dealt at the same time with the problems of American Motors, which was in a more serious situation than the schools. As a gambler might bet his final blue chip in a desperate game of chance, the corporation had sold for $10,662,000, by two offerings through Smith, Barney & Company, its 61 per cent interest in Ranco Inc., of Ohio, the world's largest maker of thermostatic controls for appliances and automobile heaters. The former Hudson body plant on Gratiot Avenue in Detroit was sold for $2,175,000. The automobile assembly plant at El Segundo, California, was sold to the Hughes Aircraft Company for $3,050,000. But even with these sales and rigorous economy, Romney had to report a net loss of $19,746,000 for American Motors for its 1956 fiscal year. "American Motors Deeper in the Red," said a *New York Times* headline of December 16, 1956.

Sales of its cars were disappointing. In 1953, the year before Hudson and Nash-Kelvinator merged, they sold between them 204,304 cars or 3.56 per cent of the industry's sales. In 1954, the year of the merger, this dropped to 118,553 cars and 2.14 per cent of the market. In 1955, when most companies did much better than the year before, American Motors' sales rose to 136,753 but its per cent of the market dropped to 1.91. In calendar 1956, sales dropped back to 115,105, much less than Nash had been selling alone prior to the merger, and the per cent of the industry sales was virtually the same at 1.93.

Buried in these gloomy figures was a small note of cheer. While total car sales were down, sales of the Rambler, American Motors' compact car, rose from .64 per cent of the industry's sales in 1954 to 1.01 in 1955 and 1.19 in 1956. Sales of the Metropolitan, a small eighty-five-inch wheel-base car made in England by Austin Motor Company, Ltd. for American Motors and imported also showed sales gains though it had been given very little promotion.

The Rambler was proving to have better resale value on used car lots than comparable Fords, Chevrolets and Plymouths. A Rambler took top honors in the 1956 Mobilgas Economy Run, completing the 1,469-mile test with a record 24.3545 miles per gallon of gasoline as compared with 21.1715 for a Chevrolet Bel Air. All participating cars were equipped with automatic transmissions. In June, two company engineers, Les Viland and Carl Chakmakian, drove another Rambler the 2,950 miles from Los Angeles to New York on just six tanks of gasoline for an average of 32.09 miles per gallon.

Romney continued to have faith in the future of the Rambler and the company and, as he later explained, "our faith gradually became knowledge." Executives and employees of the company shared Romney's faith. After an initial payment of 12½ cents a share in 1954, there had been no dividends. The price of American Motors shares dropped from $14.50 immediately after the merger to $5.25 in December of 1956. But at that time James Bratherton, a company photographer, borrowed five hundred dollars from a credit union and bought a hundred shares of American Motors stock convinced it would pay for his son's college education.

The decline in the price of the company's shares nullified stock options at $9.56 a share given executives in the fall of 1954. The next year Romney read of the new head of a company in trouble being given a "cut-loss" bonus. He devised, not for himself but for his three hundred executives, a loss reduction bonus which gave them very tangible reasons for staying with the company and working furiously for its success. After certain provisions for stockholders, he promised them, when the money would become available, 5 per cent of any reduction in loss of 1956 as compared to 1955 and 10 per cent of any profits. As losses were greater in 1956, this was academic but it was extended the following year. Whether promised a bonus or not, virtually all employees stayed on the job.

Others were not so hopeful. Some of the bankers to whom the company owed millions felt that a merger of American Motors with some other company was inevitable. Sol A. Dann, a Detroit attorney who owned nine hundred shares, organized an American Stockholders Protective Association and demanded changes in management. Bill Davidson, a perceptive magazine writer, interviewed Romney in 1956 and wrote an article for *Collier's* predicting that he just might make a success of American Motors. The editors did not publish it for fear that the company might go out of business in the interval required to print and distribute a magazine. It was no comfort to American Motors that *Collier's* itself went out of business.

Romney continued undaunted. One autumn afternoon he took his two small sons and a visiting cousin, Marion Romney of Salt Lake City, to a football game at Ann Arbor. Michigan was much the better team but one of the opposing halfbacks reeled off long gains every time he got the ball.

"How can he do that?" cried the cousin.

"Because he thinks he can," Romney answered, slapping the visitor's knee.

Romney had the same sort of faith. At meetings, he talked confidently of the impossible yielding to vision, courage and hard work. He found encouragement in a line from Harriet Beecher Stowe, the author of *Uncle Tom's Cabin,* who had said that when things are the worst that is the time and place the tide will turn.

He aroused sales gatherings by quoting the "Stouthearted Men" chorus of the Oscar Hammerstein II–Sigmund Romberg song:

> Give me some men who are stouthearted men
> Who will fight for the right they adore.
> Start me with ten, who are stouthearted men
> And I'll soon give you ten thousand more . . . [1]*

His competitors at this time termed Romney "an insufferable optimist." While he never conceded that he would not win, he was close to despair at times. He jokingly told his wife that if American Motors did not succeed they might not finish the new house they were building in Bloomfield Hills. To a Detroit newspaper friend he desperately confided: "I still have faith in this company, in this car and in the future. If I could have one wish to be granted for it by some fairy godmother, it would be for the public to have faith in American Motors."

He took so much work home that his secretary, Mrs. Margaret Little, had a company electrician devise an ingenious bedside notebook for him which would light up when he opened the cover. He took along a heavy bag of work on his frequent trips to New York to confer with the company's creditors. If a matter was unresolved at the end of the day he would sometimes telephone his executives at night to conclude it. He sometimes slept in cars as he was driven from airports to plants and offices.

He worried and prayed. At times he appeared wan and much older than his years. Some nights he awoke at 3 A.M. and was unable to return to sleep. One morning just four days before the annual American Motors stockholders meeting he awoke at that hour with an abdominal pain which he didn't think serious enough to arouse his wife. When she awoke she summoned Dr. Luther Leader, who promptly diagnosed appendicitis and took him to Detroit's Harper Hospital.

By having an immediate operation, Romney hoped to attend the stockholders meeting in a wheelchair. When Dr. Leader vetoed the

* Superior figures refer to notes found in a group beginning on page 248.

plan, Romney summoned Richard E. Cross, who was both counsel and a director of the company, and half a dozen of the principal officers to the hospital. Before the operation on Monday, February 4, 1957, Romney gave Cross the notes he had prepared for the stockholders.

Cross presided smoothly and firmly at the meeting on the following Wednesday in the American Motors building on Plymouth Road. He insisted on following the agenda in spite of hecklers, one of whom arrived equipped with an electric-powered megaphone. Sol Dann, one of Romney's most outspoken critics, was disappointed at his absence and proposed that the meeting be delayed until he could be available. Dann was not impressed by the fact that ten times as many stockholders were present as had ever attended earlier American Motors and Nash-Kelvinator meetings in Baltimore, Maryland.

"A fire will attract many people," he shouted, "especially those whose belongings are being consumed or liquidated." He denounced the management, suggesting a complete reorganization to remove many officers; urged discontinuance of the Metropolitan, Nash and Hudson cars; suggested diversification even to the extent of manufacturing disposable diapers; assailed the sale of the Ranco stock as "a sinking ship throwing the paying passengers overboard" and concluded with an essay, titled "The Monumental Failure." This proved to be a parody on Lincoln's Gettysburg Address, in which Dann threatened "a great proxy war" so "this Corporation, and other corporations, must never forget what we are about to start here." Romney listened to a tape recording of the tumultuous meeting.

Though Dann owned even less stock the next year, his proposal for cumulative voting for directors and half a dozen other suggestions were printed in the American Motors proxy statement. Other automobile companies in which he was similarly interested did not give him this consideration. AM stockholders voted down his proposals by a wide margin.

Sales figures did not yet reflect it, but at the start of 1957 Romney had made great progress in giving American Motors direction. He had anticipated critics. Costly automobile-manufacturing operations had been discontinued in Detroit and consolidated efficiently in Kenosha and Milwaukee, Wisconsin. Employee relations had been improved from probably the worst to perhaps the best in the industry. He had found effective executives within the company for nearly all departments and plants. Executives who did not favor the smaller cars had seen the light or retired.

The company began to emphasize the Rambler and, at a stormy meeting of the directors in November, 1956, decided to drop the venerable Hudson and Nash names the next year. Director A. E. Barit, the last president of Hudson, was so bitter about it that he left the board after the December meeting.

While both names had been respected in past years, the annual questionnaires the corporation's advertising agency[2] sent purchasers of new cars showed that the names had become liabilities. Some dealers considered them jinxes and resale values were poor. Hudson stood well in stock car racing circles, but recent models were not attractive and sales had slipped steadily since 1950.

Nash design had been better. Some models showed the touch of Pinin Farina, Italy's great designer, and the seats could fold into a bed. But the Nash was not popular. Billboards picturing a dog with the caption, "He'll only chase a Nash," inspired the retort: "That's because it's the only car he can catch." Nash cars had been designed for maximum torque and economy rather than horsepower.[3]

Nobody named either Hudson or Nash had been connected importantly with either enterprise for many years. The names then stood for little in the way of public service or civic enterprise. In some plant cities they actually stood for nonparticipation in civic affairs. Dropping the Nash and Hudson names permitted effective concentration of the company's advertising and promotion dollars on the Rambler. Dealers applauded the news.

At the time of this crucial decision the company had three divisions: automotive, appliance, and special products. Roy D. Chapin, Jr., headed the automotive division. Son of a founder of the Hudson Motor Car Company, he had spent his career in the industry beginning as an experimental engineer and working in production, accounting and sales. As treasurer of American Motors, he helped renegotiate the bank credits and was promoted to vice president and then executive vice president. Bernard A. Chapman, a veteran of twenty-six years in manufacturing, was executive vice president and general manager of the appliance division, which accounted for a third of sales. Stuart G. Baits, a veteran Hudson engineer, headed the special products division. Staff vice presidents included Jack J. Timpy, who handled financial matters and sat on all company policy committees; Edward L. Cushman, in charge of industrial relations and; William H. McGaughey, in charge of communications and management development.

Elmer W. Bernitt, a former Kenosha works manager, was named vice president in charge of automotive operations. Meade F. Moore, a bantam-sized engineer who had designed both the Rambler and Metropolitan, was vice president in charge of engineering and research. After retiring, he continued as a consultant, dividing his time between Detroit and Phoenix, Arizona. Ralph H. Isbrandt meanwhile became director of engineering. Ted Ulrich was executive engineer and Carl W. Cenzer, chief engineer in charge of body activities. Joseph W. Mueller, who began as a draftsman, was works manager in Kenosha and Julius Riedl, who started as a tool designer, was in charge of the Milwaukee body plant. George H. Beld, who had started with a predecessor company as a clerk, was in charge of appliance manufacturing at Grand Rapids.

After spending ten million dollars, approximately what was

realized from sale of the Ranco stock, the company began to make its own V-8 engine on a new assembly line at Kenosha in 1956. This replaced the V-8 engine which had previously been purchased from Packard as part of a projected reciprocity program with that company. The new engine was less costly and less troublesome than the old one. A lightweight four-cylinder air-cooled aluminum die-cast engine which developed sixty-two horsepower though weighing but two hundred pounds also was produced. It went into a revolutionary jeep-type vehicle, the "Mighty Mite," designed for airborne units of the armed forces. The Marine Corps ordered $5,587,720 worth of them as a starter.

A revolutionary paint-dip process for the prevention of rust and corrosion was introduced the next year at a cost of $700,000 for equipment at Kenosha and Milwaukee. Conventional spray methods were replaced by huge tanks of rustproofing primer into which car bodies were immersed completely as they came from the assembly line. Basic body shells were cut to two. There was a general improvement in manufacturing. Dealers had to do less work on cars when they received them. The cars began to receive higher ratings in magazines of consumer organizations. This improved quality was coincident with and partly a result of improved employee relations.

The day American Motors was formed, Mason and Romney employed Edward L. Cushman as industrial relations director. His background was unusual. He had studied economics at the University of Michigan under Professor William Haber, who had helped draft the Social Security law, and had married a classmate in a course in labor economics. Upon graduation, Cushman joined the Michigan Unemployment Commission as a research economist. After various government posts, he became Michigan Director of the War Manpower Commission and the U.S. Employment Service in 1943. The Junior Chamber of Commerce named him Detroit's outstanding young man of the year in 1945. After World War II, he became Professor of Public Administration at Wayne State University and one of the best-known industrial arbitrators.[4] He had been a consultant for Romney at Nash-Kelvinator and also for Walter Reuther, leader of the United Automobile Workers union. Cushman saw his new role in part as "interpreting Romney and Reuther to each other."

Cushman and Professor Haber were among ten distinguished economists Walter Reuther invited in 1953 and 1954 to advise the UAW on the impact of a guaranteed annual wage in the automobile industry. When Reuther asked for a guaranteed annual wage in 1955, Cushman turned the tables. He asked the same group to advise American Motors on the same subject, inviting Sumner H. Slichter of Harvard to take his place. Reuther had paid the economists fifty dollars a day and expenses. For fear of appearing to influence them, Cushman paid only their expenses. All served except two who were in Europe.[5]

Romney and Cushman also asked Industrial Relations Counselors, Inc. of New York to study how the UAW proposal would have affected Nash-Kelvinator and American Motors in the years 1952, 1953 and 1954. A research team headed by Howard S. Kaltenborn, later a vice president of Westinghouse, concluded that the guaranteed wage plan "would have imposed an extremely heavy burden of liability . . . so heavy . . . that it well might have jeopardized the company's solvency."

The public did not realize that unions had been extracting from the independent automobile makers higher wages and fringe benefits than were granted by the Big Three. The union would win a new contract from a major company and then demand the same, plus additional benefits, from the smaller companies. The discrimination increased the cost disadvantage of small size. For example, American Motors in 1955 paid assembly line welding operators seven to fifteen cents more an hour than Big Three companies.

On June 10, Romney testified on union contracts before the

Senate Subcommittee on Antitrust and Monopoly, then headed by Senator Harley M. Kilgore of West Virginia. "A major problem confronting the smaller manufacturer," Romney asserted, "is that occasioned by union insistence on not only following the pattern set with the largest and most successful manufacturers but also demanding even higher wage rates and more liberal employee benefits."

While the economists composing Reuther's "public advisory committee" made no formal reports either to the UAW or American Motors, they influenced the negotiations. Professor Slichter wrote an article[6] saying the proposal would have to be modified. Professor Haber publicly asserted that the guaranteed annual wage was not practical for all companies. Dr. Seymour Harris of Harvard, who had been economic adviser to Adlai Stevenson, was convinced that insistence on a guaranteed annual wage from American Motors was economically unsound and so advised Reuther.

A compromise between Reuther's plan and a counterproposal by Ford became the pattern for the union contracts in 1955. General Motors and Chrysler soon signed but American Motors refused to agree. Cigar-smoking Cushman and Leonard Woodcock, UAW vice president, negotiated through the summer, giving their arguments to the press as well as each other. At one point Woodcock said the company would be "better off if it produced more cars and fewer press releases." Cushman continued to demand a contract based on the "economic facts of American Motors and not of Ford or General Motors."

After an all-night session at the Fort Shelby Hotel in Detroit agreement was reached on September 2, 1955. The old contract had expired two weeks earlier and several hundred employees were on strike. The new three-year contract postponed for one year payment of the five cents per hour supplemental pay for the annual wage fund. Instead of providing the increases of 21 cents, 27 cents and 33 cents for the next three years won from General Motors, American Motors got the unions to accept 14 cents, 20 cents and 26 cents. This was the first off-pattern settlement ever obtained from the UAW by an end producer of automobiles. It saved American Motors millions of dollars. Subsequent contracts and improved administration brought its labor costs as low as any company's in the automobile field.

For advice before the 1958 union negotiations, the company reconvened the same economists and in addition a panel of ten nationally known clergymen. Cushman, who is active in Episcopal Church affairs, suggested this and Romney approved, in the belief that the fundamental basis for labor decisions should be moral and ethical as well as economic.

The clergy panel members were: the Right Rev. Richard S. Emrich, Bishop of Episcopal Diocese of Michigan; the Very Rev. Msgr. George C. Higgins, director, National Catholic Welfare Conference; the Rev. Dr. Cameron P. Hall, executive director, Department of the Church and Economic Life, National Council of the Churches of Christ; Rabbi Eugene J. Lipman, director, Commission on Social Action, Union of American Hebrew Congregations; the Rev. Dr. G. Merrill Lenox, executive director, Michigan and Detroit Councils of Churches; the Rev. Leo C. Brown, S.J., director, Institute of Social Order, St. Louis University; the Rev. Robert Allen, director of Social Action, Roman Catholic Archdiocese of Detroit; the Rev. G. Paul Musselman, executive secretary, Division of Urban Industrial Church Work, The National Council Protestant Episcopal Church; Rabbi Morris Adler, Congregation Shaarey Zedek, Detroit; and the Rev. Dr. Marshall L. Scott, dean, Presbyterian Institute of Industrial Relations.

After receiving a mass of printed matter about the company, the automobile industry and current business problems, the clergymen met for the first time with American Motors executives in January of 1958 at the Dearborn Inn. The sessions were opened and closed with prayer. Vice President Cushman presided and President

Romney explained American Motors' goals. The company's labor
relations director, George C. Gullen, Jr., the son of a Congregation-
alist minister, and other executives listened to the ministers' com-
ments on living standards, job security, inflation and many other
subjects. Papal encyclicals were discussed. All talked freely.

"While we cannot evaluate the benefits which may have accrued
to the company," said the clergymen in a joint statement after the
two-day meeting, "we feel strongly that the conference was a successful one. We want to express our commendation to the leaders
of the American Motors Corporation for their sincere concern for
ethical and moral values and their willingness to discuss company
policies and programs in that framework. The discussions were
notable for their total frankness and freedom."

The clergymen involved were so respected for their integrity,
competence and concern about labor relations that Walter Reuther
at once invited the entire group to advise the UAW and they
accepted. Just as American Motors followed the union with the
economists in 1955, the union followed the company with the
clergymen in 1958. There have been several meetings since, with
all concerned terming this unique development in labor relations
"a most stimulating and educational experience."

In the meantime, Romney began to give employees and their
families a preview of new products and a personal report on the
company's progress at huge gatherings in the Milwaukee Arena
and at the Lake Front Stadium in Kenosha. No other automobile
company had ever done anything like it. The workers responded
to Romney's evangelical oratory by improving the quality of their
production and becoming loyal users and volunteer salesmen of
the products they made.

Union leaders became as concerned as the management with
quality of the cars. "The cars we make could be our own," said a
Local 72 poster in Kenosha. A UAW committee urged city and
state government agencies to buy Ramblers and helped the com-

pany sell a fleet of station wagons to the Kenosha police department. Jack Beni, Tony Russo and several other officers of Local 72 bought American Motors shares, attended and spoke at stockholders meetings. At one, Beni told how employees were publicizing the cars and urged the stockholders to do the same. Russo, a truck driver with a hundred shares, won applause at the stormy 1957 meeting by asking for more dealers in Wisconsin. "It is high time," he concluded, "that we started shaking the bushes around here."

Shaking the bushes and building an almost entirely new dealer organization was Roy Abernethy, 235-pound vice president in charge of automotive marketing. The 2,800 dealers with which American Motors started dwindled by defection and franchise termination to 1,900 before Nash and Hudson sales organizations were consolidated and the trend reversed.

Many dealers did not believe in smaller cars and others were not doing a good job. Jim Moran of Chicago, who had been the top Hudson dealer, turned to Ford. On the other hand, Charles Kreisler of New York, once the biggest Nash dealer, gave up his Edsel dealership and took on the Rambler with the comment, "The Ford Motor Company laid an egg." Dealers like Morris Lipman of Hartford, Connecticut, the Boston Nash Company, and Coon Bros. of Livonia, Michigan, did even better. Some new dealers like Reedman Rambler, Inc. of Langhorne, Pennsylvania, and Cranson Rambler, Inc. of Bethesda, Maryland, also set sales marks.

Good dealers were attracted by a program Romney revealed to Senator A. S. Mike Monroney's committee investigating automobile marketing practices in January, 1956. Dealers elected their own representatives by secret ballot to exchange information and iron out difficulties with the company. On the suggestion of Senator Monroney, the dealer council was renamed the American Motors Corporation Dealer Advisory Board to distinguish it from councils set up by other companies.

The program prevented some of the inequities in dealer relations the Monroney committee uncovered. American Motors had a joint company-dealer appeals board with final authority in dealer cancellation cases and worked with it on matters affecting dealers and customers, such as unethical advertising. There also was a "volume investment" fund through which all dealers profited from the national sales effort.*

At ease before the committee, Romney concluded his testimony with a sales talk: "We are going to get away from these cars that are designed for just bulk and weight as primary considerations and move importantly into the area of lighter-weight cars that are superior in other respects, too."

"I think if this dream comes true," answered Senator Monroney, "they may build a statue to you as the man who could park two cars where one parked before."

Dealers and the automotive press were as enthusiastic as the Senator about the American Motors dealer plan. Admiral Frederick J. Bell, then executive vice president of the National Automobile Dealers Association, who followed Romney before the Monroney committee, termed it "the most progressive step taken by any manufacturer" in many years. The *Automotive News* headlined news of the Dealer Advisory Board as "AMC Gives Dealers Big Voice In Policy." Several other companies revised their dealer relations policies.

These changes largely anticipated the factory-dealer "good faith" law sponsored by Senator Joseph C. O'Mahoney of Wyoming and Representative Emanuel Celler of New York. This was opposed as unnecessary by American Motors and all other automobile manufacturers but was enacted by Congress and approved by President Eisenhower somewhat reluctantly in August of 1956. It permits dealers to take claims against manufacturers in connec-

* See Chapter XV.

tion with franchise contracts to federal court regardless of the wording of the franchise.

With manufacturing, labor and organizational difficulties solved or near solution, Romney still had the enormous problem of interesting a profitable portion of the public in the virtues of the compact car on which he had staked the future of American Motors.

II

The Dinosaur in the Driveway

Romney believed in the Rambler and he was sure he could convert the public to a good thing, but he at first did not realize the immense inertia of "big-car" mentality and the prejudice of the public against cars of independent manufacturers that had to be overcome. The Rambler was a happy medium, offering the interior space and comfort of big cars and at the same time the ease of handling and economy of small cars. In addition, it had an all-welded single-unit body which made it lighter, stronger and safer than cars of conventional separate-body-and-frame construction. Romney, the company's No. 1 salesman, illustrated the latter by comparing the weakness of a loose flat sheet of paper with the strength of the same sheet slightly shaped. In talking smallness, he sometimes employed props. Though he drank no liquor, he would exhibit and compare a tiny dining car bottle of Scotch whisky with a huge straw-wrapped bottle of Chianti wine to prove that the smaller item packed the wallop. He also compared a loaf of bread and a vitamin pill to the advantage of the latter.

Howard Hallas, American Motors public relations director, had another idea. The Detroit *News* on January 2, 1955, published an editorial criticizing the trend in automobile design. This was written by Gordon Harrison, a newspaperman with Harvard and Oxford background. "Surely there is some point at which the pyramiding of bigger bodies and bigger engines must stop," said Harrison, "or the private automobile will go the way of the dinosaur." Earlier Randall Gould, Denver *Post* columnist, wrote: "I think the bigger makers are emulating the dinosaur. There isn't much offering in the way of a car for the kind of guy the nation is packed with—except for Rambler and Metropolitan." Hallas read both items and was struck by the repetition of the word "dinosaur."

When Romney accepted an invitation to address the Motor City Traffic Club of Detroit, a few days later, Hallas suggested that he review the traffic, parking and garaging problems of big cars and title his speech "The Dinosaur in the Driveway." Romney developed the idea and tried it on his wife, who was experienced in dramatics. She endorsed its possibilities. He addressed the club the evening of January 27, 1955, illustrating his remarks with sketches by Hallas of a dinosaur, and various foxhole, elastic-back and bustle-type garages which might be required "if we continue in the dinosaur direction."

"Cars nineteen feet long, weighing two tons," he said, "are used to run a 118-pound housewife three blocks to the drugstore for a package of bobby pins and lipstick." He quoted criticism of big cars by Dr. Vannevar Bush, Frank Lloyd Wright, Raymond Loewy, Alfred Sinks[1] and others. New York Traffic Commissioner T. T. Wiley had said any further increase in car size and horsepower would be sheer madness. "I predict there will be a smaller percentage of mechanized dinosaurs in the American driveways of the future," Romney concluded. "However, if you still want them, we've got them, too, built a better way—our dinosaurs are smoother, safer and roomier!"

Dinosaurs had been mentioned only half a dozen times but the *New York Times* and other newspapers used it in headlining the story. The Automobile Manufacturers Association was moved to issue a statement saying that low-priced American automobiles had increased in length an average of "only 6.1 inches during the past fourteen years." There were many requests for copies of the speech but the idea was not immediately pursued. Romney's father, Gaskell Romney, to whom he was extremely devoted, died a few days later and he was in no mood for levity. Also American Motors continued for a time to make its own "dinosaurs."

In 1957, when American Motors quit making its Hudson and Nash monsters and the new Big Three cars were more monstrous than ever, Romney returned gleefully to the subject. The dinosaurs became "gas-guzzlers." Scientifically correct scale models of them became props for speeches and photographs. Romney had fun introducing his model menagerie to organizations like the National Parking Association:

"This fellow is called a Brontosaurus. He was about seventy feet long and dragged around mainly about the lagoons which would support his enormous body. He weighed a good many tons. His fuel consumption was tremendous. His mouth was relatively so small that he had to spend all of his waking hours eating.

"This fellow is a Triceratops. He had perhaps the largest radiator ornament in prehistoric history. It kept getting bigger and bigger until finally he could no longer hold his head up. He had a wheel base of nearly thirty feet.

"This streamlined fellow here was called Dimetrodon and is considered a predecessor of the modern horse. One of his problems was that he began developing this fin on his back to a point where it became larger and larger and finally completely upset his equilibrium.

"This handsome model was known as Stegosaurus. He perhaps represented the highest development of the dinosaur in terms of useless nonfunctional decorative treatment.

"This is the Pterodactyl, an advanced example of swept-wing design. All of these fellows perished from the earth around seventy million years ago because they were unable to adapt themselves to the changes that gradually came in their environment."

Romney predicted that most mammoth automobiles would vanish eventually. In the meantime, he suggested the parking operators charge extra for cars that take up more room and less for cars like the Rambler. After an address in Ohio, he was given a dinosaur-decorated plaque reading, "To George Romney, critic, lecturer, anthropologist, white hunter of the American dinosaur. The committee to preserve the American dinosaur. Cleveland Automobile Dealers Association." When *Time* later devoted a cover story to him, it was titled "The Dinosaur Hunter."[2]

Publicizing the single-unit construction was more difficult. A car built this way looked like any other car but there was grim evidence that it was safer. Between 1949 and 1954, Massachusetts analyzed the deaths of 1,556 persons in automobiles in the state. On the basis of the number of Nash cars in use in the state, forty-four of these should have been killed in cars of this make. But apparently thanks to its single-unit construction, only fourteen were killed. Harry Stanton of the Boston *Globe,* in fact, reported a freak accident in which a Nash was hit by a train, bounced against the base of a signal tower, thrown back into the path of the train and hit again. The driver escaped with only cuts and bruises.

Ted Ulrich, who had largely engineered the unit construction, Vice President Bernitt and Romney himself all had experienced accidents which might have been much more serious but for this construction. Romney's mishap came while driving his family from Detroit to Ann Arbor over a highway lightly covered with snow. In getting back on the pavement, the car skidded across the highway, narrowly missing an oncoming machine, turned on its side and slid forty-five feet more before coming to a stop. Nobody was hurt and they drove on into Ann Arbor.

When Ford began to advertise safety belts, which Nash had abandoned years earlier, Romney wanted the safety of unit construction dramatized. He added words to advertising copy attempting to explain this until somebody said the copy was as long as the night thoughts of a loose lady. In an effort to stimulate thinking, he staggered his colleagues by saying: "I'll challenge young Henry Ford to a crash test. I'll drive a Rambler, he'll drive one of his."

They talked him out of it and into giving away a twenty-five-thousand-dollar one-year accident insurance policy with each car covering both the owner and his wife. Studebaker immediately followed with a similar offer. Attorney General Jacob K. Javits of New York, however, ruled shortly that this violated state laws and the idea was dropped after attracting valuable attention to the Rambler. "The idea is certainly an intriguing one," said the *Wall Street Journal* in an editorial, "for nobody can say where it will lead from here on out. Ford might be induced to give away garages with every car, Chrysler might offer a year's supply of gasoline, and General Motors might be argued into providing a shelter for its Cadillacs."[3]

At this point Romney began to use cartoon strips to help explain the single-unit construction and warn the public against "gas-guzzling dinosaurs." The cartoon idea was tested in Philadelphia newspapers of November 16, 1956, with a page titled "The Story of the Man Who Bought a Dinosaur." When 43 per cent of Philadelphians interviewed at random the next day remembered the advertisement, it was repeated in seven cities with higher scores. Cartoon strips, at first drawn by anonymous advertising agency artists, but soon by well-known newspaper and magazine cartoonists, became a major part of American Motors advertising. Among those whose talents were employed were Hoff, Rube Goldberg, Charles Addams, George Price, Ted Key, George Lichty, Willard Mullen, Chon Day, Whitney Darrow, Jr. and O. Soglow.

Romney, the crusader, bought full pages of newspapers to tell the Rambler story over his own signature and with his picture. Some of his personal messages were thirty-five hundred words long. He also delivered many of the commercials on "Disneyland," a high-ranking television show which American Motors co-sponsored from 1954 to 1957 at an annual cost of three million of its five-million-dollar advertising budget.

American Motors stayed away from the big picture, and short, dreamy copy of most automobile advertisements. Some AMC advertisements heretically showed no car at all. Many were in the form of news bulletins. For the news magazines, a series of "Love Letters to Rambler" pictured and quoted owners. After Ogden Nash called the Rambler "an epigram in a world of bombast," and Bennett Cerf termed it "the greatest invention since the ice cube," testimonial letters poured in from Rambler fans. Authors of letters used received photographs of themselves and one dollar as a legal formality.

A page in *Reader's Digest* compared Rambler's higher resale value with Car "C," Car "F" and Car "P." In "X-Ray" booklets which the company began to publish in 1956, however, there were ruthless comparisons by name and picture of prices, dimensions and details of the Rambler with those of competing Chevrolet, Ford and Plymouth models. These were described as "following a beaten path toward monstrous size with excessive overhang and non-functional styling." Plymouth was reported continuing "the out-worn Forward Look" with an "antiquated" engine. Chevrolet was "more ostentatious than ever before" and its curving front pillar post could "create a definite blind spot for the driver." Ford was said to use "army-bunk" zigzag springs resulting in an "unyielding cushion that means a tiring ride on long trips." When Ford undertook to "set the record straight" on gas consumption figures, American Motors bought newspaper space to reprint a *Printers' Ink* account of the squabble and mischievously headlined it: "Now—a big competitor confirms Rambler is the modern yardstick of car value."

Detroit had never seen anything of the sort. Competitors who had been mildly amused at Romney's "gas-guzzling dinosaurs" now accused him of "doing irreparable harm to the automobile industry." An important General Motors executive bitterly protested the X-ray booklet but Romney continued it as "a new, daring and authentic comparison never published before." While Chrysler executives insisted, "We are in the business of selling cars and not booklets," all companies stepped up their sales efforts and Ford's Mercury division issued a "New Car Buyer's Guide" which applied the Romney comparisons to the medium-priced car field. "Gone," wrote Ralph R. Watts in the Detroit *News*, "is the soft, velvet glove approach of the old days when salesmen practically whispered about the superior features of their own model car against competitors' A, B or C. Sales competition between some automobile manufacturers has reached the bare-knuckle stage."[4]

Romney strained any lingering love his General Motors and Ford competitors may have felt for him in a voluntary appearance before Senator Estes Kefauver's Subcommittee on Antitrust and Monopoly.[5] It was assumed that Romney would inveigh against the growing power and increasing demands of labor unions. He did this but in addition he proposed that to preserve competition the antitrust laws be revised to curb excessive concentrations of power in industry as well as in unions. His proposal would have the effect of requiring both General Motors and Ford to divide amoeba-like into two smaller companies.* This made headlines across the country.

It was not a sudden whim on Romney's part. The idea grew out of his church work. He observed how groups in his own and other churches divided when they became large to form new groups with opportunities for greater service and leadership. He wanted to propose it two years earlier but his associates warned that he would be accused of self-interest if he suggested it while American Motors was losing money. At first, he thought only General Motors would

* See Chapter XVII.

be affected, but after consulting Victor Kramer, a Washington attorney with long experience in the Department of Justice Anti-Trust Division, on the details of the proposal, it was obvious that Ford would have to be included.

Romney explained his idea to the directors of the Automobile Manufacturers Association. Before going to Washington, he had called personally on L. L. Colbert of Chrysler, Harlow H. Curtice of General Motors, also Henry Ford II and Ernest R. Breech of Ford to tell them what he proposed. All attempted to dissuade him.

The press debated the idea. "If we are going to adopt his system of percentages," said the *Wall Street Journal,* "maybe there should be an amendment to somehow guarantee that no one is too small, either." The Urbana, Illinois, *Courier* thought the automobile industry "a good example of the benefits of bigness" and the Racine, Wisconsin, *Journal-Times* said, "Romney's viewpoint is not hard to explain.... He is wide open to a charge of self-interest." The Springfield, Missouri, *Leader & Press* and some others applauded Romney's "novel theory" and John W. Love, Scripps-Howard business columnist, said: "What made the proposal surprising was that it came from a business source."

Reports of the Subcommittee on Antitrust and Monopoly spurred the Department of Justice to a new antitrust investigation of General Motors, the nation's biggest corporation. Senator Kefauver introduced a bill to divest General Motors of its financing subsidiary, General Motors Acceptance Corporation, by forbidding automobile manufacturers insuring or financing new cars. Nothing came of either action immediately but the company was caused such expense and annoyance that it was understandable for a top General Motors executive to say privately that he "loathed" George Romney and his ideas. "Romney's running a real danger," said another automobile man, "of becoming an outcast in Detroit."[6]

Romney naturally took a different view. He felt that he was saving rather than harming the automobile industry and that he really had no choice. The public had been so brainwashed about the virtues of big companies and big cars that only challenging comparisons and language bordering on the fiery utterances of Old Testament prophets could secure attention and divert motorists from "a false concept of car value based on size, flash and power." If the American industry did not provide the sort of cars that people really needed at prices they could afford, they would turn increasingly to cars made abroad by foreign workers.

"It now costs less," he told the Senate Subcommittee, "to build automobiles in certain European countries than in Detroit, Flint, South Bend, Kenosha, Los Angeles and elsewhere in the United States. . . . This is a critical point in our country's history. Either our wage, price, inflation and monopoly problems must be wisely solved, or America will be surpassed by others." He regarded his campaign as one against inflation and in favor of the old-fashioned virtues of thrift, economy and saving.

All of this, plus an unmeasurable change in public attitude, began to cut sales of most bigger cars and push sales of Ramblers upward. American Motors helped spur the change in attitude with advertisements signed by Romney in women's magazines headlined "Bigger Car or Better Living?" But the change came only gradually. From 1956 to 1957 registrations of American Motors cars increased only from 115,105 to 117,330 and its share of the market only from 1.93 to 1.96 per cent. For fiscal 1957, the company had a loss of $11,833,200. Meanwhile Romney had to deal with Louis E. Wolfson.

III

Stockholder Louis E. Wolfson

As the price of American Motors stock plummeted to six dollars in the summer of 1956, Vice President Jack Timpy remarked at the meeting of the company's policy board that with a book value of more than twenty dollars a share the company was likely target for a "raider." Even a small automobile company is huge by usual business standards. On the basis of sales, American Motors was eighty-fifth in *Fortune* magazine's ranking of the five hundred American industrial corporations, ahead of National Cash Register, Coca-Cola and many other well-known companies. In addition it had piled up a tax loss of more than $33,000,000, which could have been used to offset profits in a merger with another company.

A few days later Romney received a letter from Louis E. Wolfson, then an ominous Wall Street figure, saying that he was "a substantial stockholder" in American Motors and would "like to arrange a meeting with you to discuss some matters that may be important to the company." Two banks also informed Romney that Wolfson was buying stock. He had owned sixteen thousand shares of Hudson Motor Car Company stock prior to the merger but was known principally for a series of shrewd financial coups following World War II. He made millions in the liquidation of two Florida shipyards and more in the capture and operation of Capital Transit in Washington, D.C. He lost a bitter proxy fight in 1955 for control of

Montgomery Ward but forced the big mail-order house to modernize its policies. He headed a business empire which included Merritt-Chapman & Scott, Devoe and Raynolds, a chain of Florida theaters and other enterprises. He regarded business as an exciting game to be played intensely.

Wolfson wrote Romney on July 16 but both men were moving at such a frantic pace that their meeting was delayed. Though the loan agreement had a year to run, Romney that month asked a two-year extension of the bank credit arrangements. As representatives of the twenty-seven banks involved met at the Chase Manhattan in New York, they expressed confidence in Kelvinator but had their doubts about the automobile business. After hearing Romney tell the American Motors story at morning and afternoon meetings, they agreed to back the company with a new revolving bank credit reduced from $73,000,000 to $45,000,000. To follow American Motors affairs, the bankers formed a seven-man steering committee headed by Henry J. MacTavish, a Chase Manhattan loan review officer as Scotch as his name.[1] The Prudential Insurance Company of America deferred $2,569,000 due on its long-term debt. Romney flew to England in the fall on Kelvinator and Metropolitan business. After his return, he met Wolfson for the first time on October 31, 1956, in Room 925 of the Ambassador Hotel (later Sheraton East) in New York.

An immaculate, conservatively dressed six feet two inches, Wolfson was as personable in his way as Romney. The forty-four-year-old financier was accompanied by one of his principal associates, Elkin "Buddy" Gerbert. With Romney was Richard E. Cross, a partner in the Detroit law firm of Cook, Beake, Miller, Wrock & Cross. He was counsel as well as a director of American Motors. Wolfson at once made it plain that he was a forceful, supremely self-confident individual and that he knew a lot about American Motors.

Wolfson explained he had bought more than 200,000 shares of

American Motors stock with the idea that the company be at least partially liquidated. He said he had received letters from many stockholders suggesting that he "move in or take over" but that he would not do that to Romney without talking to him. He had investigated Romney and the company and felt he was trying to do a good job and would need time to do it. Wolfson had attempted to buy some of the company's notes from the banks at thirty-five cents on the dollar and said he had found two willing to sell at fifty cents if the others agreed. They had not agreed and Wolfson congratulated Romney on being able to work out a new banking agreement. Wolfson hadn't thought it possible.

But the point of the meeting was that his Universal Corporation at the moment had $8,000,000 in cash to invest. The money came from the sale the previous August of the transit properties in Washington, D.C., for $13,540,000, of which $9,662,000 had been paid in cash.

"Before I leave this hotel room," announced Wolfson, "I am going to decide whether to have Buddy Gerbert here buy through A. M. Kidder & Company one million shares of American Motors stock at up to eight dollars a share." The stock was then being traded at six to seven dollars. With what they already held, a million shares would have given Wolfson and his associates more than 20 per cent of the 5,587,000 shares outstanding and almost certainly enough for control of the company.

Wolfson questioned Romney sharply about the operating figures for the fiscal year just ended. Like the bankers, Wolfson was especially interested in Kelvinator. Romney explained that while the company as a whole had an operating loss of more than $30,000,000, Kelvinator had earned $3,600,000. Wolfson asked Romney to consider a certain young man as a possible director of the company. Romney agreed to do so and launched into an earnest explanation of his plans for American Motors. Wolfson gradually warmed to this.

"Buddy, I've made up my mind," he told his associate. "I'm going to back Romney. You take that eight million and go off on the other deal."

While it was not identified at the time, the other deal was the purchase of the Marion Power Shovel Company and the Osgood Company for $16,873,000. This took place a few days later on November 7, 1956, and Universal became the Universal Marion Corporation.

Wolfson said it was necessary to be competitive, unorthodox and aggressive in business. He urged Romney not to be afraid of public opinion and to get rid of the Hudson cars, "or all of the cars," if he felt it necessary. Wolfson was critical of the company's four-year employment contract with A. E. Barit, former president of Hudson, under which he received $141,666 as a consultant in 1955 while Romney was paid only $125,772 as head of the company. Wolfson thought it "outrageous" that Barit did not relieve the money-losing company of some of its obligations to him. Cross defended the contract as having been negotiated and approved at arm's length by both boards of directors at the time of the merger and said Barit's experience was such that a consulting arrangement was reasonable.[2] Wolfson insisted that his first concern in any enterprise was fair play for stockholders. Romney concurred heartily in this.

By the time the hour-and-a-half meeting ended, Romney and Wolfson were calling each other "Lou" and "George." They found they had something in common. Both had been school athletes, Wolfson an end on the University of Georgia football team. Both were abstemious, neither smoking nor drinking. Both were hardworking men of fierce energy.

Wolfson promised to support Romney as long as he was cooperative and emphasized that he wanted no information that Romney would not give to other stockholders. They agreed to meet again in December at the time of the National Automobile Show in New York. In the meantime, Romney said he would investigate

Wolfson and his nominee for the board as Wolfson already had investigated American Motors. Wolfson welcomed this. He insisted his word was his bond and, despite what people said about him, that he was always a square shooter. He volunteered that he was a member of a Southern Jewish family with thirty million dollars and that he felt American Motors could be taken over with an investment of less than sixteen million.

"I had more than $100,000,000 behind me in the Montgomery Ward fight," he boasted.

Romney obviously faced a grave problem, perhaps as serious as any in his business career. He interviewed Wolfson's nominee for the board and personally investigated Wolfson in Chicago, New York and Washington. At their November meeting, the American Motors directors agreed to oppose any effort by Wolfson to take control of the company. One of them, Harcourt Amory of Smith, Barney & Company, said he would leave the board if Wolfson came on it.

On December 6, Romney and Wolfson met again in New York at the Ambassador Hotel, this time in Room 1001. After half an hour, Dick Cross joined them in a meeting that lasted almost two hours.

Romney began by reporting that his investigation had confirmed that Wolfson was a man of his word and that even his most bitter opponents agreed to this. But he had received so much "unfortunate publicity" as a raider and liquidator of laggard companies that Romney felt any identification of Wolfson with American Motors would raise doubts as to its future in the minds of some people. Public confidence in a company is more important in the automobile field than in any other. No motorist wants to buy a car that is likely to become an "orphan." Wolfson's nominee for the board, though a personable young man, Romney felt had nothing definite to offer it.

He proposed four alternatives: (1) That Wolfson withdraw his request and be satisfied with being given information by a director; (2) that Wolfson himself become a director, though neither Romney nor the other directors felt this would be wise; (3) that they select somebody mutually agreeable; (4) that they add a public figure as a director. Romney suggested Wolfson study the suggestions for a week but he answered at once.

"I've made up my mind," he said. "I don't want to do anything to embarrass American Motors or you. I withdraw my request. I don't want to interfere with management but I want to study the company and what you are doing and make any suggestions I think may be helpful. I would like to be kept informed and I would rather you did it." As Wolfson's stockholdings were large enough for him to have access to the company's books, Romney readily agreed to this.

Wolfson had several suggestions. If there was a possibility of a merger with Chrysler, he suggested that it be explored before Chrysler spent money tooling for the manufacture of small cars. He believed that his newly acquired Marion Shovel Company and American Motors special products division might do business with each other. He said he and his associates had 400,000 shares of American Motors stock and would support Romney for two more years and then "move in" if the company did not become profitable. He added that he thought highly of Romney and would like to have him for Merritt-Chapman & Scott if any misfortune befell American Motors.

They agreed to meet again in March in Miami Beach, where Wolfson had a home overlooking Biscayne Bay, and at Romney's invitation later in Detroit for Wolfson and his associates to see the American Motors operations and to meet the executives. Wolfson took Romney up on his promise to supply information with a December 31 letter asking twenty-three questions about the company. In addition to financial, tax and sales matters of the company and its subsidiaries, these asked the ages of key executives and a list of all tools and equipment in each plant. All information except the last was supplied promptly. For the annual stockholders meeting in February, Wolfson sent a proxy for 240,000 shares held by his wife and himself to Romney.

Wolfson's investment in American Motors became known at this time, with the late Leo Donovan of the Detroit *Free Press,* the *Wall Street Journal* and the Associated Press reporting the fact. The effect was as Romney expected. Trading increased in the shares on the New York Stock Exchange but sales of cars dropped and franchising of new dealers became difficult. Under the headline "Wolfson's AMC Plan Disclosed," the *Free Press* on February 11, 1957, published a syndicated column of Sylvia Porter saying he proposed to get rid of American Motors' unprofitable automobile operations, sell the Rambler to another company, retain the profitable appliance division and merge it with Marion Power Shovel or other Wolfson property. That month Marion people inspected American Motors plants and Vice President Stuart G. Baits, manager of the company's special products division, visited the Marion plant but found the products too different for co-operative manufacturing.

In a March 3 letter, Wolfson said he believed American Motors affairs were "growing more critical each day." He urged Romney to do something to take advantage of the $3,083,000 tax-loss carry-over expiring in 1957. Wolfson suggested it would be better to save the jobs of seven thousand employees by sale of part of the company than for all twenty-two thousand to be jobless "because it is inevitable that the corporation will go out of business based on both its past and current record." He offered to help, saying: "I have never seen anything accomplished unless somebody reached out for the responsibility and followed through to make sure of its fulfillment."

Some of the figures in this letter turned up in another Sylvia Porter column two days before Romney and Wolfson met in Miami Beach. "Is Chrysler Buying AMC Car Division? 22,000 Jobs Are

Riding on Wolfson-Romney Talk," said the *Free Press* headlines over the Porter column, which said a plan to sell all American Motors automobile assets to Chrysler for $100,000,000 in stock was being weighed. *Time* appeared that week with an AMC story headed "Wolfson at the Door" and *Newsweek* had one labeled "Wolfson Rides In" and he was quoted as saying, "Certainly some overhauling of American Motors is indicated."[3]

Romney dined with Wolfson and Charles Block, one of his aides, at the Fontainebleau Hotel the evening of March 19 and for the next two days, accompanied by Vice President Timpy, discussed American Motors plans and problems with Wolfson and his aides at the Seaview Hotel. Wolfson suggested possible sales and mergers. At a joint press conference afterward, Romney denied any project to sell the company's automobile business. Wolfson disclosed he had increased his holdings in American Motors stock to 350,000 shares, said he had declined the offer of a directorship and voiced his confidence in Romney.

Sylvia Porter heralded Wolfson's visit to Detroit with an April 8 column starting: "A crucial stage is nearing in the dramatic and inevitable overhaul of the American Motors Corporation." Accompanied by Gerbert, Alexander Rittmaster, Joseph M. Glickstein and Charles Block, Wolfson spent April 11 at the American Motors offices. Romney, Chapin and Chapman explained their plans and showed mock-ups of future cars and displays of new appliances. At the end of the day, Wolfson told another press conference that he was just a stockholder and that Romney spoke for the company.

While Wolfson felt better about the automobile side of the business after seeing the 1958 designs at this time, he continued to be most interested in Kelvinator. He had approached Don Mitchell of Sylvania with the idea of a deal and had proposed negotiations with Norge and York Air Conditioning. In the summer of 1957, Wolfson offered four million dollars for a ninety-day option to buy

Kelvinator for forty million dollars for resale. Romney and his directors refused the option.

Romney was confronted at the same time by an intricate proposal from A. M. Sonnabend, the Boston industrialist, for utilizing American Motors tax credits by acquiring profitable companies in various industries. At a time when American Motors stock was selling at eight dollars a share, Sonnabend offered nine dollars a share on a deferred payment basis for the 360,000 shares then held by Wolfson if Romney would approve the project. Wolfson said he would not sell without Romney's approval. Sonnabend proposed deals involving a shoe company, a woman's knitwear firm, a dress manufacturer, an engineering company, a fluorescent lighting company and a musical toy company. Directors called them the "brassière companies." Romney was rather appalled at the idea and when it developed that Sonnabend did not want to pay cash for at least 110,000 shares, the proposal came to nothing, with Wolfson using harsh language about Sonnabend. The latter later worked out a similar deal, however, with Studebaker-Packard.

In the course of his turbulent career, Wolfson often had found company executives meeting his proposals with prejudice and close-mouthed hostility. He was surprised and pleased at the courtesy, dignity and respect with which Romney dealt with him and soon began to reciprocate. Wolfson's backing of the management undoubtedly spared it some stockholder trouble and may have protected it from forays by others. He rejected many suggestions of dissident stockholders that he lead a proxy fight. In acknowledging the offer of a proxy for 100,000 shares held by a Dutch holding company Wolfson on September 30, 1957, wrote: "I have found Mr. George Romney to be very sincere, honest and conscientious in his dealings with me. He and I may have had differences of opinion on many matters but . . . there has been no breach between us." He and Mrs. Wolfson then had 404,500 shares of American Motors stock.

Wolfson was impressed by Romney's effecting another ten-million-dollar reduction in operating expenses in fiscal 1957 and especially by Romney and the four other highest paid officers voluntarily cutting their salaries an average of 25.9 per cent. Wolfson was gratified to discover that Romney was in no sense a tool of the bankers. Bankers and directors and executives with little or no investments in their enterprises were anathema to Wolfson.

He assailed them for "not putting their money where their mouth is" and for being callously indifferent to the interests of stockholders, "the small people" Wolfson felt he represented along with his own interests. The bank creditors of American Motors, in Wolfson's opinion, "didn't give a hoot about stockholders" and were only interested in getting their money out "fustest and mostest." Rather than allow them to take over American Motors, Wolfson reiterated that he would take it over himself or find additional working capital for it.

Though their loans had been greatly reduced, some bankers still were dubious of the future of American Motors in the fall of 1957. Besides forbidding the payment of dividends, the credit agreement then in effect required that a minimum working capital of $42,000,000 had to be maintained. Costs of preparing the 1958 Ramblers were so great that capital had dropped close to this figure. Wolfson went to work on another proposal for American Motors.

Sylvia Porter syndicated a gloomy column about the situation on September 11, which the Detroit *Free Press* headlined "Crucial Days Are Ahead for AMC." As a result of the column a $1,200,000 ice-cream cabinet deal fell through in California, a joint automobile promotion with *Sports Illustrated* was canceled by the magazine and several dealers about to sign contracts to sell Ramblers backed out. As the column seemed to be based on information from the Wolfson organization, Romney wrote Wolfson a letter of protest. But car sales increased, bankers were inclined to modify the credit agreement if necessary, and Wm. C. Roney & Co., a Detroit brokerage house, in its September 27 letter said American Motors had a "strong case" for a profitable 1958 and that the stock at seven dollars a share appeared attractive for speculative commitments. The company ended the month with working capital of $46,238,000.

Romney and Wolfson met to hear the latter's proposals on October 10 in a conference room of Merritt-Chapman & Scott at 261 Park Avenue in New York City. With Romney were Timpy, Chapin, Chapman and Cross. Present with Wolfson were Rittmaster, Gerbert, Glickstein and two men new to the American Motors group. These were William A. Shea of New York and Martin Segal of Jacksonville, Florida. Shea was a partner in the law firm of Manning, Hollinger & Shea and later was chairman of the baseball committee of Mayor Robert Wagner of New York which spurred formation of the Continental League. Segal was an officer in several Wolfson enterprises.

Early in the meeting there was a sharp exchange about the Sylvia Porter column. Wolfson suggested that she obtained her information as a result of the steering committee of bankers lunching at the Chase Manhattan Bank. He indignantly said Romney should retract any suggestion that any Wolfson man had given her the information or he, Wolfson, would walk out of the room. Romney did not retract and said it was ridiculous to blame the bank when what the columnist wrote about had been known only to Wolfson and Romney and their associates at the time. Wolfson moved on to other subjects.

Wolfson explained he had considered a merger of American Motors and Merritt-Chapman & Scott, had gone as far as to have Shea talk to the Chase Manhattan Bank about it, but had abandoned the idea. He now proposed that American Motors acquire Universal Marion properties at their book value of $15,130,000. He offered to accept 850,000 new shares of American Motors stock at $6.50 a share for $5,520,000, with the remaining $9,610,000 to be paid after payment of all bank loans by a series of 5 per cent notes.

Among the conditions would be the naming of Shea, Segal and Gerbert as American Motors directors.

American Motors working capital would be increased to about $64,000,000, Wolfson calculated, and the four-million-dollar profits that year of the Marion-Osgood operations could utilize that much of the American Motors accumulated tax loss. Wolfson also felt Romney and his staff might effect economies in the Marion manufacture of power shovels, pile drivers and similar equipment in Ohio. Wolfson asked for an immediate decision and repeated that he was receiving almost daily letters from American Motors stockholders asking him to represent them. He said he could muster a million and a half shares in any proxy fight but did not want control of the company.

The American Motors men discussed the proposals that night with three directors, Harcourt Amory, Howard A. Lewis and Eustace Seligman, the last a member of the Sullivan & Cromwell law firm, joining the group. With the stock that he already held, the additional shares obviously would give Wolfson control of the company any time he wanted it. Though it might mean a proxy fight, Romney was determined to refuse the proposals. He telephoned Wolfson and suggested that they meet as a smaller group. With only Cross and three Wolfson aides present, they met again next day at Merritt-Chapman & Scott.

Romney refused the proposals but offered to let Wolfson or a mutually acceptable nominee fill the director's seat then vacant because of the death on August 26 of Dean George Granger Brown of the University of Michigan. He had been dean of the College of Engineering and a noted engineering consultant.

"We are going to be in the black this month, this quarter, and this year," said Romney. "We don't need additional capital for a renewal of our banking agreement. It would be contrary to the interest of our stockholders generally to dilute their stock values by giving you this much stock for these properties because there's no need of them."

"Lou, let's go caucus," proposed Shea. "No, no," said Wolfson very calmly. "There's no need to caucus. I think George is right. Things are more favorable than our bank contacts led us to believe."

They compromised by Wolfson naming two men to the Board of Directors, "to help you, not heckle you," Wolfson promised Romney. Shea became a director on October 24 and Segal, president of Wolfson's Continental Enterprises in Florida, at the next stockholders meeting on February 5, 1958. Wolfson gave a proxy for 415,200 shares to Romney for this meeting and in response to a stockholder's question about Wolfson's stock, Segal that day said:

"As a long-time personal associate, and a business associate of Mr. Wolfson, I think that this would be the proper forum to scotch a rumor. . . . Mr. Wolfson has had no discussions with General Dynamics, or with anyone, for that matter, on the sale of even a share of his stock in American Motors. He has great faith in Mr. George Romney, and the management of American Motors, and will continue to co-operate as called upon as a shareholder in anything for the benefit of the company.

"This, by the way, is a unique departure in his method of doing business, for he has only spent his time and his energies heretofore in companies in which he had direct operational responsibility."

Wolfson, Segal and Shea became among the most loyal supporters of American Motors. They put Ramblers in Florida hotel lobbies. They bought cars for their families and Wolfson encouraged several of his companies to buy whole fleets of Ramblers. He helped sell so many cars that the management on April 8 gave a dinner for him at the Sheraton East Hotel in New York, presented him with a new white Ambassador car and Roy Abernethy formally awarded him a "top salesman" plaque.

In its account of the Merritt-Chapman & Scott stockholders meeting, the *Wall Street Journal* that day quoted Wolfson as saying that he and associates owned about 460,000 shares of American Motors stock and was "perfectly satisfied" with the company's progress. He appeared preoccupied at the dinner and made some cryptic remarks about feeling that his contribution to the country was identifying companies that needed help and new life, giving it to them, and then moving on to other companies needing the same thing.

American Motors continued in the black as Romney had promised. The stock which Wolfson had bought at around six dollars a share in 1956, early in 1958 was soon worth nine dollars, eleven dollars and fourteen dollars a share. But the earnings in the quarter ending in March were less than the previous quarter and all Wall Street commentators did not share the optimism of Wm. C. Roney & Company. In answering a reader's query, *The U.S. Investor* of Boston, in June, for example, termed American Motors a speculation that should be sold "ahead of the mob."

On the morning of June 20, a Friday, Romney received a long-distance call at his home from Shea, one of the Wolfson directors, saying that Wolfson was selling some of his stock and wanted Romney to be told about it. When he reached his office, Romney found a spokesman for Wolfson, quoted in that morning's *New York Times* as saying, "Frankly the stock looks fully priced on the basis of the immediate outlook." He was reported "a third of the way home" in disposing of his holdings in American Motors. The *Wall Street Journal,* which does not publish on the weekend, on Monday had a story from Wolfson confirming that he was selling but saying that the *Times* figure was wrong. The stock, which had closed Thursday at $12.75, dropped on this news to $11.00.

As anyone with stock or anything else to sell usually does not deprecate it, the Securities and Exchange Commission at once investigated. At the time Rittmaster, one of Wolfson's aides, gave the *New York Times* the information on which it based its story, the SEC found Wolfson had not only sold all of his stock but was buying to cover a short position of 137,400 shares! His accounts bought 10,000 shares on Friday and 8,300 more on Monday for this purpose.

Some Wolfson shares had been sold as early as February and by the time of the April dinner, he had sold 173,400 shares. On Tuesday, June 24, Federal Judge Frederick Van Pelt Bryan on complaint of the SEC restrained and enjoined Wolfson from "false and misleading" statements and transactions that would "operate as a fraud or deceit" on buyers or sellers of American Motors stock.

"As the SEC has already made clear," Romney said on June 27, "neither the company nor its management is involved in this development in any way. . . . Mr. Wolfson's relationship with American Motors has been that of a stockholder. He did not determine policy nor did he have any hand in company operations. The basic policies and programs that have produced our present success were developed before he became a major stockholder and his stock ownership did not change them." Romney announced earnings for the quarter would be more than five million dollars.

On July 1, Wolfson telephoned Romney to say that Shea and Segal had not known of the stock sale and to ask that no action be taken against them. Wolfson said he felt "bearish" about the whole market but had not intended to sell all his American Motors stock. He had many accounts and had not realized that he was completely out but that people who had acted were responsible to him and he was responsible. Shea and Segal were required to resign as directors at the July meeting of the board.

The last of the bank debt was paid in that month and the stock sold for more than $15 for the first time in the history of the company. On August 1, Wolfson denied the SEC allegations but assented to the injunction being made permanent. That month the stock reached $17.50. It passed $20 in September, $36 in October and soared past $43 before the end of the year and over $95 in 1959.

Wall Street circles estimated that Wolfson sold his American Motors stock at a profit of some $2,000,000 and even after paying as high as $28 a share to cover his short sales may have had the better part of a million dollars for his two years in American Motors.

But his decision to sell was one of the most egregious errors of history, one comparable with the prediction of the *Literary Digest* that Alfred Landon would be President and the pollsters' choice of Thomas Dewey for the same office. If he had held on for a few months longer, he could have made one of the most fabulous profits in the history of Wall Street and would have enjoyed an unassailable position in the financial world. If he had held until 1959 he would have had a profit of more than $40,000,000!

"You are the men of faith," Richard Cross told a Dearborn Inn dinner of American Motors directors and executives celebrating the company's first year of profitable operation. "There is one other who if he had had faith just a few months more would be here." This was the tragedy of Louis Wolfson.

Once the tide turned, everything seemed to go well for Romney and American Motors. It was the only automobile company in the country to sell more cars in 1958 than the year before. In calendar 1958, it increased its percentage of industry sales from 1.94 to 4.66. It produced and sold 217,332 cars in 1958 compared with 114,084 in 1957. One-fifth of them were the small hundred-inch wheel-base Rambler American. It had been discontinued in 1955 because a slightly bigger Rambler sold better, then successfully reintroduced almost unchanged in the fall of 1957. The comeback of a discontinued model was without precedent in automobile history.

Figures tell the story of the extraordinary management job Romney and his executives did in three years. In 1958, when the company sold 217,332 cars, the overhead of the automotive division was $28,088,000; in the red-ink year 1955, overhead was $38,036,000 on sales of 137,000. Engineering and styling expense had been cut from $6,036,000 to $3,459,000. Advertising and selling expenses had been reduced from $28,065,000 to $20,400,000. The $3.87 advertising expense per car for the Metropolitan was the lowest in the industry. The 1958 record car total was sold by 2,636 dealers, slightly fewer but much better than the 1955 organization.

Profits for fiscal 1958 were $26,085,134 or $4.65 per share on sales of $470,349,420, a welcome change from four straight years of losses. There was every reason for employees to carol spontaneously at Christmas. Cuts in executive salaries were restored and some of them, including Romney's, were increased. On December 15, some 275 executives received $759,784 in "cut-loss" bonuses for 1957. A month later, 329 shared $1,911,485 as their share of the 1958 profits. As Romney, Chapin and Chapman were not in the plan, directors voted them a total of $190,000. By way of contrast, officers of most other automobile companies received less in 1958 than in 1957. Romney picked up his five-year-old stock options to become the company's biggest individual stockholder.

Ward's Automotive Reports called the comeback the "surprise package" of the year. American Motors was the most heavily traded stock on the New York Stock Exchange in 1958. At the end of the year a 5 per cent stock dividend was declared. As profits continued, sixty-cent quarterly dividends were started. The company's profits were so much higher than expected that the men in the executive bonus plan voluntarily reduced their bonuses by 40 per cent to keep them in line with those of Ford and General Motors. For the 1959 fiscal year, earnings were about $60,000,000 on sales of more than $869,000,000 after payment of $45,000,000 income taxes. No income tax was paid in 1958 because of previous losses.

Truckloads of new Rambler bodies directed by radio telephone were then moving every five minutes around the clock from the Milwaukee to the Kenosha plant, which became the busiest automobile plant in the country. Facilities were expanded at a cost of ten million dollars to meet higher production schedules. Kenosha renamed Sixtieth Street "Rambler Drive." When employment doubled at the American Motors plant there, Mayor Gene Hammond announced: "George Romney is a hero here."

He was praised and honored on all sides. Mayor Louis C. Miriani of Detroit gave Romney a key to the city and proclaimed an American Motors Day. David J. Wilkie, automobile editor of the Associated Press, wrote a dispatch starting: "If George Romney wanted to, he justifiably could say 'I told you so . . .' " and Associated Press editors voted him industry's "Man of the Year" for 1958. He was the *Saturday Review's* "Businessman of the Year" and the National Management Association's "Management Man of the Year." The Franklin Institute gave him its Vermilye Medal.

He was chosen by a committee of Michigan college presidents to receive one of the state's Wolverine Frontiersman awards, as a modern-day pioneer "who has left a trail of leadership in industry, joined with a devotion to God, and a love for mankind." Brigham Young University and Wayne State University gave him Doctor of Laws degrees. He also received awards for achievement in business from the University of Michigan, University of Utah and the Drexel Institute of Technology. A Detroit insurance man formed a "Citizens Committee to Draft George Romney for Governor." Inez Robb, the syndicated columnist, proposed him for President.

In an article, "The Man Who Surprised Detroit," Arthur W. Baum, *Saturday Evening Post* editor, compared Romney with Frank Merriwell, Jack Armstrong and all other nick-of-time, victory-when-all-is-lost heroes and said he snugly fitted the part of a dime-novel hero except for one point: "He is handsome, strong-jawed, clean-living, and he has scored the necessary brilliant achievement. But he is not fun-loving." Romney's intimates agreed with all of this except the last.

His activities outside his business and his church may be too strenuous to be considered fun by the timorous but he loves them. Until he was fifty, he played basketball with the teen-agers in the neighborhood of the Romney summer home on Lake Huron at

Grand Bend, Ontario. After half an hour's ski instruction, he once rode the lift to the top and with only a few falls came down the hazardous Wild Cat run at Snow Basin in Utah. He also has indulged strenuously in water skiing, tennis and horseback riding, once being tossed by a wild Palomino into the back of an automobile with force enough to dent it.

Romney's regular exercise is solo early morning golf on the course of the Bloomfield Hills Country Club adjoining his home. He arises at dawn, a lifelong habit, and hits two or three balls for six to nine holes before anybody else arrives. Friends have found golfing with Romney like competing in a track meet. He walks fast, addresses the ball, wallops it and moves on with little time spent in contemplation. Only extremely bad weather keeps him from the course. In cold weather he wears an Abercrombie & Fitch plastic zipper outfit similar to Winston Churchill's wartime siren suit. If there is snow on the ground, Romney uses balls colored with a luminous red paint developed by Russ Streeter of the Kelvinator laboratory.

The answers to problems, Romney says, sometimes come to him while he golfs. In any case, he finds the early morning hours profitable. His mind is clear, there are no interruptions and no telephone calls. He then drives to work at a speed that sometimes attracts the attention of the police.

While he may take time and seek the advice of many people on a problem, once his decision has been made, he has no regrets and concentrates on carrying it out. He does not worry about what people may say. The usual social conversation has little appeal for him. When he is not working at something, he usually is reading a book, mostly serious works on problems of modern life. He also makes repairs around his home and works in his rock garden with its artificial waterfall. He always has a home project of some kind.

The Romney parties are mostly family gatherings. He devotes a great deal of time and thought to planning surprises for his wife and children and enjoys photographing their surprise. For his wife's birthday in 1956, the year of their twenty-fifth wedding anniversary, he arranged a surprise party with an elaborate This-Is-Your-Life program, "Lenore, a New Operetta." One anniversary, he arrived at their summer home with enough Saks Fifth Avenue dresses for a family fashion show. One Christmas he gave his daughters, Lynn, later Mrs. Larry Keenan, and Jane, later Mrs. Bruce Robinson, tickets to Europe in travel folders. He once hid a huge sideboard in a neighbor's garage until Christmas Day and all the males in the neighborhood had to be enlisted to carry it home. If he has to be away when Lenore appears in a little theater show, he attends the dress rehearsal.

When the children were younger, the family took a long automobile trip every other summer, singing on the way with Romney's voice as loud as any. His favorite tune for driving is a Spanish song, "Me gustan todas las muchachas, pero me gusta una más," which can be translated, "I like all the girls but I like one best of all." They would pack lunches, start out at 5 A.M. and, stopping only for gasoline, drive six or seven hundred miles in a day.

Romney is a fast driver, though he attempts to stay under seventy miles an hour, and also likes to try short cuts which look promising on road maps. These don't always work out. He once wound up in an actual Western ghost town and had to spend eight hours traveling fifty miles over boulder-strewn dirt roads to get back on his route. On these trips, they would often rent motel accommodations only for the distaff side of the family, while Romney and his sons, Mitt and Scott, slept in their bed-seated Ambassador.

Success of the Rambler added compact cars made by the Big Three to the Studebaker Lark and the great array of foreign cars already competing with American Motors in the general small-car area. Romney was undismayed. Members of the Romney family have been competing with rivals, danger and adversity of all sorts for centuries.

IV

Dragon-Slaying Heritage

An eighteenth-century member of George Romney's family was the famous portrait painter of the identical name. With Sir Joshua Reynolds and Thomas Gainsborough, he composed a famous triumvirate in English art. If the ancestry which painter Romney worked out for the family is accepted, both his rebellious truculence and the Detroit Romney's war against driveway dinosaurs may be explained by inheritance. According to this account both descended from that noted fourth-century slayer of dragons, St. George, the patron saint of England. The Detroit *Free Press* reported a 1959 speech of the American Motors executive under the headline: "Sir Romney Challenges 'Dragons.'"

Early settlers in Utah thought enough of the dragon legend to name a town in Washington County near the Arizona border "St. George." George Romney's father was born there and the family tree definitely connects with Thomas Romney, one of the three brothers of the father of the painter. Some prints of his paintings hang on the walls of the Romney home in Bloomfield Hills.

For some years Romney also had as his secretary in Detroit a highly efficient English girl named Muriel Willoughby. When another secretary in the office vacationed in Washington, she saw in the National Gallery a portrait of a young girl titled "Miss Willoughby" and mailed a postcard copy of it to Detroit. It was then noted that it was a 1783 work of Romney the painter and Miss Willoughby of American Motors revealed she was a member of the family of the young subject of the painting. George Romney owns a print of it.

William Romney, a sixteenth-century member of the family, which at that time sometimes spelled its name "Romeny" or even "Rumley," was Lord Mayor of London and later knighted by the King. It was John Romney, father of the artist and ten other children, however, who established something of an occupational pattern for the family. Born in 1704, he became an expert carpenter, joiner and cabinetmaker at Dalton-in-Furness, Lancashire.

He was the first, at least in his part of the world, to replace clog or solid wheels with spoke-wheels, "which being lighter in their construction, and in every respect better fitted for use, were soon afterwards universally adopted."[1] George Romney of Detroit points out that even then Romneys were saving weight. John Romney also developed an improved plow and built engines for raising water from neighboring iron mines. Many later Romneys have been carpenters and builders.

"Mental and emotional characteristics peculiarly noticeable in the family," according to one of its historians,[2] "are an indomitable will and a bull-dogged determination, which is reinforced by a courage and an honesty of purpose, admired even by those who disagree with them in matters of judgment. Intensely frank and aggressive, almost to the point of combativeness, they have been thought by some to be opinionated and dictatorial, but fundamentally they are democratic and possess a fair measure of humility.

"Important and distinctive physical characteristics of the male members of the family are a large square head with a massive under-jaw, with blue eyes and light hair predominating. The figure is usually inclined to be stocky and somewhat above medium in height."

One of Thomas Romney's great-grandsons, Miles Romney, born

at Dalton-in-Furness in 1806 and a carpenter who specialized in circular stair building, emigrated to America. He and his wife, who had been Elizabeth Gaskell, were attracted by a street meeting of Orson Hyde, one of the first Mormon missionaries to England, and in 1839 were baptized.

With other converts from Preston and Manchester, they sailed February 7, 1841 from Liverpool for New Orleans in the *Sheffield*. There were 235 aboard. The voyage required fifty-one days and was marked by three deaths and an attempted mutiny. The passengers helped quell this and conducted religious services en route. From New Orleans, they traveled by boat up the Mississippi River to Nauvoo, Illinois, at that time the largest city in the state thanks to Mormon thrift and industry. When Chicago had a population of only five thousand, Nauvoo had more than twenty thousand.[3]

There they traded a Paisley shawl for a small house and Miles Romney worked on the big Nauvoo temple then under construction. On August 18, 1843, their third son was born and named Miles Park Romney. The next summer an angry mob murdered Joseph and Hyrum Smith, the Church leaders, in a nearby jail. Early in 1846 the persecuted Mormons, led by Brigham Young, began their great overland trek from Illinois to Utah. The weak died on the way, leaving the survivors an unusually hardy lot. In part because of their respect for physical health and exercise, their descendants have had higher birth rates and lower death rates than their neighbors ever since.

The Romneys were too poor to make the long journey at once. They moved first to Burlington, Iowa, then to St. Louis, Missouri, where all had smallpox, and next to Council Bluffs, Iowa. They left there in March, 1850, and traveled by ox team to Salt Lake City, where they arrived on October 13. Seven-year-old Miles Park walked much of the way. His father became foreman of the public workshop in Salt Lake City, visited England as a missionary, and helped settle St. George, Utah. There he directed building of a redstone tabernacle and in 1877 was fatally hurt in a fall from a window of the structure while working on it.

His son, Miles Park Romney, followed him as a carpenter and builder, as a missionary to England, and as a colonizer in St. George. In 1862, Miles Park married Hannah Hood Hill, a nineteen-year-old Canadian-born girl, who like himself had made the long journey from Nauvoo to Salt Lake City as a child. Five years later he became one of the never more than 3 per cent of the Mormon men who embraced "plural" marriage.

When Congress outlawed polygamy in 1885, Miles Park Romney, three of his wives and their children were living in St. Johns, Arizona.[4] He was a contractor and builder, had a contract for hauling mail and was editor and publisher of the *Orion Era,* a local weekly newspaper. Overnight he was reduced from the leading citizen of the community to a hounded and hunted man. He and others in the same plight sought asylum in Mexico.

Heading a Mormon mission in Mexico City at this time was Helaman Pratt. He had been born on the march from Nauvoo to Utah and was a son of Parley Parker Pratt, an important early Church leader who traveled widely as a missionary and composed the hymn, "The Morning Breaks, the Shadows Flee," first published in the *Millennial Star,* British missionary magazine which he founded. In his missionary role, Helaman Pratt presented the *Book of Mormon* to President Porfirio Díaz of Mexico and became a frequent guest at Chapultepec Castle. With others, Helaman Pratt obtained permission from Díaz for Miles Park Romney and other Mormon refugees to buy lands and establish colonies in Mexico.

Partly with funds advanced by the Church, they purchased large, mostly undeveloped tracts in Sonora and Chihuahua. Díaz was happy to have colonists there as buffers against the Apache Indians. Mormon authorities themselves banned the controversial plural marriages beginning in 1890 but the economic opportunities spurred more emigration to the colonies in Mexico. Three permanent settlements were established in Sonora and seven in western Chihuahua. All except one of the latter were along the Piedras Verdes River. The largest were Colonia Juárez, Colonia Dublan, and Colonia Díaz. Title to most of the property was held by the Mexican Colonization and Agricultural Company, organized by the leaders of the Church. This first leased, then sold tracts and lots to the colonists.

Helaman Pratt bought a wild tract of land in the Sierra Madre Mountains known as Cliff Ranch. It was thirty-two miles west of Colonia Juárez. He and Miles Park Romney and part of their families jointly occupied the ranch. It was a beautiful but lonely place where subsequent tenants were massacred by Apache Indians. After one year Romney moved back into Colonia Juárez to resume his trade of carpenter and builder. A year later, the Pratts also left. The arrangement lasted long enough, however, for one of his sons, Gaskell Romney, who had been born September 22, 1871, in St. George, to become acquainted with Anna Amelia Pratt, one of Helaman Pratt's ten daughters.

Gaskell, as a boy of fourteen, had helped drive the horses when his mother Hannah and some of her other children made their way from Arizona into Mexico in 1886. They braved snowstorms and at one point Gaskell removed shoes from U.S. Army horses slain by Indians for use on their own poorly shod animals. A carpenter in the family tradition, he helped his father at Cliff Ranch and also returned to the United States to study. After a year at the old Latter-day Saints College in Salt Lake City, he returned and married Miss Pratt February 20, 1895 in Colonia Juárez. The bride's mother was Anna Johanna Dorothea Wilcken, who had been born in Schleswig-Holstein, the daughter of C. H. Wilcken, a picturesque German-born early Utah figure. The couple lived first in a little house outside of Casas Grandes but soon moved to another in Colonia Dublan.

Their first son, named Gaskell Maurice, but known by the latter

52

name to distinguish him from his father, was born in 1897. A second boy, Douglas Pratt, was born in 1899. The next year the father was assigned to a Mormon mission in Pennsylvania and New York. During his two-year absence, the young wife sent him funds and supported herself and two sons by making peanut brittle and cream-filled candies for stores in Colonia Dublan, Casas Grandes and elsewhere.

Gaskell Romney prospered on his return. He made furniture, built houses and set up a planing mill which was the only one in a wide area. He supplied sash and doors to the colonists, to mining companies and to the ranches of venerable Luis Terrazas, the great Chihuahua cattle and land king. A third son, Miles Pratt, was born in 1903 and to house his growing family the father soon built a handsome two-story red brick house, the most substantial in Colonia Dublan and one which still was standing half a century later.

In this house a fourth son, George Wilcken, the future president of American Motors, was ushered into the world by Aunt Aggie Thurber, a cousin of the Pratt family who was the leading local midwife, on July 8, 1907. As his parents had retained their American citizenship, experts on constitutional law believe his birth in Mexico is no bar to George Romney becoming a candidate for President regardless of the U.S. Constitution's clause: "No person except a natural-born citizen, or a citizen of the United States at the time of the adoption of this Constitution, shall be eligible for the office of President." No court has interpreted this clause but children born abroad or at sea have been considered "natural-born" citizens for passports and other privileges. If astrology is to be believed, those born in July are receptive to new ideas and adapted to catering to public needs.[5]

The colonies were remarkable communities. They had no crime. There were no saloons but numerous schools, churches and tithing houses, many of them built by Romneys. The population was numerous enough by 1895 for organization of the Juárez Stake of the Church.[6] Junius Romney, a twenty-nine-year-old uncle of George and the other children of Gaskell Romney, was elected president of the Stake in 1908.

Orchards bloomed. The farms yielded great quantities of food, enough to ship to other parts of the country. Many had herds of cattle and horses. Helaman Pratt once delivered a load of cheese of such fine quality in Chihuahua City that authorities believed it smuggled from Switzerland or Wisconsin and arrested him. He was held incommunicado until he smuggled a note out to Don Luis Terrazas, who had him freed. Later Pratt received a certificate at a government fair for producing the best cheese in Mexico.

The Romney family was largely self-sufficient. Anna Romney baked bread and cooked or prepared everything to feed the family. She also made all of her own clothes, being talented enough to work from pictures in fashion magazines, all of the boys' clothes and even some of her husband's. The father cut the boys' hair and made virtually everything required. He made baseballs and bats for them and organized a baseball team on which he was catcher. This team defeated one sponsored by Henry Bowman, a storekeeper who owned the first local automobile, a much rebuilt machine in which he hauled his ballplayers, sometimes even bouncing over the roadless desert as far as El Paso.

George Romney's earliest memory was of a train trip with his father to El Paso when he was about four years old. There he saw his first bakery bread—"It tasted like cake"—also his first bottled milk, and saw his first motion picture, an early nickelodeon. It was a devout family and by this time George was praying morning and evening along with his brothers. At breakfast they knelt at the side of their chairs.

The family had a farm about two miles from town in addition to the other enterprises and by the time he was four George was riding a handsome gray horse, Monte, between home and the farm.

He fell off Monte one day when riding bareback and was unconscious four hours. As he regained his senses, his mother left the room to make some ice cream for him. By the time she returned with it, he was again out riding Monte! There were other mishaps among the boys. Miles, the next older brother, was kicked in the face by a horse. His face also was torn when he slipped off the galvanized-iron roof of his father's planing mill. He bore the scar for life.

A spark fell one day into the sawdust at the Romney planing mill, smoldered undetected for hours and at midnight burst into flames which destroyed the place. Before it could be rebuilt, more serious troubles from causes beyond their control beset all the colonists, and all Mexico.

V

Exodus from Mexico

In a memorable interview with a magazine writer,[1] President Porfirio Díaz, who had ruled Mexico so long, said he would not seek re-election in 1910. Francisco I. Madero, a wealthy young idealist, became a candidate. But Díaz ran again despite his eighty years and jailed Madero. The latter escaped, and with the aid of adventurers from the United States and many other countries, began a revolution in which most of the fighting took place in Chihuahua.

When Madero and his men attacked Casas Grandes on March 5, 1911, the firing was heard in Colonia Dublan, six miles away, and several of the defeated rebels, heavily draped with belts of cartridges, rode through the colony. Nevertheless, Miss Amy Pratt, a schoolteacher sister of Mrs. Romney, and other instructors taught classes as usual that day and the older Romney boys attended. The area was held first by rebels, then federals, then rebels again. Madero emerged victorious after capturing Ciudad Juárez, across the Rio Grande from El Paso, on May 10, 1911, and traveled triumphantly by way of the Northwestern Railroad southward to be inaugurated as president.

The Romney family was in the crowd that gathered at the station to see the little man who had just overthrown what had seemed an impregnable regime. Madero responded with a speech and patted the heads of George Romney and other children. Peace was restored but not for long. Pascual Orozco, a dissatisfied follower of Madero, led a counterrevolution in February, 1912, adopted a red flag as his emblem and soon held most of Chihuahua. "Red Flaggers" confiscated from the Mormons supplies, cattle and horses, including the Romneys' Monte. There were robberies and murders on outlying farms, nine Mormons in all eventually being killed. To safeguard lives, President Junius Romney had rifles and ammunition smuggled to the colonies.[2]

Anti-American feeling flared in the area when President William Howard Taft on March 2 proclaimed an embargo on shipments of arms from the United States, thus cutting off rebel supplies. Two days later the State Department urged all American citizens to leave Chihuahua "without delay." With the exception of a dozen who had become naturalized, all four thousand of the Mormon colonists were American citizens but their only homes were in Mexico and they remained. Junius Romney pledged their neutrality and obtained from General José Inez Salazar, the rebel commander at Casas Grandes, assurances of protection. These promises were ignored increasingly after the Red Flaggers lost battles and the federals occupied Chihuahua City on July 9. Salazar asked for a list of arms in the hands of the colonists.

While George and the other children slept, a conference took place at the Gaskell Romney house in Colonia Dublan, the night of July 12. A messenger had ridden sixty miles with word that a rebel colonel at La Ascension had looted a Mormon grist mill and announced he would attack Colonia Díaz next day unless the colonists there surrendered their arms to him by 10 A.M. Informed by telephone at 9:30 P.M. in Colonia Juárez, Junius Romney and his counselor, Hyrum S. Harris, rushed ten miles by buckboard to Casas Grandes.

Though it was nearly midnight, Junius Romney with the plea that it was "a matter of life or death" induced guards to awaken

Salazar. The sleepy general cursed the colonel, said he was not supposed to demand the arms and, apparently involuntarily, added *"todavia no,"* ("not yet" in Spanish, which Romney understood). Junius Romney and Harris drove on six miles to Colonia Dublan with Salazar's written message countermanding the La Ascension order. The messenger from Colonia Díaz, who had been put to bed, set off with it at 3 A.M. and the colony leaders spent the remainder of the night debating what to do.

Salazar's *"todavia no"* sent a cold chill up Junius Romney's spine. To the council, which lasted until dawn in the front room of the Gaskell Romney home, Bishop A. D. Thurber of Colonia Dublan brought another alarming message. A friendly Mexican, who had been in the councils of the rebels, warned they were planning to loot the colonies. When he made a quick trip to the border to consult Church officials about the situation, Junius Romney encountered Salazar on the train. He threatened vengeance for the arms embargo, saying the United States was killing his men without risking its own, and boasted that the rebels could defeat all of the United States, "except maybe Texas."

"To attempt to retain our arms and ammunition," Junius Romney advised Church authorities, "means to engage in an armed conflict with the rebels with odds of twenty to one against us; and to surrender our arms means to have our families at the mercy of demons." Depredations increased. More cattle and horses were seized. Rebels walked streets begging and looting. Events came to a climax on July 27, a Saturday, when Salazar ordered Henry Bowman, the storekeeper, to bring Junius Romney to rebel headquarters at Casas Grandes.

In a stormy interview, the general demanded that Romney order the colonists to surrender their guns, saying previous promises were "words carried away by the wind." When Romney objected that he lacked authority, Salazar said his men would search the Mormon homes and take the arms by force if they were not surrendered. Romney agreed to discuss with colony leaders surrender of the arms at a central point, if Salazar would allow the women and children to be evacuated and would not invade the Mormon homes. Salazar agreed and a guard of soldiers accompanied Romney and those with him to Colonia Dublan.

There they found rebels looting a store, cavalry on three sides of the town and four cannon and seven machine guns trained on it from the cattle yards to the northeast. Armed rebels surrounded Bishop Thurber's house as Junius and Gaskell Romney and other leaders discussed their plight. There was no alternative but to appear to comply with the demands. Keeping their forty-seven new long-range rifles concealed, the colonists yielded pistols, shotguns, hunting rifles and rusting old weapons of many kinds to the rebels at the schoolhouse. Other colonies followed the same procedure.

Preparations began to send women and children to the border. Money in the local bank was divided among the families. Some took the Mexico Northwestern train that night. One man went with every ten families while the others remained. Colonists, some of whom lived seventy-five miles away in the mountains, began to stream afoot and in wagons and buggies toward stations on the railroad. Some on the way to Pearson were held up and robbed by drunken soldiers. Every train north was crowded.

The Gaskell Romney family and other women and children of the colony were scheduled to leave Colonia Dublan Sunday evening on a special train. Several hundred persons gathered in a drizzling summer rain at the station and in front of the Bowman store but a damaged bridge to the south delayed the train. The Romneys returned home and slept. When the train pulled in early Monday its passenger and freight cars were jammed already with refugees and additional cars had to be added.

As an expectant mother, Mrs. Romney was given a seat in a coach. With her were Miles, young George, who had just celebrated his fifth birthday, and Lawrence, his two-year-old brother; two of her sisters, Miss Amy Pratt, the schoolteacher, and Mrs. Verde Pratt Cardon, wife of Clarence Cardon, then a missionary in Paris, France. Ahead in a freight car were the older Romney boys, Maurice and Douglas. They were cheerful as they arrived in El Paso that afternoon.

In all 2,300 Mormon refugees reached El Paso within three days, to become, in the later words of George Romney, "the first displaced persons of the twentieth century." Half a dozen babies were born en route and the El Paso *Herald*[3] compared their flight to the exodus of the Jews from Egypt and the hegira of the early Mormons from Nauvoo to Utah sixty-five years earlier. Those unable to pay were carried without tickets by the railroad and their fares billed to the Church.

The Romney family crowded into a taxicab and, after being turned away by several places, found temporary quarters in a small hotel. They had just twenty-five dollars, two suitcases and three bedrolls. Many families were installed in vacant tenements and several hundred were quartered in huge empty lumber sheds on Magoffin Avenue which the Long Lumber Company made available. The U.S. Army supplied rations and loaned tents from Fort Bliss. Mayor C. E. Kelly and city officials joined Church leaders in finding homes and jobs for the refugees. Congress voted $100,000 for their transportation and relief.

Looting and abuse of Americans, meanwhile, increased in the colonies and Junius Romney ordered the Mormon men to rendezvous with their guns and horses at "The Stairs," a hidden mountain spot seven miles from Colonia Juárez. Gaskell Romney buried some valuables beneath the floor of his home. He brought away his wife's hard-used sewing machine but had to abandon it when the rebels pursued and opened fire. A young man named William Smith was hit in the leg by a bullet. When the colonists returned the fire, the pursuers turned back. A military organization was formed with Gaskell Romney as quartermaster and the party of 235 men, 500 horses and a commissary wagon started north between a federal force to the west and the rebels to the east. Marching under a blazing sun, the Mormons covered the 150 miles to the border in two days and entered New Mexico at Dog Springs, southeast of Hachita.

With a beard of several days still on his face, Gaskell Romney rejoined his family in El Paso that night and moved them to better quarters in a house near Fort Bliss owned by an absent friend of Helaman Pratt. A big Army truck delivered the government rations of bread, Post Toasties, peanut butter and similar items.

There Charles Wilcken Romney, the family's sixth son, was born, on August 26, 1912, with Aunt Aggie Thurber, the Colonia Dublan midwife, again in attendance. Charles grew up to be a Salt Lake City attorney, businessman, director of the Salt Lake Baseball Corporation, member of the Utah Legislature and, unlike most of his family, a member of the Democratic party.

Foreseeing no early peace in Mexico, Gaskell Romney sold his brick home in Colonia Dublan to one of his brothers-in-law, Wilford Farnsworth, the husband of Eleanor Romney, and saw it only once more years later. The colonists eventually in 1938 received from Mexico $2.65 for each $100 of loss during the revolutionary disorders. Gaskell Romney's losses were so great that he received enough to purchase a comfortable house in Salt Lake City in which he lived his last years.

In the meantime, Colonia Díaz was burned to the ground. Several tides of revolution swept over Colonia Dublan and it was headquarters for General John J. Pershing's expedition in pursuit of Pancho Villa, most famous of the bandits of the region. Paradoxically that genial killer favored the colonies and spared Colonia Dublan both before and after his 1916 raid on Columbus, New Mexico.

Even General Salazar, who caused the exodus, eventually regarded the colonists with friendship. A Villista in his last years, he camped in 1917 on the river above Colonia Juárez and was invited by young women of the Mutual Improvement Association to a picnic lunch. He accepted and enjoyed himself. A few weeks later he was ambushed and slain near Nogales.[4]

To support his family in El Paso, Gaskell Romney obtained tools and returned to his old trade of carpenter. Maurice, the eldest son, became a Western Union messenger. Douglas obtained a newspaper route and even Miles went to work at $2.50 a week as a department store cashboy. But the city was crowded and work limited.

Gaskell and his brother, George Samuel Romney, a refugee from Colonia Juárez, that fall moved their families to Los Angeles in the hope of greater opportunities. Grandmother Hannah Hood Hill Romney, then seventy years old, accompanied the two families. In all, five of her sons had come out of Mexico in the exodus and she had gone from Arizona, where she had been living, to El Paso to help care for new babies and those who had become ill because of the hardships. They arrived in Los Angeles in time for nine-year-old Miles to sell newspaper extras announcing the election of President Woodrow Wilson.

The two families were so large that they had difficulty in finding houses within their means and landlords willing to rent to them. With the birth of young Charles, there were six sons in the Gaskell Romney family. His brother, George Samuel, then had two sons and five daughters. A sixth girl, Maurine, was born in Los Angeles December 12, 1912.

After promising to repair any damage their children might do, the families rented houses a block apart. The fathers at once went to work as carpenters. Gaskell's eldest son, Maurice, and George Samuel's son, Marion, went to work also as carpenter's helpers. The younger children attended school.

To get to school from the Gaskell Romney home at Twenty-first and Main, they had to walk through abandoned Luna Park and were a little frightened by mysterious-appearing Japanese boys who frequented the place. Sensing this, one pushed young George. Miles came to his aid and knocked down the other youth. This ended the Oriental menace in the neighborhood. About this time young George rode in an automobile for the first time.

C. H. Wilcken, the colorful 6 feet 4 inch great-grandfather of the boys, paid Los Angeles a visit and took them to their first vaudeville show. For the first time they saw trained ponies and dogs. As the Romneys were not used to such entertainment, it was a memorable occasion. Wilcken also fascinated the youngsters with recollections of his life in Germany, how he served in both the German and American armies and how he had been a personal bodyguard for the Kaiser in Germany and for Brigham Young in Utah.

Besides his carpentry, George Samuel Romney had been a science teacher in Mexico. When he had a chance to return to teaching in the fall of 1913 in the Oakley Academy, a Church school at Oakley, Idaho, he accepted and moved his family there. The Gaskell Romneys followed, stopping for a short stay in the old Wilcken home in Salt Lake City, and the brothers were reunited in Oakley, a town of six hundred in the southern part of the state near the Utah border. They bought a farm in an area that was to be benefited by water from a dam being constructed on Goose Creek and Gaskell Romney built a frame house in Oakley.

25538

VI

Idaho-Utah Boyhood

Even seven-year-old George Romney took a hand in work on the farm outside Oakley. There he had one of the narrowest escapes of his life. After a field was plowed, a heavy metal-shod leveler was pulled by horses over the ground to break up the big clods of dirt. One day George fell off a leveler just in front of the heavy device and the horses pulled it over him. He was scraped slightly but the fact that he fell into a furrow saved his life.

The farm proved to be poorly located and because of the subnormal snow and rainfall there was not as much water as had been expected. Idaho potatoes, not then as popular as later, were the principal crop and also the leading article of diet of the family. Potato prices tumbled and, despite everybody's efforts, the farm was not a success. Both families moved back to Salt Lake City in 1916, George Samuel to earn a degree at the University of Utah and Gaskell to resume construction work with his older boys as helpers.

On a snowy Christmas eve, the father returned from a job in Magna, twenty-five miles to the west, and was distressed to find homemade candy and little else for the Christmas of George and the other youngsters. As he could not afford the carfare, the father walked through the snow from the Romney home in the Forest Dale section to the Sugar House business district and back, a distance of more than four miles, to return with two Flexible Flyer sleds for the youngsters. It was one of the happiest Christmases of their lives.

A farmer for whom the father did some construction in the summer was unable to pay but offered a wagonload of tomatoes. As these were already overripe, Anna Romney worked frantically, day and night, for several days canning or converting them into chili sauce, ketchup and other tomato products. Meanwhile, the whole family ate fresh tomatoes as they had potatoes earlier in Oakley. The next year the family had a sizable war garden plot and it was part of young George's chores to take care of this garden.

In the fall of 1917, Gaskell Romney and his brother, George Samuel, made another move together, this time to Rexburg, Idaho, a city of four thousand in the eastern part of the state. The educator became president of the local Ricks Academy, a Church school which grew into a junior college. When his brother was ill, Gaskell taught his classes in history, English and mathematics. By this time there was a tenth child, Merlyn, the eighth daughter, in the schoolman's family, and a seventh child, Meryl, the first and only daughter, in the Gaskell Romney family. She was born before they left Salt Lake City and grew up to become Mrs. LaVell Ward of Bloomington, Idaho.

Gaskell Romney designed and built in the foothills east of the college scores of homes which the Rexburg Home Builders, of which he was a director, sold to local residents prospering from a World War I boom in sugar and wheat. Under the impetus of the boom, the enterprise was consolidated along with the Rexburg Investment Company and Hyrum Ricks and Company, an old real estate firm, into the Rexburg Building and Loan Company, which was capitalized at a million dollars. It owned homes, farms, lots, a hotel and planned to build a five-story office building.

The family bought its first car, a secondhand Maxwell. When

it was replaced by a new Studebaker, Douglas Romney, second of the sons, stripped and rebuilt the Maxwell into a racing car. He entered this in county fair races in the neighborhood and won several events.

Young George early gave evidence of alertness and shrewdness. When pursuing his brothers in a variety of hide-and-seek, he would take off his necktie and pin it to the corner of the house. While they watched the tie, he would run around the house and pounce upon them from the rear. George also trained a small part-collie dog named Bill to pull him in a small wagon. He taught Bill to follow him down a sledding hill. Harnessed to the sled, the dog then pulled it back up the hill. "The rest of us had to drag our sleds up the hill," recalled a brother, "but George had his dog trained to do it and didn't have to bother."

George H. Blunck, a fellow classmate at the Washington Grade School in Rexburg, later recalled George in their carpentry class. "He showed unusual ability in the use of tools," recalled Blunck. "We made cedar chests, stands and then, as the winter progressed, many of us made skis and George even made a toboggan which compared favorably with factory products." George had some help from his father in making the toboggan.

At Rexburg, George earned his first money at age eleven, shocking wheat at a dollar a day and thinning sugar beets at the same rate per acre. There also was systematic work at home. As each boy became twelve, the mother designated him as her helper. It became George's turn in 1919 and, as his brothers had done before, he assumed dishwashing, table-setting and other chores in his turn. But there was play as well as work for the six sons and baby girl at Rexburg. The mother always had candy and cake for the children and their friends. She also had novels, religious books, histories, books of all kinds. "She read them herself," recalled her son Miles, "then left them where she hoped some of us would pick them up. All of us did, too, but no one read so avidly as

George." He read a biography of Theodore Roosevelt and ever afterward remembered the Rough Rider's advice that "the best road to success is to do your present job well."

Father and sons went camping and fished and swam in the Teton River and irrigation canals. George became an expert swimmer and diver. He also was a Boy Scout in Rexburg Troop No. 2, of which his brother, Miles, was senior patrol leader and Andrew M. Andersen, a Marine veteran, was scoutmaster. The troop hiked to an extinct volcano southwest of Rexburg and to many mountain lakes. Andersen remembered George as a "quiet, unassuming, and slightly aloof" boy who seemed to smile with his eyes.[1]

The father's construction of homes went well for a time but the collapse of farm prices after the war hit the project hard. Miles of paved streets were abandoned to jack rabbits and the project for the five-story office building advanced no farther than an excavation for the foundation, a gaping hole on College Avenue that remained unfilled for many years. Farmers began to move away, leaving their property for creditors. On February 12, 1921, Lawrence Romney, George's twelve-year-old younger brother, died of rheumatic fever and was buried on Valentine's Day.

On the brighter side, George graduated that spring from grammar school as valedictorian. He asked his parents what he should talk about at the exercises but before they could answer decided to make the decision entirely his own.

"If you told me," he said, "then the speech wouldn't be mine, would it?" He spoke to an audience of eleven hundred.

While the educator's family remained in Rexburg, the Gaskell Romneys and their children moved back to Salt Lake City in the summer of 1921. The father and older boys continued in the construction business, eventually building many residences along Gilmer Drive in one project. George and the younger brothers attended school but soon were lending a hand with hammers and nails after classes and during vacations.

George and his brother Miles became expert lathers, filling their mouths with nails and "spitting" them out point first so fast that they could place three thousand lathes a day when the standard was only sixteen hundred. Sometimes Charles, who could handle a thousand, went along and the three brothers could lathe an ordinary house in a day. Friends called them "the lightning lathers." George was weak on ceilings but good on walls and explained that the secret of being a good lather was to consider the work "a race against time." His life since then has been largely a race against time. The boys also shingled roofs, laid floors and were subcontractors on the Temple Square Hotel and other sizable buildings. The father and his workers once completed in a week a temporary chapel for the Yale Ward in Salt Lake City and later erected an imposing church building for it.

Young George first attended Roosevelt Junior High School and then the old Latter-day Saints University high school and junior college in Salt Lake City. The Romneys were a family of athletes and he wanted to uphold the tradition. His older brothers had played high school football and his brother Miles was Inter-Mountain Amateur Welterweight boxing champion in 1922. One of his 165 first cousins, Mitt Romney, had been an All-American football player for the University of Chicago, while another, Elwood Romney, was to be an All-American basketball man for Brigham Young University. Dick, Ott, Lon and Floyd Romney were All-Conference stars in one sport or another and some became coaches.

George was too light for some teams and too heavy for others. His first success came through reducing enough by starvation, steam baths and exercise to win a place on a basketball team with a weight limit of 108 pounds. He and three others with the same problem were so weak that they almost had to be lifted on the scales for the weighing in required only for the initial game. They then wolfed a bag of sandwiches and played so sluggishly that they lost the contest.

Coach Vadal Peterson almost laughed when George first reported for football. There was no uniform small enough for him but he took the smallest, tied up the sleeves and pant legs with shoelaces and joined the squad. "It was just plain grit," recalled Peterson, who later coached champion University of Utah teams. After three years of effort as a scrub tackle, during which he became taller and heavier, George in 1924 was a halfback on the high school team which won six games, two of them by a score of 60 to 0, and played a scoreless tie with the Carbon County High School eleven for the state championship. The team had piled up 151 points to 21 for its opponents.

He began the following basketball season still a guard on the second-string team. A younger friend, Gerald Smith, also was on it. The first game of the season was with Bear River City, sixty miles to the north. As is sometimes the strategy, Coach Peterson started his second team to absorb the initial shock and wear down the opposition. As the starting players gathered in a circle, George, who was acting captain, threw his arm around Smith's shoulder and said: "Now let's play so well, he can't take us out of here!" They did exactly that, and without cheering support—a snowstorm delayed the Salt Lake rooters until the closing minutes—remained in the game and won.[2] The team triumphed in nine of eleven games. George also played right field on the baseball team, which won six and lost four games, and earned letters in all three sports. The school yearbook captioned his photograph: "Serious, high minded, of noble nature—a real fellow."

The most important 1924 event for George Romney, however, was an automobile ride that he chanced to take with one of his teammates, Occie Evans. The latter invited George to come along with another boy as they drove twenty miles south to pick up

Occie's girl at an autumn picnic. There they loaded a dozen girls into Evans' battered car, a Nash, and took them home. The group was soon reduced to Occie, his girl, Genevieve Bird, George and Lenore LaFount, a pretty fifteen-year-old brunette high school junior who was strumming a ukulele.

Like George, who had just passed his seventeenth birthday, Lenore was of a pioneer family. Her maternal grandmother, Rosetta Berry, had walked from Nauvoo to Salt Lake City with a handcart party. Her English-born father, Harold Arundel LaFount, had come with missionaries from England to Utah as a boy. From small beginnings in a hardware store at Logan, he had become a land developer and a manufacturer of earphones for the early crystal radio receivers. He was a bishop in the Church and a friend of President Heber J. Grant, Senator Reed Smoot and other leaders. Mrs. LaFount, the former Alma Robinson, was a church worker, society leader, and known for her dramatic readings. Besides Lenore, there were three other LaFount daughters, Elsie, Constance and Ruth. All were so popular that on Sunday evenings, when they were not allowed to go out, the LaFount home at Fifteenth South and Ninth East was crowded with boys.

Lenore made a deep impression on George. He wanted to see her again but—and this is difficult to believe in the perspective of years—was too timorous to approach her directly. In the manner of Miles Standish of early New England history, George had one of his friends convey to Lenore his invitation to a dance of the Ciceronia Club, a school speaking organization to which he belonged. Lenore was a bit surprised when he and not the other youth called for her but went along and found George "a marvelous dancer."

Courtship of Lenore took precedence over George's other activities. Because the Evans' Nash was usually available, they often double-dated with Genevieve and Occie. If it was not, George walked or rode over on the bicycle of his brother Charles and took his chances at the LaFount home. Whenever they were blooming,

George plucked a rose from the bushes of the Romneys' next-door neighbors, a family named Mollerup, and presented it to Lenore. At school he passed notes to her in the halls and each noon brought her a piece of cake from the cafeteria. While she was uncommitted and Mrs. LaFount counseled delay, Lenore soon was George's girl as far as the students were concerned. At one dance, when he thought she had danced too long with another boy, he pulled her away and literally carried her off the floor. "It was the most exciting thing we had ever seen," said her sister Constance.

Partly because of Lenore, who was a year behind him, George continued in the school the next year as a junior college student instead of pursuing ambitions to work his way through some Eastern university. He was elected president of the student body. When Lenore, who had dramatic talent and ambitions, was cast in the class play, Miss Marion Redd, the sympathetic dramatic coach, also found a role in it for George. This retarded rather than advanced their romance. The play was Edward Childs Carpenter's *Bab,* based on a novel by Mary Roberts Rinehart. Helen Hayes had starred in the Broadway production. Vilate Crane had this role in the student cast.

Lenore had the second most important feminine part, that of Leila Archibald, the eloping daughter of James Archibald, who was played by George. The plot called for kissing scenes between Lenore and a character played by Frank O'Brien. These were not practiced until the dress rehearsal but then Frank and Lenore kissed so enthusiastically that George, who had not yet attained such privileges, exploded. The show was presented with all the kisses to a packed house at the Salt Lake Theatre on the evening of December 14, 1925. "A night apart," said the school yearbook of the comedy. "It will be long remembered; a performance in which much will be recalled and but little forgotten; an epoch in the lives of the players; a memory poignant with all those who saw it."

Lenore cheered George to a measure of basketball glory later in

71

the winter. The junior college had no football team but its basket-ballers usually were among the best in the area. George played guard. The school won three games and lost the same number. The team then entered the Utah-Idaho Junior College tournament at Ogden. Their first opponent was Branch Agricultural College. As basketball was then played, guards were not supposed to score but George shot a goal and it proved the margin of victory, LDSU winning 28 to 26. He made one point as LDS defeated Brigham Young College 26 to 24 and then three points as LDS bested Weber College 26 to 22 to win the tournament. Both of these teams had previously defeated LDS.[3]

As student president, George accompanied the school's unde-feated high school basketball team of that year to the national championship tournament in Chicago and from there sent Lenore a pair of slippers filled with candy. The team won a consolation trophy. As president of the school's Booster Club, formed to adver-tise college activities, he also had some experience that year in salesmanship.

Many of George's classmates were destined for fame. Frank E. Moss, son of physical education director James E. Moss, was elected United States Senator. Principal Guy Wilson, who had come out of Mexico with the Romneys, had a son, Owen Meredith Wilson, who became dean of the University of Utah and president of the Uni-versity of Oregon. Richard Evans, editor of the school newspaper, produced the weekly Mormon Tabernacle choir radio program and became an Apostle of the Mormon Church. Occie Evans mar-ried Genevieve Bird and, after a fling at professional baseball, was for many years a deputy sheriff in Salt Lake City.

Inscriptions in George's copies of the 1925 and 1926 school year-books indicated he was making progress in what he considered the most important campaign of his life, his courtship of Lenore. While she signed only as "a sincere friend," she wrote at length on several pages in both volumes. "Don't let it be your banner year at all," she said on one page. "This year has just been the start." She ended another: "You can do with the future as you will—and George I know that you will be all that I want you to be and more!"

The one note of sadness during the year was the death of George's mother. His father had just been chosen Bishop of the Yale Ward and the Romneys were dressing the evening of February 3, 1926, to attend a party in honor of the outgoing bishop, Edward Ashton, when Mrs. Romney was stricken with a cerebral hemorrhage as she combed her hair. She was only forty-nine but had endured the hardships of Mexico and half a dozen states in rearing her seven children. She and George were especially close and, without his knowing it, she often came to the school to hear him speak.

He had decided already to go on a mission that fall and his mother's death turned him more to religion. An important factor in the growth of the Church of Jesus Christ of Latter-day Saints, to which five generations of Romneys have belonged, is the six thousand missionaries which it sends forth each year. All pay or have their families and friends pay their expenses. The usual tour is two years. The Church chooses those to go and assigns them where needed. Some travel only from Salt Lake City to Denver but others go to Europe, Australia and South Africa. Those selected may decline but this is rare.

Young men are eligible for missions when they are twenty years of age and after they attain the rank of elder. This follows deacon, teacher and priest and usually is obtained at age nineteen. Women hold no priesthood rank but must be twenty-three years of age and qualified. Bishops recommend prospective missionaries. The recommendation is studied by the Stake president and, if approved, passed along to Church authorities. If they too approve, another missionary sets out.

As his grandfather, father and two of his brothers had gone on missions, George Romney obviously was destined for one. But when he became nineteen, and an elder, in 1926, his father was his bishop and wanted to defer George's leaving until the return of his brother Miles, then in South Africa and winning acclaim for his faith by using his American football experience to become an expert Rugby player. The family couldn't afford two missionaries at once.

"How much money would I need to start on a mission in October?" George asked his father at the beginning of the summer.

"Well," replied Gaskell Romney, "I'd say at least five hundred dollars."

While taking Lenore LaFount out nearly every evening in his father's car, by then a Chrysler, George worked furiously as a lather all summer. After the death of his mother, the Maurice Romneys returned to the home and Mrs. Romney kept house for the family. To avoid disturbing her and to get an early start on his lathing or shingling, George arose at dawn and made his own breakfast. He sometimes worked after dark.

At the end of the summer, George handed his father seventy dollars "for tithing" and reported that he had $630 toward mission expenses. Printed invitations announced a farewell party for Elder George Romney, "who leaves Oct. 22, 1926, for the British mission." On the evening of October 8, the Yale Ward Chapel at Fourteenth East and Gilmer Drive, not far from the Romney home at 1337 Gilmer, was crowded with George's family and friends. They contributed a few dollars, heard Mrs. Lola Leonard Sols sing, Bob Stafford play the cornet and listened to talks by George, former Bishop Edward M. Ashton, George's father and others. Dancing followed.

Lenore, then a freshman at the University of Utah, naturally was present. The day he left she also was at the train looking marvelous in a brown coat and black hat. He noted this in a laconic diary that he attempted to keep at the time.

VII

Missionary Years

Missionary work is often character-building and it proved so for George Romney. He found his mission the best training that he received and later said that it meant more to him in his work than any other single experience that he ever had. "The first thing you find out," he once explained, "is that you have to decide what you really think, what you really believe. Secondly, you have to acquire the ability to explain what you believe to others and to do it in various manners. The third aspect is exposure to people of all types of religious, economic and social conviction. This is stimulating."

George had begun to think about his future and hoped that his missionary experience would help resolve his ambitions. He had been debating medicine, the law and business. After talking to lawyers and doctors in Salt Lake City, he had narrowed the decision to law or business. He thought of attending George Washington University, where one of his cousins, Isaac M. Stewart, was then studying law. His missionary work might help him decide and he was eager to be on his way.

The group with which he left Salt Lake City stopped in Chicago for passports. George bought a pen and pencil set at Marshall Field's for Lenore's birthday, November 9. The party also stopped at Niagara Falls and, like his father forty years earlier, George marveled at the water tumbling into the gorge. Grown to thirty, the missionary party sailed from Montreal on October 29 in the *Mont-clare,* a 16,400-ton Canadian Pacific liner, and after a stormy, sea-sickness-producing voyage landed on November 4 at Liverpool.

At the great port city, they were welcomed by Dr. James Edward Talmage, an Apostle of the Church and president of its European missions. He took them to its headquarters at 296 Edge Lane in Durham House, which somebody described as "a gentleman's house of ancient and unmodern vintage." George was greatly impressed and influenced by Dr. Talmage. A native of Berkshire, England, he had emigrated to America as a boy and studied chem-istry and geology at Lehigh University, Johns Hopkins and other institutions. He had been president of the Latter-day Saints College and also of the University of Utah. He had earned fame in both theology and science and was a member of the Royal Society and many other learned organizations. He had written books on both minerals and religion.

While some of his companions of the voyage went on to Ger-many and Scandinavia, George was sent to Scotland. Despite the difficulties of Great Britain's first general strike, he made his way to Glasgow, where one of his great-grandmothers, Mary Wood Pratt, had been born. The district president assigned him to work with J. R. Smith, an older missionary who had been there some time. The missionaries were required to keep diaries and account on printed forms for their time. Much of this was spent in door-to-door "tracting."

"Good morning," was the proper greeting, "I am a missionary of the Church of Jesus Christ of Latter-day Saints and I have a very important message about the restoration of the Gospel that I would like to explain to you. Would you care to accept a tract?"

The tracts explained the beliefs and story of the Church, how Joseph Smith, prophet and founder, started it at Fayette, New York, in 1830 after the *Book of Mormon* was revealed to him; how its members believe theirs a restoration of the true church. Tracts also listed its articles of faith,[1] the belief of its followers in work for all and explained Mormon precepts, such as the avoidance of alcohol, coffee, tea and tobacco; its unpaid, robeless, lay ministry.

If the missionary was invited inside, or conversation developed, he expounded further, invited the householder to a meeting and perhaps sold him a pamphlet or the *Book of Mormon*. Householders usually accepted the tracts politely but sometimes they angrily slammed doors. When this happened often, a weary missionary was inclined to get rid of his tracts by leaving them in mailboxes without attempting to talk to the residents.

George yielded to "box-stuffing" only rarely. He liked to talk. He talked to barbers, fishermen, a gas lamp lighter and the officers at the police station where he had to report as an alien. But there were times of discouragement. "Four people at Sunday School," he once noted, "was little to cheer one who is spending money and time to bring a gift to these people."

He saw a great deal of the Scottish coal miners. Some of the church members lived out in the coal districts and the missionaries visited them and also proselyted among their neighbors. George's habit of early rising proved useful. He found it much easier to distribute tracts to miners as they went to work in the morning than to induce them to give him time in the evenings. The missionaries also worked in the slums of Glasgow, among the worst in Europe.

After three months in Glasgow, George was transferred on February 21, 1927, to Edinburgh. There he had as his companion Bob White, another youth from Utah. Companions worked together and also lived together, either boarding or cooking their own meals. George and Bob did both. George later in this period had as a companion M. B. Langford.

With White, George conducted on April 3, 1927, his first street meeting on the "Mound" in Edinburgh. Public speaking is part of Mormon education, with small children making two-and-a-half-minute talks as part of their Sunday-school training. But speaking to an indifferent or hostile public street meeting is more difficult than talking to friends. The street meeting, in the course of which the speaker is likely to be heckled by any bystander and must compete with other speakers talking at the same time, is an institution better established in the British Isles than in the United States. The "Mound" had been created in the nineteenth century from earth displaced in the construction of that attractive part of Edinburgh known as the New Town. The East and West Princes Street gardens were separated by the Mound and it was overlooked from the south by beautiful Edinburgh Castle.

While the Mound had its hecklers, it sometimes held unexpected pleasures. One night when young Romney and Langford concluded their speaking, a man named Goodman stepped up, introduced himself and said that he played golf. He asked them if they would care to borrow his clubs and play on one of the public courses. On August 1, 1927, George noted: "Went down and had a try at golf this morning for the first time, made it around in 130. Not so bad!" On August 3, he added: "Out again bright and early for another chase after the little white pellet. Batted it around this morning in 116." Next day, he played eighteen holes in 109 at Craighertiny and thirty-six in the afternoon at Braid Hills, shooting 105 on both rounds. The fifty-four holes left him "stiff as a flagpole" and it was weeks before he played again.

The young missionaries were not allowed to dance or to date girls but enjoyed a bit of horseplay among themselves and on occasion were permitted to attend sporting events and to see the sights of the country. With Bob White, George saw Scotland defeat England at Rugby. With a later companion, Golden W. Stewart of Venice, Utah, George made a memorable bicycle trip from Aberdeen to Inverness and along the Caledonian Canal. Even the fact they had to push their machines twelve miles up Glencoe Pass in a pouring rain to reach Glencoe failed to dampen their spirits.

Dr. John A. Widtsoe, also an Apostle of the Church, in the

autumn of 1927 succeeded Dr. Talmage as head of the European missions. Dr. Widtsoe, a native of Norway, had emigrated to Utah and married a granddaughter of Brigham Young. After study at Harvard, he won fame as a chemist and authority on dry farming and served as president of the Utah State Agricultural College and then the University of Utah. When a power company doubled its charges to the college, Dr. Widtsoe found a site on the Logan River and had the state build a hydroelectric plant to supply the electricity. He was the author of many books and later recorded his career in one titled *In a Sunlit Land*.[2]

"Live mightily today," Dr. Widtsoe urged George and other young men. "The greatest day of all time is today. It is the product of all the past and the portent of all the future."

Dr. Widtsoe transferred George to London the following February. There he worked for a time with Milford H. Piggott. The *Daily Mirror* on April 16, 1928, published a photograph of Dr. Widtsoe; Elder Clinton L. Mills, president of the London district of the Church; George Romney and a score of others gathered for a conference of missionaries at Masonic Hall, Camberwell, London. Soon afterward Romney was chosen by Mills to be his clerk and they roomed together. They took turns preparing meals but, as Mills later recalled, George sometimes would say, "Let's go out and eat a good meal," and they would do so.

They lived at 22 Doughty Street, not far from the Old Curiosity Shop immortalized by Charles Dickens. Nearby also was the British Museum with its huge collection of books. There George spent many hours studying economics as well as religion and reading Scottish and English history.

As clerk or secretary of the district, Romney handled the receipts and disbursements of money from thirteen branches in the area. He once remarked that he couldn't see why the British couldn't change their pounds and shillings to the dollar system as he "liked to count dollars better."

This was in addition to the usual missionary duties of preaching and teaching, visits to the poor and the sick and helping the unfortunate. In London, preaching involved street meetings and evening oratory in Hyde Park, the traditional forum of advocates of all sorts of causes. The missionaries also spoke to workers of the financial district as they ate their lunches in Tower Hill Square, opposite the Tower of London. It was often difficult to attract an audience in the square.

On one of his first appearances there, he found an unexpected ally in a big red-bearded socialist who was denouncing religion from a stand a few yards away. Observing that Romney's audience was small, the red-bearded man came over. "Sonny," he said, "I don't agree with anything you've got to say, but I think you have a right to get your message across. The best way to draw crowds around here is to have a bit of heckling. Suppose, when I see you ain't doing too well, I come over and heckle you. That'll bring the people around here for sure. Then you can heckle me when I need it." They helped each other this way but Romney soon required no aid.

"George was a great preacher," recalled Mills, a resident of Woods Cross, Utah, in later years. "Besides our Church speaking assignments, we would have invitations to speak to various clubs and organizations. These always went to George because he could handle them better than any other man we had."

While official permission was required to speak from the Nelson Monument, Trafalgar Square also was the scene of Mormon efforts. In a column "The Talk of London by the Dragoman," the *Daily Express* of May 28, 1928, reported: "Trafalgar Square provided me with my first sight of Mormons on the platform. An earnest young man, perched on the base of the Column, was describing the delights of Utah, and denying the existence there of polygamy. It was too serious a subject for a hot, happy day: so I passed on."

The earnest young man, of course, was George Romney. A companion snapped a picture of him that day as he stood in the sun, just behind the tail of one of the lions of the monument, and addressed a crowd of perhaps seventy-five, including a woman with a parasol and a London bobby who seemed to be listening intently.

"George's deep voice could be heard ringing out a block away," recalled Mills. "He was fearless and spoke with such clarity that everyone could understand. The hecklers never disturbed him for a moment. He was determined to have the right answer for any question. With his sound reasoning and charm, he won the hearts of many people."

Confronted with the often-asked question, "How many wives did Brigham Young have?" Romney's usual answer was that "he had enough that he didn't have to bother with any other man's wife."

One day he came into the office asking what "of" meant. This arose over a line in the *Book of Mormon* saying, "Christ was born of Jerusalem." A questioner had said, "Is this an error? Christ was born in Bethlehem." George found that "of" meant near by or close to and that Jerusalem and Bethlehem were separated by approximately three miles. This satisfied the party asking this question.

While in London, George received news of events at home. In 1927, his father remarried, taking for his second wife, Amy Wilcken Pratt. She was a younger sister of George's mother and had taught school in Mexico and Davis County, Utah, and been a librarian at the Utah State Agricultural College. His elder brother, Douglas Pratt Romney, had died in Denver. He was stricken with appendicitis and delayed an operation for a few hours to attend to a business project. He left a seven-year-old daughter and a son born three weeks after his death.

Lenore LaFount was one of six pretty girls chosen to welcome

Charles Lindbergh when he visited Salt Lake City in the course of his triumphal tour following his flight from New York to Paris. The six beauties had their pictures across the front page of the Salt Lake *Telegram* and several of his friends sent the paper to George. More importantly, Lenore wrote him that the LaFount family was moving to Washington. On the recommendation of his friend, Senator Reed Smoot, her father had been appointed by President Calvin Coolidge as one of the original members of the Federal Radio Commission, a forerunner of the Federal Communications Commission.

On arriving in Washington, LaFount paid two hundred dollars for a morning suit and wearing it called at the White House only to be received coolly and briefly. The austere Coolidge shook hands and said: "In case of doubt read the law. Good-day, sir."

Despite this start it was an interesting and important appointment, which brought LaFount into contact with important government people as well as leaders of the growing broadcasting industry. For Lenore it promptly earned a ride in an Army airplane at Bolling Field with Octavia Sykes, daughter of another member of the Federal Radio Commission. In consequence, the Washington *Herald* published on its front page a picture of the two young ladies wearing the long beads and short skirts of the day. This clipping was relayed to George in England. At this time he and Lenore were writing to each other twice a week and he was sending her frequent presents. One of these was a blue satin robe with a fur collar. She was photographed in it and sent him the picture.

Perhaps a trifle homesick, Romney wandered one evening into London's old Drury Lane Theatre to see a new 1928 American musical comedy. Titled *New Moon,* it was the work of Oscar Hammerstein II, Laurence Schwab and Frank Mandel. The music was by Sigmund Romberg and the high point of the show for George and most others was a roaring male chorus number "Stout-hearted Men," with words by Hammerstein. Romney left the

Drury Lane humming it and years later in Detroit had it played whenever he needed music to bring cheer and hope to an audience.

In his sight-seeing about Trafalgar Square, he visited the National Gallery and admired the work of his eighteenth-century kinsman, George Romney, the painter. His masterpieces there include "Lady Hamilton as a Bacchante," "The Parson's Daughter," "Lady Craven," "Lady and Child," and "Mrs. Mark Currie." The artist also painted the beautiful Lady Hamilton, who had been born Emma Lyon, as Cassandra, Circle, Magdalene and Joan of Arc.

George Romney was one of the thousands who saw the running of the 1928 Derby at Epsom Downs. His interest in sports also drew him to a soccer game between the Sheffield and the Tottenham Spurs. He watched Oxford defeat Cambridge in a boat race and pulled an oar himself in a river outing.

As Romney and a companion wearily concluded an evening of preaching in Hyde Park, a well-dressed man stepped up and insisted on carrying their stand for them. He introduced himself as William Goodair and took them to dinner at the Royal Automobile Club. He was the son of an English gentleman and a Polish noblewoman related to the last royal house of Poland.

Through Goodair, George Romney met a number of titled people. One of these was Lady Beecham. She was interested then in the Oxford Movement and he joined university young people in attending several of its meetings. Goodair gave a party for Romney on his twenty-first birthday. A month later in August, 1928, when Clinton L. Mills left for America and Romney was made president of the Scottish District, Goodair gave a farewell dinner for his two friends.

Scotland was a difficult field for the Mormons. With whisky-making a national industry, a sect which opposed drinking could not expect popularity and many new adherents to the Church emigrated to America as soon as they were able to do so. At the time a lurid motion picture called *Through Death Valley, or the Mormon Peril* was being shown and one nationally circulating newspaper had published a series of outdated anti-Mormon canards. Romney returned to Glasgow, lodged with a family named Dunn at 33 Great Western Road and undertook a new approach.

Instead of traveling about in pairs, he decided to lead all of his seven or eight missionaries into one community at a time in a task force approach. They would call on the mayor and visit the office of the leading newspaper. This usually resulted in the surprised editor publishing a story about them and often photographing them. They would then distribute tracts, show motion pictures of Utah and conduct for ten days or so a series of indoor and outdoor meetings. These would sometimes be advertised in newspapers and always would be announced by signs chalked on sidewalks, for example: "Stop! Look! Mormons Give Free Lecture Co-op Hall," with the date and hour.

Permission from local authorities was required for some meetings. When officials disputed over granting this, the Mormons received further notice. To carry his campaign into Perth, "the fair city" on the River Tay, Romney had to obtain from the police a "pedlar's certificate." It authorized him "to act as a pedlar within any part of the United Kingdom for a year from the date," which was August 17, 1928. He kept it as a souvenir.

Under the leadline "Mormonism Exposed," the Perthshire *Constitutional & Journal* ten days later reported:

> Before an audience of nearly two hundred, three of the missionaries of the Church of the Latter-day Saints gave testimony to their doctrines in the Co-operative Hall on Friday evening. Men predominated, but the fair sex, mainly of the younger generation, were also well represented. The missionaries all through had a most attentive hearing, and at the close, when questions were invited, there was a good response, many showing that the testimonies had created an impression . . . . One speaker said there was no unemployment problem in Utah. Everyone who be-

came a member of the Church of the Latter-day Saints was fully provided for, the rich helping the poor. It is one of the richest of states and in health and education showed a better return than the states as a whole.

Seven earnest young missionaries, rather solemn in their stiff derby hats, the next month visited Saltcoats, a town of ten thousand on the River Clyde. Besides Romney, the group included Golden W. Stewart, district clerk; William F. McKelvey of Kansas City, Missouri; Lawrence S. Crosby and Alva L. Ritchie, Ogden; Kelvin L. Baldwin and Lewis S. Leatham, Salt Lake City; and Melvin L. Condie, Preston, Idaho. The foray received notice in at least one London newspaper.

As a result of the visit of seven Mormon missionaries to Saltcoats [noted the *Sunday Mail* on September 30], the Clydeside town is at present in the throes of a religious war, and as the gentlemen from "over the pond" are not having matters all their own way, a certain amount of liveliness seems bound to follow. . . . They are desirous of having a permanent missionary settled in the district. A local gentleman, however, has taken up the cudgels against Mormonism, and has held a series of open-air meetings. . . . It has been many years since such lively interest has been aroused in a religious campaign in Saltcoats.

This earned Romney congratulations from Dr. Widtsoe. "I wish you would write," asked the mission president, "before it is all out of your mind, your methods of approach, with the plans, as you carry them out, and everything else of interest, with respect to the campaign to be used in other places when we undertake similar work there." The missionaries moved to Alloa, Aberdeen and Glasgow.

At Alloa, a whisky-making town on the River Forth, they received permission, over protests of the chief constable, for meetings in Station Square. As it turned out, bad weather forced them into a hall. At Aberdeen, Alvin G. Pack spoke and George Romney showed lantern slides. They encountered the usual polygamous argument. "You are over here to take girls away," shouted somebody in the crowd, "that's all you have to do for a living."

In Glasgow, they were better prepared for this. Under the headline "Bachelor Mormons," the *Daily Express* on November 14 reported that in the McLelland Galleries the previous night two men from Salt Lake City had endeavored to clear up misunderstandings which existed in the average citizen's mind regarding the Mormon faith.

"Lecturer Alvin G. Pack and Mr. George Romney, the chairman, both claim to be Mormons," said the *Express,* "otherwise one might have been pardoned for mistaking them for American college youths. Both are in their early twenties, and neither can claim even one wife so far." They explained the end of polygamy in 1890.

"We do not come to this country with any idea of decoying young girls away to Salt Lake City," shouted Romney. "You will agree with me that there is nothing wrong with our girls out there."

He then showed the audience a picture of Lenore LaFount, who by then was a senior at George Washington University in Washington, D.C. "It was easy to agree with him in the face of such conclusive evidence," said the *Express* account. The *Daily Mail* also reported the meeting.

Somewhat to the annoyance of larger denominations, the Mormons received notice far out of proportion to their numbers. There were few Latter-day Saints in Scotland—250 in Glasgow, 100 in Edinburgh, only 20 in Aberdeen at the time of the meeting there. But partly as a result of the notice steady progress was made with some hundred conversions in 1928.

As his two years of missionary work ended, Romney sought advice from Dr. Widtsoe and made a special trip to Liverpool. They discussed the possibilities of law and business. Dr. Widtsoe advised the latter. "I had the inner assurance when he was talking that he was right," recalled Romney later.

Dr. Widtsoe urged him to continue his education. "You have

made a success of your mission," he said. "Go on and get your education. Cost what it will, stay with it." With a warm letter of appreciation and advice, Dr. Widtsoe formally released George from his mission on November 26, 1928. "You have done splendid work," wrote the mission president. "I hate to part with you. . . . If you will keep the spirit that you have had the last few months in your heart, the doors of this earth will open to you everywhere, and ultimately the doors of heaven will open to you also. You cannot do better than to go through life with the true missionary spirit actuating you always."

George Romney undertook to do so. Until 1944, his role in his church continued to be only that of an elder. In that year, Darrel Ensign, district president of three small Mormon branches in Detroit, consolidated them into one large branch of five hundred members and asked Romney to head it. "There were plenty of reasons for me to say 'no,'" he wrote his father, "but all of them were business reasons and I therefore had to accept." It subsequently became a Stake and, as noted, he led in the building of a tabernacle and the administration of its affairs. This has kept him in touch with David C. McKay, president of the Church, Ezra Taft Benson, Secretary of Agriculture, and other Mormon leaders.

Romney's religion has given him moral courage that has contributed importantly to his success. From this stems his belief that the majority is not necessarily right, the biggest companies not necessarily the soundest, nor the biggest cars the best. His faith's belief in self-reliance, its system of farms and storehouses to take care of the needs of any member, and its dislike of government doles account for these qualities in Romney.

He does not force his religious beliefs on anybody. There are as many coffee machines in American Motors plants as in any others and executives who feel like drinking something stronger in moments of relaxation do so. Nor do Mormons receive any special favors from American Motors. When one of Romney's brothers-in-law, for example, mentioned that his wife wanted a Rambler and he'd get her one if he could buy one at a "good" price, Romney cut him short. "If you want a Rambler," he said, "you know where to get it—go to your nearest dealer."

But Romney takes a Bible with him on his travels and his faith is no secret. "My religion is my most precious possession," he wrote in an article for the Detroit *Free Press*.[3] "It teaches me the purpose of life, and answers life's greatest questions: Where we come from, Why we are here, and Where we are going. It provides me with yardsticks for life based on eternal values."

Among the values he listed were:

The end of all Learning is to know God. And knowing Him to love Him and strive to be like Him . . .

When we serve our fellow men, we serve our God.

Marriage and the family ties can and should be eternal.

Man is that he might have joy.

Freedom of choice is man's great privilege . . . .

We cannot be saved in ignorance; we cannot be saved any faster than we gain knowledge.

That America is the "Land of Promise" and the "Everlasting Hills" referred to in Israel's blessing to Joseph who was sold unto Egypt.

That the Constitution of the United States is a divinely inspired document whose purpose is to free Americans and through their example and assistance free men everywhere from bondage of all forms . . . .

Above all, Romney said, his religion "has taught me to honor the convictions and personal rights of others, to accept truth wherever I find it, and to seek everywhere for 'anything virtuous, lovely, or of good report or praiseworthy.' " He has been active in the Detroit Round Table of Catholics, Jews and Protestants and received the 1959 Action for Democratic Living Award from the Michigan Regional Board of the B'nai B'rith Anti-Defamation League.

VIII

Washington and Aluminum

George didn't have the money for the European tour which many missionaries to Great Britain take at the end of their service. After a brief visit to Paris, he returned to America in December of 1928 aboard the *Leviathan,* the former German liner which for many years was the largest ship in the world.

From New York, he rushed to Washington and spent the Christmas-New Year's week with the LaFounts, then living on Twenty-ninth Street in the northwest part of the city. On New Year's Eve, he and Lenore borrowed the family Nash, and with George driving started for a dance at the fashionable Wardman Park Hotel. Impatient to get there, they were speeding along Connecticut Avenue when a motorcycle policeman, siren blaring, waved them to the curb.

"Let's have your license," he ordered. George handed over the papers in the glove compartment of the car.

"This says Harold LaFount, forty-nine years old," said the policeman, studying the papers. "You are not forty-nine years old!"

George and Lenore explained.

"Well," concluded the officer, "I have you for speeding, driving without a license and maybe for a few other things but it's New Year's Eve. You kids go on and have a good time!"

Their haste was in vain. At the Wardman Park a stern headwaiter refused to let them in because George was not in formal attire. Instead of dancing they spent the evening driving.

When he departed for the west two days later, George didn't want the LaFounts to know but, besides his railroad ticket to Salt Lake City, he had just thirty-five cents in his pockets. He spent this for peanuts and subsisted on them during the train ride.

With Lenore living in Washington, George's plans to go to college there became definite. He and his brother Miles planned to move there in the fall and work their way at George Washington University. Their cousin, Isaac M. Stewart, whose mother was Katherine Romney, had just graduated there and gone to work as secretary to Senator Reed Smoot. J. Willard Marriott, another young man from Salt Lake City, was starting a chain of restaurants in the capital.

Meanwhile in Salt Lake City, George resumed his part-time work and enrolled in the University of Utah. There he renewed his friendship with Gerald Smith, the basketball teammate of his high school days. Smith was a member of Sigma Chi and George pledged this famous fraternity but was not at Utah long enough to be initiated. He worked that summer with his father and brother and took an evening course in speedwriting at the local Latter-day Saints Business College.[1] He had learned typing in high school and believed a knowledge of shorthand would help him in Washington, where secretarial jobs were reported abundant.

The LaFounts returned to Salt Lake City for the summer. Completing college in three years, Lenore had graduated in June from George Washington University. "I had seen her only two weeks in two and a half years," George recalled later, "so I was really more interested in courting her than going to those night classes in speedwriting. I got to only six classes all summer long." In his father's car, George also took Lenore on long desert and mountain drives. They swam at Saltair and Lagoon and danced at many places, often in company with Lenore's sister Constance and her date, who was as serious about her as George was about Lenore. Neither liked to trade dances.

In the fall of 1929, George and Miles drove to Washington in the latter's new Chrysler 50. As he had work for them, their father was sorry to see them go but gave them his blessing. They lodged at a rooming house and enrolled for night classes at George Washington. Miles obtained a construction job and George studied the classified columns of the newspapers. One morning he noticed a male-help-wanted advertisement in the Washington *Post*. It simply said "stenographer" at a room in the Senate Office Building.

When he arrived there, he found it to be the office of Senator David I. Walsh, the first Democrat sent by Massachusetts to the Senate since the Civil War.[2] There were more than a score of applicants ahead of him and a stack of letters from others on the receptionist's desk. As there were nearly a hundred candidates for the job, she suggested that he might not want to wait but he insisted and was interviewed by both a secretary and the Senator. Senator Walsh liked George and hired him at $120 a month. It proved an important turning point in his career.

Senator Walsh was a large, kindly, gentle bachelor. He was one of a large family whose Irish immigrant parents had died early leaving three boys and eight girls. He had been reared by two older sisters, a dressmaker and a schoolteacher, and had worked as a newsboy to help pay his tuition at Holy Cross and Boston University Law School. He was lieutenant governor and then governor of Massachusetts before serving twenty-seven years in the U.S. Senate. He was then a member of the Senate Committee on Naval Affairs and a ranking member of the powerful Senate Finance Committee, which deals with taxation, tariff legislation and revenue problems. He was a Roman Catholic and a personal friend of Cardinal O'Connell of Boston.

Because of his faith and his membership on the Naval Affairs Committee, Walsh recently had engaged in a sharp exchange with

Catholic-baiting Tom Heflin of Alabama. Senator Heflin wanted to end the Navy's custom of hoisting a church pennant above other flags during divine service aboard ship. Speaking for his Navy and his God, Walsh said: "In my own Commonwealth of Massachusetts there is not a public assembly begun or ended in the Legislature, in the courts, without a prayer 'God save the Commonwealth of Massachusetts,' a custom that came down from the old Pilgrims, a custom that the children of emigrants, whatever their religion may be, have followed. . . . From the very earliest days of the founding of our government, the word of God, respect for God, reverence for God, and love of God have been paramount. . . . We have proudly placed God first and country next. . . . During divine service in the Navy we raise, not a flag but a pennant, to remind all of the worship of God. . . . I refuse to put even the flag of my country above the emblem of God and I want my country to continue to teach its children in the service . . . that we are a God believing people . . . that we need His guidance." The Senate voted overwhelmingly with Walsh on the issue.[3]

When George reported for work, the Senator dictated letters to him for two days and his speedwriting, while slow, was adequate. Then the Senator undertook to dictate a speech and George's speedwriting proved far too slow. It looked as if the young man from Utah might be out of a job. Instead, the Senator consulted with his private secretary, young James T. Clark, who had previously taken his dictation but who was then working for him on pending legislation, especially tariff matters. Clark, who was then saving his pennies for law school, suggested that he and Romney exchange jobs. This was done and George fared much better.

The Hawley-Smoot tariff bill was pending at the time. While Senator Walsh was a critic of Republican high tariff measures, he was interested in protecting New England textile and shoe industries against inroads of imports. It was in George Romney's assignment to analyze each item of the bill in its relationship to the national interest and also to summarize all of the arguments that the Senator's office received from any source. This often involved receiving and interviewing constituents. Some of these thought tariff changes would halt the business depression triggered by the stock market crash of October. Romney's work also involved obtaining information from the Tariff Commission, the Library of Congress and from foreign embassies.

It involved considerable work with his cousin, Isaac M. Stewart, who was clerk of the Senate Finance Committee as well as secretary to Senator Smoot, chairman of the committee and sponsor of the tariff measure in the upper house. Besides Walsh the committee included Henry F. Keyes of New Hampshire, husband of the novelist, Frances Parkinson Keyes; "Young Bob" La Follette of Wisconsin; Pat Harrison of Mississippi; Walter F. George of Georgia; Tom Connally of Texas and Alben W. Barkley of Kentucky. Young Romney met all of them.

He attended numerous hearings of the Finance Committee and its subcommittees and finally sat at the side of Senator Walsh on the Senate floor during debate. As Walsh spoke, Romney passed him notes and papers. He listened at close range to Jim Watson of Indiana, David A. Reed of Pennsylvania, George Norris of Nebraska, and other colorful figures. He became personally acquainted with Leslie M. Biffle and Felton M. Johnson, each of whom served as Secretary of the Senate.

Work on the floor of the U.S. Senate at twenty-two was heady adventure and the day-to-day tasks of Senator Walsh's office a priceless education in the intricacies of government and the art of winning and keeping friends. There was a Napoleonic attention to details. Every visitor was received with courtesy. Any information a constituent asked was dispatched promptly. All incoming letters were answered at once and Senator Walsh at times had three clerks handling his messages of condolence, congratulation and thanks.

The experience gave George Romney a lifelong assurance and

confidence in dealing with Congress. While most businessmen dread and avoid appearing before Congressional committees, Romney, when he became head of American Motors, several times appeared voluntarily. It was no ordeal, but a chance to use another forum for his ideas and an opportunity to revisit the scenes of his youth. Once when he was testifying before a Senate committee, a secretary came in and whispered a message to Senator Alexander Wiley, just as young Romney had sometimes summoned Senator Walsh.

"Just a minute, Senator Wiley," said Romney as the Senator started to leave. "I want you to hear this point." Somewhat surprised, Senator Wiley waited for Romney to make his point.

When he went to work for Senator Walsh, George and Miles moved into the Dodge Hotel at North Capitol and E Street, Northwest. It advertised "no tipping" and was only three blocks from the Capitol. In addition to his night school and work for Senator Walsh, George joined his brother Miles in a small business venture. This was the construction of a drive-in eating place across the Francis Scott Key Bridge over the Potomac River in Rosslyn, Virginia. It was principally a venture of Miles but George invested a little time and money. The building was a curious structure, with a big knob and handle hanging down in the manner of an old-fashioned home ice cream freezer. It did enough business to encourage Miles to open a second establishment out Rhode Island Avenue not far from one of the first Hot Shoppes of J. W. Marriott.

Lenore LaFount, one of George's reasons for being in Washington, meanwhile moved to New York to study acting at the American Laboratory School of the Theatre. She shared a small apartment at Eighty-sixth Street and Park Avenue with Daryl Bagley, another student at the school. George worked on Saturday but every other weekend would take a night train and show up early Sunday morning at the apartment. As Daryl was popular and often out late, she usually was asleep and George and Lenore would have to visit in the hall. George would take an evening train back to Washington.

Lenore had talent and the school was inspiring. Madame Maria Ouspenskaya, a tiny dynamic actress previously with the Moscow Art Theatre and the Provincetown Players, was the leading spirit of the enterprise. She was an exponent of the Constantin Stanislavsky method of acting. In this the actor is supposed to live the part, to throw himself into the role so as to lose his identity for the time being. The students were taught to be uninhibited. One exercise was to act like a fish under water. Another was to be a melting chocolate ice cream cone. One exercise for the girl students was to play the role of a mother with an ill child praying to the Madonna. They worked at it until Madame Ouspenskaya tapped them on the shoulder. Lenore did this so well that she wept and forever afterward could cry easily.

Talent scouts attended the student productions of famous plays. Lenore played Ophelia in *Hamlet,* also Portia in *Julius Caesar* and also had roles in Ibsen's *Doll's House,* Chekov's *Uncle Vanya, The Three Sisters* and *The Cherry Orchard,* some of these the same roles that Madame Ouspenskaya had played in Russia. In consequence of her success in them, Lenore received offers of jobs from the National Broadcasting Company to act in a series of Shakespearian programs, and from Metro-Goldwyn-Mayer to come to Hollywood. As her father was a member of the Federal Radio Commission, Lenore hesitated about the NBC offer but was inclined to go to Hollywood.

News of this upset George. Without waiting for permission from Senator Walsh, he rushed up to New York and attempted to dissuade her. They argued over a period of weeks. In the course of the argument, he had one of the most embarrassing moments of his life. Some youths from Utah lived in the building where Lenore and Daryl Bagley had a room. All lunched together one day when George was visiting. He and Lenore excused themselves, saying they were going for a walk, and went back to the girls' room to talk about her Hollywood offer. In a few minutes, Daryl led the other youths back to the room. As they approached, Lenore and George jumped into a closet. They stood helplessly there for two hours and listened to the Utahans argue that Lenore should accept the Hollywood offer. She eventually did so.

George's chagrin was mitigated by an opportunity with the Aluminum Company of America, which developed for himself at the same time. Alcoa was interested in tariffs and, in the course of his work for Senator Walsh, George met J. E. S. Thorpe and Vice President Safford K. Colby of the company. They were impressed with him and also by his refusal to accept any pay for assembling some information they requested. They offered him a job with the company as an apprentice trainee at $125 a month, with the expectation of twice this after the end of his apprenticeship, and a job in the company's Washington office.

It meant an end to his plans to go to the Harvard School of Business Administration but offered the hope of soon earning enough to marry Lenore. After his usual prayerful consideration, he accepted. Senator Walsh gave him a silver tray and on June 10, 1930, he became an Alcoa employee. As Lenore went to Hollywood, he reported at the company's plant and laboratories at New Kensington, Pennsylvania.

Congress enacted the long debated Hawley-Smoot tariff bill five days later. Though he had successfully included in it protective measures for New England industry, Senator Walsh, as a good Democrat, finally voted against the bill. Like an earlier measure, it was termed "the tariff of abominations." Its record-high duties provoked foreign reprisals and President Hoover was not happy with it.

At New Kensington, George roomed with a fellow apprentice, Mylo M. Dean, later a Ford Motor Company executive. They learned the manufacture and processing of aluminum, its use in pots and pans, airplanes, automobiles, bicycles and other applications. M. M. Anderson, then head of apprentice training and later a vice president of Alcoa, was much impressed with George as was Vice President Colby. This encouraged George at this time to visit the LaFounts and formally ask for Lenore's hand. They were favorably inclined but Mrs. LaFount suggested that George defer such plans until he was employed permanently.

To be near Lenore, George asked and obtained a sales assignment, the last part of his apprentice training, in the Los Angeles office of the company. He arrived there September 15 and began to sell aluminum foil against lead foil for food containers and wrappings, also aluminum sheathing for houses and, less successfully, as a centerline strip for highways. He obtained a brush and painted a number of lampposts on fashionable Wilshire Boulevard to show the efficacy of aluminum paint. He also enrolled in night accounting and public speaking courses at the University of Southern California and resumed courting Lenore.

She had a variety of jobs in the movies. She was a stand-in for Lili Damita and had bit parts in films with Greta Garbo, Ramon Navarro, William Haines and others. She also dubbed in sounds for animated cartoons, in some cases conversation for dogs and cats. Talking pictures were just beginning and there were many assignments for an actress with a trained voice. To get to work, to classes and to drive Lenore home from the studios in Culver City, young Romney bought a 1925 Oldsmobile coupé that had been driven twenty thousand miles. Its first and second gears failed and it was restricted to downhill parking and starting. George spent many evenings watching Lenore work on movie sets and waiting for her to finish so he could drive her home.

They had become engaged as soon as he arrived in Los Angeles but a misunderstanding threatened to break the romance. While George was out of town, an Aluminum Company man named George Stanley arrived in Los Angeles and telephoned Lenore. She went out with him and Romney was furious with jealousy on his return. As Lenore thought she had been doing him a favor by being friendly with his colleague, she decided that she would "never marry him." But there was soon a reconciliation. Stanley later became a brigadier general in the Army Air Force.

A few months later Metro-Goldwyn-Mayer offered Lenore a three-year contract. If all of the various options had been picked up it would have meant fifty thousand dollars to her. But there were certain things about the movies which were distasteful to a girl of her upbringing. Instead of signing the contract, she capitulated to George's pleas that they delay their marriage no longer. She flew home to Washington and the LaFounts planned a wedding in Salt Lake City.

Bill Lynch, the understanding manager of the Alcoa sales office in Los Angeles, gave Romney two weeks off for a honeymoon on condition that he try to sell some aluminum on the way. He had not been with the company long enough for a vacation. With a friend, Romney left Los Angeles at 4 P.M. in the old Oldsmobile. They drove all night and next day, a blazing summer day, the fan belt of the old car parted and they limped into St. George, Utah. It was 5 A.M. when George reached his father's house. But after two hours' sleep, he borrowed his father's Chrysler and met Lenore's train at Ogden. They went to a dance that night.

In the traditional and private Mormon marriage ceremony, they were married "for time and all eternity" in the Salt Lake City Temple on the morning of July 2, 1931. A reception for some four hundred guests followed at the Chi Omega sorority house at the University of Utah. Lenore had been a member there. Her attendants included her sisters and Daryl Bagley. George's brother Miles was best man. His restaurants in Washington had fallen victim to the depression and he had returned to the West to study geology.

George and Lenore started their honeymoon at Pinecrest, a mountain resort a few miles east of Salt Lake City, driving there in a borrowed Ford. George neglected to turn off the ignition and they had to push the car into the canyon when they left on July 4. In Salt Lake City, they picked up George's old Oldsmobile and started west on Highway 40. They were driving after midnight when the car suddenly stopped and all its lights went out, leaving them in blackness in the middle of the Nevada desert. George locked his bride in the car for safety and walked back along the highway for help. He managed to flag down a motorist who had a flashlight. The battery had dropped out of the Oldsmobile. They snipped some barbed wire from a fence, fastened the battery back with it and made Winnemucca at 2 A.M. From there they went on to Reno, Lake Tahoe, and through the Tioga Pass into Yosemite Park, which they found sweltering and as crowded as Times Square. They cut short their visit and drove through Merced and then to Santa Monica. The next day the car wouldn't start at all and George sold it for junk.

In the course of their honeymoon, they had been refused quarters at a resort because they looked young and hadn't bothered to bring their marriage license. In one of his pronouncements, Brigham Young had once said "an unmarried man twenty-five years of age is a dangerous element in a community." Romney escaped becoming a dangerous element by a little more than a year. He was not yet twenty-four and Lenore was two years younger.

At Santa Monica they set up housekeeping in a one-room apartment with a pull-down bed and spent most of their spare time at the beach. Lenore did not return to the studio. In the fall George's apprenticeship came to an end and he was assigned to Washington. His salary was doubled to $250 a month but he was broke at the moment, the Oldsmobile had not been replaced, and Lenore bought their railroad tickets back to the capital.

Romney reported to the Alcoa office, then in the Southern Building at 1425 H Street Northwest, on October 1 and he and Lenore moved into a ninety-dollar-a-month two-room apartment at the

new Kennedy-Warren. Except for a radio set and a few other wedding presents, they had no furniture so they bought a used bedroom
set for twenty-five dollars. After two years, they moved to larger
space in the older Westchester Apartments. There they entertained
an increasing number of friends from many segments of Washington life.

Part of the Alcoa office sold aluminum to the government but
George Romney and his superior, Fred J. Gauntlett, were concerned with keeping up with Washington developments, legislative or otherwise, that might affect the Aluminum Company of
America and, at times, to attempt to influence these to favor the
company. Only a small part of their time was devoted to this, and
executives from Pittsburgh did any testifying before Congressional
committees, but if later legislation had been in effect, Romney
would have had to register as a lobbyist.

He read the *Congressional Record* for developments affecting
Alcoa's affairs. Because cheap electric power is essential for making
aluminum and aluminum also is sold for electrical equipment, the
company was deeply concerned with all hydroelectric power development. It owned steamship lines and small railroads and had
to deal with agencies regulating these. It reported bauxite mining
figures to the Bureau of Mines. It also was involved in international
trade and concerned with tariffs.

The company was under intermittent attack as a monopoly. A
1924 Federal Trade Commission report declared it a monopoly but
another in 1930 exonerated Alcoa. However, criticism continued,
with Oswald F. Schuette, a representative of a number of small companies buying aluminum, inspiring publicity designed to stimulate
Department of Justice action. Romney had to counteract this with
the Washington correspondents. He pointed out that Alcoa had
been founded by the man who discovered the commercial process
for making aluminum, that the company earned only 6 per cent on

its capital, and that, while it produced all of the aluminum, this was in competition with copper, steel and other metals.

In fact, the warfare between copper and aluminum in the electric cable field was continual in Washington, with Western senators often putting pressure on government agencies to buy copper. Young Romney attempted to do the same with senators from states with aluminum interests and asked the help of Senator Otis S. Glenn, then newly elected from Illinois, where Alcoa has a huge bauxite-processing plant in East St. Louis. They met between the Capitol and the Senate Office Building.

"Young man," said Senator Glenn, "I didn't come to Washington to run errands for the business interests of my state. I came to concern myself with national policy and national problems so I am not going to do anything."

The presence of Andrew Mellon in Washington as Secretary of the Treasury under Presidents Harding, Coolidge and Hoover created a special problem for Alcoa. Mellon was only a minority stockholder in the company, Arthur Vining Davis having the controlling interest, and during his government service Mellon had turned his shares over to a family holding company. This itself caused criticism and Senator James Couzens of Michigan accused Mellon of using his cabinet position to further the sale of aluminum for his personal benefit. The reverse was true. Washington bureaucrats leaned over backward to avoid buying aluminum for fear of criticism. When he joined Alcoa, Romney was sent by his office to meet Secretary Mellon but they had no other contacts. The election of President Franklin D. Roosevelt removed Secretary Mellon but the advent of the New Deal and its feverish activities created new problems for Alcoa and an immense volume of work for its Washington office.

While handling his share of this, young Romney managed to have considerable fun. In the winter of 1932-33, he joined other former Salt Lake City athletes in a Utah basketball team in the city's recreational league. On the team was his old teammate, Gerald Smith, then a law student at George Washington University. The manager was David Kennedy, a young bank examiner who later became chairman of the Continental National Bank in Chicago. With Romney playing guard, the Utah team was beaten only by the team of J. Edgar Hoover's Federal Bureau of Investigation. In the shower after one of the games, Smith congratulated George on his progress in life. He replied: "You know, Gerry, you've got to have confidence—enough to bet every last dollar on yourself."

At this time Romney took up golf seriously enough to read a book about it and take two lessons. Alcoa wanted him to join a club but he didn't want to play with important people until his game was better. He worked at it. "Golf," he has explained, "is a most exasperating game. It doesn't look it but it is a very difficult game. There are so many things that you have to do right to play well and you are always making some little mistake that exasperates you. Golf keeps me humble and in physical shape."

While playing the Congressional Country Club course one morning, Albert L. Warner, then of the New York *Herald Tribune,*[4] and Raymond Clapper of the United Press noticed a solitary player on an adjacent fairway, whacking first one ball and then another and practically running between shots. "There goes a young man in a hurry," said Warner. "And with a purpose," added Clapper. In the clubhouse, they made a point of speaking to him and met George Romney. He improved his dancing as well as his golf at this club. Wives of members organized a dancing class and he and Lenore learned the rhumba with Supreme Court Justice Robert Jackson, the Warners and others.

Romney later joined the Burning Tree Country Club, so called because it is located in Bethesda, Maryland, where legend says Indians once made smoke signals. In this refuge of masculinity, where women are allowed only for a New Year's Eve party, Romney met many Congressional and government leaders through the club's rotating Sunday morning foursomes. By this time, his golf was good enough to win shares of the pool for the best scores.

He also joined the National Press Club and at least once a week lunched there at a round table with Willard Kiplinger, newsletter publisher, and others. Romney became acquainted with Senator Arthur Vandenberg, Representative Charles A. Halleck, Paul Wooton of McGraw-Hill, Ernest Lindley, the commentator, Bernard Kilgore of the *Wall Street Journal,* Harry Butcher of the Columbia Broadcasting System, Ray Tucker, George Holmes, Raymond P. Brandt, Ellsworth C. Alvord, Stephen Early, Donald Richberg and many others.

When the Romneys set up housekeeping in Washington, Lenore resumed her career to the extent of directing plays for student groups at George Washington University and conducting a fifteen-minute weekly poetry program, "Poetical Hitchhiking," over radio station WRC. Lenore chose and read the poems. She had majored in English literature at George Washington. The relaxed red-haired young man who announced the program was Arthur Godfrey.

But young Mrs. Romney soon settled into the role of hostess, an important one in Washington, and did much to advance her husband's fortunes. "I'm bringing thirty men up for supper," he telephoned late one afternoon. She fed them. They entertained or went out five or six nights a week, often to cocktail parties, and both were so animated and enthusiastic that very few noticed they drank only water or soft drinks. At home, they served nothing during prohibition. They attempted to continue this after repeal but found many of their guests fortifying themselves so heavily before arriving that the Romneys, in the interest of moderation, began to keep a few bottles for thirsty callers.

One way or another they met most of the figures who flashed across the Washington scene. They met the Hoovers and the Roosevelts at White House parties. A man in charge of Alcoa mining in Arkansas, who had been a battery mate of Senator Harry Truman in World War I, introduced them to him. They saw something of Marriner Eccles, of the Federal Reserve Bank, and Elbert Thomas, who had succeeded Reed Smoot in the Senate. Commissioner LaFount continued on the Federal Radio Commission until 1935, when he resigned to head the broadcasting interests of the Bulova Watch Company. Through the LaFounts, the Romneys met the Louis B. Caldwells. Caldwell, first counsel to the Radio Commission, was known as "the father of radio law." His wife, Irene, was an important capital hostess. For a "dark horse" party in honor of Senator Vandenberg, she once transformed her home at 2900 Cleveland Avenue into an English tavern named Dark Horse Inn. The Romneys were present along with the George Allens, Alice Roosevelt Longworth, Chief Justice Harlan F. Stone, Jesse Jones and sixty others.

The Romneys worked loyally for Alcoa. For a Beaux Arts ball, Mrs. Romney made an armored knight's costume for her husband by dipping washrags into aluminum paint. On June 6, 1935, their first daughter, Margo Lynn, was born and they began to plan a house for the growing family. When a second daughter, Jane LaFount, was born March 18, 1938, the house took shape in Wesley Heights, with Romney drawing the plans and acting as his own contractor. It had aluminum window frames and was sheathed with aluminum so bright that it alarmed the neighbors until painted.

When Professor Edwin G. Nourse of the Brookings Institution in Washington made a study of aluminum pricing, Romney was designated to supply the information from the company. Obtaining it involved him in Pittsburgh conferences with the top people of Alcoa, Chairman Davis, President Roy A. Hunt, Vice President Irving W. Wilson and others.

At this time the Alcoa sales manager in Washington retired and the company decided to combine the two parts of the office under one man. Though he was only twenty-nine, Romney, who already had succeeded Gauntlett, felt he was the man for the job and pointed out that young men headed CBS and NBC operations in Washington. Alcoa did not agree and moved in Edward Bell Wilbur, an older man without Washington experience, from Texas. He subsequently became treasurer of the company. Frustrated for once, Romney resolved to keep his eyes open for a job where seniority was less important. His chance came as a result of the activity generated in Washington by the National Recovery Administration.

In addition to representing Alcoa, he also was the Washington representative of the Aluminum Wares Association, a small group of cooking utensil manufacturers. In the latter role, he was invited to the Monday Club, an informal group of trade association men who lunched weekly on that day at the Press Club or the Washington Club to exchange information. There Romney met another Westerner, Pyke Johnson, Washington representative and vice president of the Automobile Manufacturers Association, and they became friends.

Until he had been brought into the AMA's highway construction promotion activities, by Roy Chapin of the Hudson Motor Car Company, one of the organization's presidents, Johnson had been a Denver newspaperman of the generation of Damon Runyon and Gene Fowler. As sports editor of the *Rocky Mountain News,* Johnson had selected many Romneys on his all-conference teams and knew the family. He believed in voluntary co-operation and often said, "When you get men on a common basis of fact, you narrow the area of controversy between them."

When asked to form a Trade Association Advisory Committee to NRA, Johnson chose Romney as one of the members. It proved so useful that it was continued after NRA was declared unconstitutional in 1935 and the original reason for the committee vanished. In the meantime, Johnson observed at close range Romney's work for Alcoa. The electrical manufacturers tried to include aluminum in the NRA copper cable code but eventually there was a code for aluminum, one on its fabrication and another on cooking utensils. These codes were no sooner buried than Alcoa had more government troubles.

Attorney General Homer S. Cummings on April 23, 1937, slapped the company with a sweeping antitrust suit, making some 140 complaints of monopoly and asked that Alcoa be dissolved. Thus began possibly the longest and most voluminous law case on record. With only brief recesses, the trial lasted from June 1, 1938 to August 14, 1940, a matter of twenty-six months and some fifteen million words. Platoons of lawyers were involved. Alcoa won in federal court in New York and the Department of Justice appealed. Because four Supreme Court justices disqualified themselves, the Court of Appeals became the court of last resort.

While approving dismissal of many complaints, Judge Learned Hand in 1945 ruled in strong language that Alcoa at the time of the trial violated the Sherman Anti-Trust Law by having more than 90 per cent of the aluminum ingot business. He ridiculed the idea of a monopoly being achieved innocently and said he believed Alcoa's position had been attained "as though based on a thousand mergers." He said the power to control prices meant that prices are under control. But by the time another court entered a final decree, Kaiser and the Reynolds Metals Company had bought surplus aluminum plants and Alcoa no longer had a monopoly. It was not broken up, but was required to sever connections with Aluminium Ltd. of Canada, to license competitors under certain patents, and to refrain from squeezing its competitors by its control of raw materials.[5]

Thanks to Pyke Johnson, George Romney by then was in Detroit.

IX

Detroit Goes to War

The initials AMA mean American Medical Association to the man in the street but in automobile circles they stand for the Automobile Manufacturers Association, a trade association which under varying names has included nearly all of the important makers of passenger cars and trucks since 1903. It began as the Association of Licensed Automobile Manufacturers and was composed of those paying royalties under the famous engine patent of George Baldwin Selden of Rochester, New York, then considered by many to dominate the automobile industry. Two-fifths of its income was retained by the Association for litigation and service to the industry.

A mechanical branch began a program of parts standardization and conducted metallurgical research until 1909, when equipment and records were given to the new Society of Automobile (later Automotive) Engineers. In that year a federal court upheld the Selden patent and Alfred Reeves, who had been organizing automobile shows for a group attacking the patent, came to the Association as general manager when the other organization disbanded. Reeves had been automobile editor of the New York *Mail* and New York *Globe* and earlier "cycling editor" of the New York *Press*.

Henry Ford continued to fight the Selden patent and won

in 1911, when the Circuit Court of Appeals ruled that the patent covered only Selden's improvements on the obsolete engine with which he had worked back in 1877 when he filed his patent application. The ALAM dissolved but the members reorganized the same year as the Automobile Board of Trade. In 1913, this became the National Automobile Chamber of Commerce and in 1934 the Automobile Manufacturers Association.

Colonel Charles L. Clifton of Pierce-Arrow served as president of the group from 1905 to 1926. Roy D. Chapin of Hudson served the next two years and later became Secretary of Commerce in President Hoover's cabinet. Alvan Macauley of Packard became president of the group in 1928. For years its principal activity was the cross-licensing of patents and it assembled and maintained the largest library of automobile patents in existence. It also staged automobile shows, assembled statistics, advocated good roads, conducted a public relations program, followed legislation, kept a registry of proposed car names, and worked for highway safety.[1]

Alfred Reeves, except for an interval as vice president and sales manager of the ill-fated United States Motor Company, had been the leading spirit of the Association and its headquarters in New York. At the start of the century many automobile companies were in the East and the Electric Vehicle Company, which bought the Selden patent, had offices there. Several later companies had New York financing and manufacturers found it convenient to attend AMA meetings and at the same time see their bankers.

All of this was changed in 1939. Directors voted to move the New York staff and activities to Detroit. Alfred Reeves retired to an emeritus status. Pyke Johnson, Washington representative and vice president, was made executive vice president and general manager. As he wished to remain in Washington, Johnson had to find a manager for the Detroit office. While some Detroit names were suggested to him, his first and only choice was George Romney.

George went to Detroit with Johnson to be looked over by officers of the Association. President Macauley, a courtly old-school gentleman, entertained them at the Detroit Golf Club and at his home. They also met B. E. Hutchinson, treasurer both of Chrysler and of the Association, and, at South Bend, Paul G. Hoffman of Studebaker, vice president of the Association. The thirty-two-year-old Romney impressed everybody and he was offered the job. Alcoa offered to meet the twelve-thousand-dollar salary, only a little more than he was earning, and Romney was concerned as to the effect of the just beginning war on the automobile industry. But after his usual prayerful consideration, he chose Detroit and on September 28, 1939, attended an AMA directors meeting there and was voted the job.

As he had only a motorist's knowledge of the automobile business, Romney spent the next two months in a furious indoctrination. He met more automobile people in Washington, Detroit and New York. He brought home and read voluminous files. Gerald Smith lunched with Romney at the National Press Club just before he moved to Detroit. At nearly every table, friends stood up to shake his hand and wish him luck. Senator Walsh wrote him a letter of congratulation.

Romney and the AMA staff from New York opened offices in Detroit's New Center Building in January of 1940. The organization had a budget of about a million dollars a year for its activities and Romney's first assignment from Johnson was to revise the dues structure. Dues were in proportion to cars produced but there was a ceiling of forty thousand dollars for any one line. This was somewhat unfair to the smaller companies and also limited AMA revenues. William S. Knudsen of General Motors and Hutchinson of Chrysler had been named a subcommittee on the problem.

While he had been used to senators and Alcoa officials, Romney was nervous when he called for the first time on President Knudsen of General Motors. Sensing this, the great Danish-American pulled from his desk drawer a picture of a big rawboned man with a black mustache standing by an old car.

"Young man," he asked, in his heavy accent, "who do you tink that is?"

Romney confessed he didn't know.

"That is me standing beside my first Chevrolet," explained Knudsen. He soon put Romney at ease.

The Romneys became friends of the Knudsen family, especially of Semon E. "Bunky" Knudsen, the son who later headed General Motors Pontiac Division, and his wife. The Romneys were godparents of Christina Knudsen, one of their daughters.

The ceiling on dues was removed and both Knudsen and Romney moved on to graver problems. As the Nazis overran Western Europe in the spring, the AMA soon became involved in defense work. In May, President Roosevelt named Knudsen to the National Defense Advisory Commission to supervise industrial production. He gave up his General Motors connections and served without pay as a matter of patriotism.

Knudsen was soon suggesting that the automobile manufacturers make no model changes that required additional scarce machine tools. In June, he induced the Ford Motor Company to undertake the building of nine thousand complex Rolls-Royce Merlin airplane engines, three thousand for the United States and six thousand for England. Irritated by Lord Beaverbrook's announcement of the contract, which was to be with the U.S. government, Henry Ford, as a man "with a whim of iron," suddenly refused to make the engines. Purple with rage, Knudsen left and invited Packard executives to his Grosse Isle home on June 24. They were happy to take over building the vital twelve-cylinder engines.[2]

Henry E. Bodman, Packard and AMA counsel, drawing the engine contract, and Clifford Durr, Reconstruction Finance Corporation counsel, worked out a formula which became a pattern for all war industry. The essential part was that the RFC subsidiary, the Defense Plant Corporation, should pay for and own the new facilities required. Packard received Plancor No. 1. Using this agreement as a model, the Defense Plant Corporation eventually negotiated contracts of more than sixteen billion dollars with war contractors.

On October 15, 1940 the AMA directors invited Knudsen to a meeting in New York coincident with the National Automobile Show to receive an autographed set of Carl Sandburg's multi-volume biography of Abraham Lincoln as a token of their appreciation of his service to the organization and to honor him in his new role. Before the books could be presented, the guest of honor launched into a confidential and desperate plea to the automobile manufacturers to help the aircraft production program.

"I was at the White House yesterday," said Knudsen, "and the President has asked me to make a request of you. General Arnold, the head of the Air Force, has just returned from England where he saw the results of the bombing of Coventry and Plymouth. He has concluded that the side that is going to win the war is the side with the most medium and heavy bombers.

"In the months that I've been in this new job, I've visited every aircraft plant in the country. They are expanded from ten to twenty times their earlier capacity. They can't expand any more without help. I'd like you men—the President would like you men, and I'd like you to agree to subordinate your new model changes and subordinate everything else to the production of subassemblies for medium and heavy bombers.

"What I want to do is get the aircraft industry to meet with you and have you take on the manufacture of the subassemblies for certain planes that will then be shipped to new plants to be erected where the aircraft companies will assemble these subassemblies."[3]

The automobile men were impressed and moved by Knudsen's

plea. While Alfred P. Sloan, Jr., presided at a General Motors luncheon, George Romney, James Cope, a Washington AMA public relations man, and others drafted a formal pledge of support for the Knudsen program. After lunch this was approved unanimously as a resolution offering automotive industry facilities for mass production of airplane parts. President Macauley at once invited not only the AMA member companies but also the Ford Motor Company, which was not a member, and also the nonmember body companies, tool and die companies and parts makers to a meeting in Detroit on October 25.

As the AMA offices were too small the meeting was held on the ground floor of the New Center Building in space recently vacated by a fancy grocery and meat market. An undertaker provided folding chairs for the eighty-five men present in the bare room. Knudsen, Major General George Brett, Major James Doolittle, J. H. Kindelberger, president of North American Aviation, Inc., and others outlined the problems. Out of this meeting developed the Automotive Committee for Air Defense and the AMA advanced $100,000 for its expenses.

With Romney handling many of the details, the committee took space in the Graham-Paige Building and five days later Major Doolittle unloaded there two planeloads of parts—one from Wright Field and the other from the Glenn L. Martin plant. Soon DeSoto, Chrysler, Hudson and Goodyear were subcontracting parts for the Martin Company. Nash-Kelvinator contracted to make propellers. Others undertook a variety of items. At an important December meeting of the committee, Knudsen revealed the government's greatly expanded production program and several huge contracts were undertaken. When the committee after four months completed the liaison introductory task assigned it, all automobile makers were working on airplane parts and the Ford Motor Company near Ypsilanti, on land where Henry Ford had previously grown soybeans, was building the great Willow Run plant to build whole bombing planes on an assembly line.

But despite the pressure of increasing work, Romney found time for his family. Principally for the benefit of his father, who retired in 1940 after a quarter of a century of contracting in the Salt Lake area, George produced a mimeographed family newsletter at intervals and mailed it to his widely scattered relatives. In the summer of 1941, he flew west to join a family reunion organized by his brother Miles in honor of their father's seventieth birthday.

They met at St. George, Utah, Gaskell Romney's birthplace, and for the next six days retraced with their father and Aunt Amy by automobile and train the route traveled half a century earlier by the father in going from Utah to Arizona and then Mexico. At Colonia Dublan in Mexico they found several of their old neighbors and the group was photographed in front of the brick house in which George had been born.

When the Romneys first moved to Detroit they rented a house in Grosse Pointe. But soon afterward they found a big three-story house at 1860 Balmoral Drive in the Palmer Woods section of Detroit, bought it, and again acting as his own contractor, Romney began to remodel the place. Between the details of this and learning the intricacies of his new job, he sometimes worked fifteen hours a day. The house provided ample quarters for two more children, both sons, George Scott born June 7, 1941, and Willard Mitt born March 12, 1947. It also provided a home for a tiny Chihuahua dog, kittens, rabbits, and, until the neighbors complained, a flock of carrier pigeons.

On December 7, 1941, the Romneys attended a Sunday afternoon party at the Bloomfield Hills home of Semon E. "Bunky" Knudsen. As they were driving in their Chrysler along Eight-Mile Road on their way home, the Romneys heard over their car radio that Pearl Harbor had been attacked. In Washington, meanwhile, the Defense Commission had given way to the Office of Production Management. After Pearl Harbor this became Donald Nelson's War Production Board and Bill Knudsen became War Department trouble shooter with the rank of lieutenant general.

To handle the industry's total conversion to war production, the AMA organized within a few days the Automotive Council for War Production along the line of the earlier Automotive Committee for Air Defense. Despite a telegram from the Department of Justice warning that it might violate antitrust laws, this took formal shape at a meeting of the board of directors on December 30, 1941, and at another meeting the following day, gloomy and dark in Detroit, work began with representatives in attendance also from tool and die and parts makers. In telegrams to President Roosevelt and all members of the Cabinet, the Council explained its aims.

"The Council," said the messages,

pledges its unlimited effort and facilities in aiding all plants in the industry to get out the mass-production of war material that will win the war.

We pledge, on behalf of the entire automotive industry, not only a cooperative spirit in the common task, but complete interchange of mass-production information, time-saving techniques, product improvements, tooling shortcuts and developments which the individual concerns have now effected or will bring about in doing their portions of the work.

We know that this mutual readiness to assist one another will bring telling results, for it has been tried and tested in the war work already given the industry, and it will be increasingly effective on the enlarged scale which coming war requirements will inevitably bring.

The nation will not lack for one gun, one tank, one engine, that the capacity and ingenuity of this industry's producers can add to the forces of our nation and its friends on all the fighting fronts.

George Romney was named managing director of the Council on January 23 by President Macauley at the suggestion of General Motors men. The next day he was one of the speakers at a meeting of two thousand executives at which leaders of the industry pledged co-operation to Ernest C. Kanzler, chief of the WPB Automotive Branch. Charles E. Wilson, O. E. Hunt, Paul G. Hoffman, K. T. Keller, R. G. Waldron and others spoke. Civilian car production ended on February 10.

In his new role, Romney saw more of the heads of the automobile companies than ever and had a job which Malcolm W. Bingay, Detroit editor, compared to Clyde Beatty dealing with lions and tigers. One day he invited K. T. Keller, the rugged president of Chrysler, to discuss a problem at luncheon. "Luncheon!" snorted Keller. "That's the trouble with this country—too many people think they're going to win this war with their teeth." Unperturbed, Romney said, "All right, we'll get together on ice water." And they did.

On March 4, Romney also was named general manager of AMA when Pyke Johnson resigned to become president of the Automotive Safety Foundation in Washington. This had been organized and until then headed by Paul G. Hoffman. He had been chairman of the AMA Safety Committee in 1935 when the *Reader's Digest* published J. C. Furnas' grim article on accidents, "—And Sudden Death," a title taken from the Book of Common Prayer. "The public furor caused by that article," Hoffman said, "frightened us into action."

As a separate organization it raised funds from many sources and inaugurated a program of improved highway engineering, traffic law enforcement and driver education, which has since helped American motorists to achieve the best safety record in the world. With far more cars in use, there were fifteen hundred fewer traffic deaths in 1957, for example, than in 1941. Johnson credits much of this to a reduction in "exposure" by the elimination of crossings and intersections on throughways. On a mileage basis, traffic deaths have been cut in half since 1937.

The Automotive Council for War Production supported itself by dues of 1/100th of 1 percent of the net sales of war articles, which, with a discount of 10 per cent for prompt payment, would be 9 cents per $1,000; with, however, minimum dues of $50 for one year. There were 654 members, though some belonged for only a few months. One of the first and most important ACWP activities was a census of machine tools and similar equipment in all of the plants. This located and made available 198,000 pieces of equipment. It sponsored an industry-wide drive which turned up huge quantities of scrap metal.

The ACWP organized committees on tanks, propellers, artillery, ammunition, aircraft engines and other items, through which what experienced producers had learned was passed along to newer contractors. Later a manpower division was organized and information exchanged on worker morale, incentives, hiring of new workers, training and upgrading, safety and health, housing and transportation, personnel policies, and other phases of human relations.

As the program got under way, Romney conducted a series of regional meetings to explain the Council to all automotive concerns and enlist their support. The first was held April 7, 1942 in Detroit's Hotel Statler, the second at the Palmer House in Chicago the next day. The third was in the Cleveland Statler on April 14 and the fourth on April 16 in the Roosevelt at New York. The Council was the AMA for the duration of the war and occupied its New Center Building offices.

A large part of the industry's early war work had been given no notice and Romney had to spend a lot of time answering critics who felt that conversion to war work should have been faster. There were many reasons why it did not go faster. Back in 1940 the aircraft manufacturers were reluctant to share their business

George's father, Gaskell Romney,
photographed in Salt Lake City in 1917.

George Romney with his mother,
Anna Romney, in Mexico, 1908.

Brick house in which George Romney was born in Colonia Dublan, Chihuahua, pictured as
the family visited it in 1941 to celebrate his father's seventieth birthday. George holds his
nephew, Miles P. Romney, Jr., at right. In the group are Gaskell and Amy Romney,
Meryl Romney Ward, Miles P. and Janice Romney, also her mother, Mrs. Cahoon.

George Romney at age ten.

As knight and lady, the Romneys set of
to a Beaux Arts ball at the Willard Hote
in Washington in 1934. She made hi
costume from washrags and aluminum pain

Cast of the play *Bab*, as presented at the Salt Lake Theatre December 14, 1925
George Romney and Lenore LaFount are seated at right in front rov

Missionary Romney, "an earnest young man," preaching from the base of the Nelson Monument in London's Trafalgar Square in May, 1928.

An Automotive Council for War Production meeting on tanks. Left to right, George W. Mason, John Anderson, George Romney, Brig. Gen. Alfred R. Glancy and Chairman Alvan Macauley.

George W. Mason and
Charles Nash.

George W. Mason rides a tiny
motorcycle, one of many small
vehicles studied by Nash in
developing the Rambler and
Metropolitan.

Pinin Farina, dean of Italian
automobile designers, and
George W. Mason in
a Nash-Healey.

As new president of the Automobile Manufacturers Association, Romney welcomes the Ford Motor Company to membership. L. L. Colbert of Chrysler, Harlow Curtice of General Motors, and Romney greet Henry Ford II in 1956.

Roy Abernethy, George Romney and Elmer W. Bernitt with 1902 and 1959 Ramblers in front of the American Motors offices.

Ollie Atkins, Saturday Evening Post

George Romney and Louis E. Wolfson confer in Miami Beach on March 20, 1957.

Vice President Richard Nixon (left) and George Romney, President of American Motors Corporation and AMA, shown at the Annual National Automobile Show Dinner at Hotel Waldorf-Astoria in New York, December 6, 1956. The Vice President was the principal speaker.

Ollie Atkins, Saturday Evening Post

Chairman Romney presents report of the Citizens Advisory Committee on School Needs to Dr. Remus G. Robinson, president of the Detroit Board of Education, and Dr. Samuel M. Brownell, Detroit Superintendent of Schools.

United Press International

President David O. McKay of The Church of Latter-day Saints and George Romney, president of its Detroit Stake, in front of new Stake Tabernacle in Bloomfield Hills, Michigan, as the $700,000 structure was dedicated on April 26, 1959.

The George Romney family and sons-in-law pictured in 1959. Left to right, Lynn, Larry and Jody Keenan; George, Mitt and Lenore Romney; Jane and Bruce Robinson; Scott Romney.

with the automotive industry and Clarence C. Carlton, director
of the Automotive Committee for Air Defense, felt obliged to
pledge that when the war was over not one of the automobile
manufacturers would continue in the manufacture of aircraft.

The "Reuther Plan" was another subject of controversy. This
was a proposal first drawn up by Walter Reuther, the UAW
leader, in December, 1940. He argued that "500 Planes a Day"
could be produced by following his proposal. This called for
conversion of the automotive industry's "unused capacity" to war
work; pooling of the industry's manpower and equipment into a
single, co-ordinated organization; and management of this by a
board of nine, three representing government, three representing
management, and three representing labor.

As Knudsen's effort through the AMA was already started, the
Office of Production Management ignored the Reuther Plan when
it was presented at the time of its formulation. After Pearl Harbor and more than a year later, the CIO revived the plan in full-
page advertisements in Washington newspapers of January 3,
1942. An open letter demanded that the government consider it
and argued that in return for its no-strike pledge for the duration
of the war, labor should be given a voice in the management of
war plants. By this time there was no "unused capacity" in the
automobile plants, equipment was being pooled and industry
leaders like Charles E. Wilson of General Motors declared that such
a division of management responsibility would destroy the foundation of American industrial accomplishment. A committee was
named but its short-lived role was only advisory.

Though the Reuther Plan was never adopted, labor received
much recognition in the war effort. Donald Nelson's WPB suggested nationally plant labor-management committees to encourage suggestions from employees for saving material or speeding
war production. This idea originated in the Detroit Packard plant,
which by the end of the war produced 55,523 Rolls-Royce aircraft

engines, more than were turned out by all five British factories producing them. More than five thousand plants eventually had such committees. Labor also received recognition in the Detroit Victory Council.

On Sunday, June 20, 1943, a fist fight between a Negro and a white man on the bridge to Belle Isle touched off a race riot in Detroit. Within a few hours, thirty-four persons were killed, seven hundred injured and thirteen hundred persons arrested. To deal with the tensions indirectly responsible for the riot and other community war problems, Romney and Victor Reuther, brother of the proposer of the plan, organized the Detroit Victory Council. It was composed of representatives of companies in the Automotive Council, the UAW, professional groups, schools, retailers and other elements in the community. Dr. William Stirton, a local educator, headed the Council. He later became a university of Michigan vice president and a director of American Motors. One of the Council members was Edward Cushman, then Michigan director for the War Manpower Commission and later an American Motors vice president.

"Detroit's problems," said Cushman in a formal statement at the time, "should be solved in Detroit by Detroiters."

With an initial eighty thousand dollars from the War Council of the Community Chest, the Victory Council undertook to do this. Romney and Victor Reuther went together to Washington and jointly persuaded Paul McNutt not to place the industry under rigid manpower controls, while a war-worker training program, directed by Dr. Stirton and already under way, was tremendously expanded. This eventually trained 337,000 men and women, including a whole burlesque troupe from a local theater, for war production. Classes in welding were conducted around the clock, seven days a week.

To free mothers for war work, the Council set up child care centers in Sunday school auditoriums hitherto idle during the

week. The Council dealt with housing shortages, organized car
pools, extended bus routes forty miles to outlying war plants and
even changed the hours of Detroit markets and stores to accom-
modate late-working war-plant employees.

During the war, Romney made countless speeches, debated war
problems with Richard T. Frankensteen and other labor leaders,
and disputed Walter Reuther's testimony before Senator James
M. Mead's War Investigating Committee when it held hearings
in Detroit. At the conclusion of one of these sessions on a Saturday, it was proposed to continue on Sunday. "I take my family
to church on Sunday," said Romney. Senator Mead set the next
session for Monday.

In his prepared statement to the committee, Romney urged decentralization of union power and "an end to the privileged status
of unions . . . and their exemption from basic laws" and analyzed,
with detailed exhibits, scores of union disputes that had delayed
war production in Detroit.[4]

"We believe no international industrial union organization
should have," he said, "any more authority to direct and control
the collective bargaining of unions representing employees of
separate employers than the Automotive Council has to direct and
control the position of its member companies. Neither an international union nor a national trade association is as well qualified
. . . as the particular union and employer directly concerned. These
are the people who know the specific problems and conditions
firsthand." It was a theme to which he returned often in later
years.

Romney and Walter Reuther frequently exchanged harsh words
during these years but gradually developed great respect for each
other. They were similar in personal habits, sincerity and voluble
articulateness. "Ask Reuther what time it is," somebody once said,
"and he will tell you how to put together a watch." The same thing
could be said of Romney. He naturally was pleased later when

Reuther bought a Rambler as part of his unostentatious way of life.

Work was hard and hours long at the ACWP during the war but morale was high. If a new mailboy was hired, the general manager looked him up in the mailroom and said, "I'm George Romney." He arranged Christmas parties for children of employees and brought his own. If something had to be finished there was no question as to who stayed. Everybody volunteered. Romney inspired great loyalty. "I had heard the words 'Christian gentleman' all my life," recalled a veteran of those days, "but I didn't know what they meant until I worked with George Romney."

Thanks to the Automotive Council for War Production, America's automobile industry early achieved a mutual association and voluntary co-operation in programs that totalitarian Germany was still seeking after years of war. Members produced literally mountains of war products. In the final totaling, the industry produced all of the motorized units, some 3,250,000 in number; 80 per cent of all tanks and tank parts, 75 per cent of the aircraft engines, half the Diesel engines, and a third of the machine guns.

When victory was in sight, the Council turned to methods of speeding contract termination so as to clear plants promptly of government tools and materials. Ernest R. Breech, then president of Bendix Aviation Corporation and later executive vice president and chairman of Ford, headed the Council's contract termination committee. Its secretary was Romney's administrative assistant, Richard T. Purdy, who a decade later became treasurer of American Motors.

"We created motion pictures," recalls Romney of this activity. "We made talks. We created publicity, appeared before Congressional committees, did everything we could to bring about a realization of the need of finding some short cuts. Every day lost would be a day lost in getting people back to work." Permission was obtained for engineers and other technical people not required in armament production to prepare for resumption of car production. This was done so successfully that reconversion was swift in Detroit and gloomy predictions of many millions of unemployed at the end of the war proved baseless. Several companies were producing cars before the end of 1945.

The Automotive Council for War Production ended its existence on October 1, 1945. Exactly five years after General Knudsen's first appeal to the industry, President Macauley on the following October 15 presided in Detroit at a Victory Dinner celebrating its achievements. Lieutenant Generals Knudsen, James H. Doolittle and Levin H. Campbell were present along with Commodore Dixie Kiefer. Messages of congratulations came from Bernard Baruch, General H. H. Arnold and George C. Marshall and many others. In his book, *Arsenal of Democracy,* Donald M. Nelson credited the automotive industry with turning out more than a fifth of all production and doing "a good job" of it.[5] With some leftover funds Romney had the records of the Automotive Council of War Production carefully indexed and filed. They have since been studied many times by both historians and government officials concerned with keeping industrial mobilization plans up to date.

X

The Automotive Golden Jubilee

As the war ended, Romney proposed that the Automobile Manufacturers Association continue a high volume of co-operative activities and take a positive public stand on many problems. He felt the
industry made a mistake in not preventing dealers from over-
charging and forcing motorists to buy unwanted accessories during
the postwar car shortage. He believed the organization should work
for a new national labor policy that would decentralize union
power. But the member companies, especially General Motors and
Chrysler, were eager to get back to competition and the Association
reverted to its prewar form.

A proposal by Romney and his staff for a celebration in 1946 of
the fiftieth anniversary of the automobile industry with an Automotive Golden Jubilee, however, was approved with enthusiasm.[1]
When a local historian, George Washington Stark of the Detroit
News, pointed out that it also was the 150th anniversary of the first
raising of the American flag in Detroit by Colonel John F. Ham-
tramck, this also was celebrated.

General Knudsen was chairman of the industry committee and
Prentiss M. Brown, chairman of Detroit Edison and former United
States Senator, led the civic celebration. Romney was managing
director of the automobile part and Dr. William Stirton had the
same role on the civic side. Together they induced the Detroit

Common Council to appropriate $100,000 toward the celebration. William McGaughey, AMA public relations director, was publicity chairman and Alfred Reeves came from New York to direct an Antique Automobile Show and help with the historical lore.

In addition to publicizing the accomplishments of the automobile industry, the Jubilee had the aim of erasing scars of the race riot. "The objective," said Romney, "is to shift the focus of the national publicity spotlight from Detroit contention and strife to her great characters, accomplishments, contributions and co-operation." Dr. Stirton termed it "an educational undertaking" to call attention to areas of agreement among all segments of the community and to prepare a basis for "solution of our community problems."

There was little time for planning. The Detroit basis for the Jubilee rested on two dates, March 6, the fiftieth anniversary of Charles B. King driving the first car, one built by himself, in the city, and June 4, when Henry Ford half a century earlier completed and drove his first car there.[2] The first date had passed in 1946 before planning began but by ten weeks of day and night work, and enlistment of the help of hundreds of persons, Romney and his staff had a ten-day program ready for the second. The Ford company still was not an AMA member but co-operated.

President Truman couldn't come and there wasn't time for a commemorative postage stamp, though one later honored the trucking industry. Frank Sinatra arrived but refused to sing in return for a Nash car. A score of persons were slightly hurt in the collapse of a grandstand. The heaviest downpour of rain in thirty years dampened some events and forced a plane bringing James Melton to land at Toledo. He arrived in Detroit by bus late for a pageant in which he sang the leading role without rehearsal. But the Jubilee triumphed over its mishaps and proved a memorable event in Detroit history.

A sketch outlining an old and new car, a wheel and the path of a split atom was chosen as the symbol of the Jubilee. It was the work of Art Radebaugh, a local artist. Massive reproductions of this lined streets. Woodward Avenue was painted gold from Grand Circus Park to the City Hall and the special nontoxic paint was even applied to the hoofs of the police horses. "Woodward Avenue Dazzles in Coat of Gold," said a banner headline in the Detroit *Times*.[3] There was a golden ramp also along the four blocks of Washington Boulevard.

There Mary Grace Simescu, a twenty-two-year-old stenographer of Rumanian descent who had been chosen Jubilee Queen, on the evening of May 29 opened the event with atomic power by waving a wand of beryllium over a tube of boron. Two thousand tagged helium-filled balloons were released, with one traveling as far as Newport News, Virginia. Over the ramp paraded new cars carrying old-timers like Barney Oldfield and Tyrus Raymond Cobb and current celebrities such as Jane Pickens, Fred Waring, Art Linkletter, Lowell Thomas and Ed Wynn. Bands played and there was dancing in the streets.

Romney was master of ceremonies at a May 31 dinner honoring fourteen pioneers chosen for an Automotive Hall of Fame. Alfred P. Sloan and William C. Durant, General Motors greats, were ill but all others were present. They included J. Frank Duryea, credited with selling the first American-made automobile in 1896; Charles B. King, Henry Ford, Charles W. Nash, Ransom E. Olds, Barney Oldfield, Edgar Apperson and George Holley, the last a pioneer maker of carburetors. Also honored were two dealers, John Van Benschoten of Poughkeepsie, New York, and Charles S. Snyder of York, Pennsylvania, and two workers, John Zaugg of Cleveland, an employee half a century for the White Motor Company, and Frank Kwilinski, who had worked sixty years for Studebaker.

In answer to published criticism over omission of the Fisher brothers and others from the list, Romney explained those chosen had been selected because they made their contributions at the start of the fifty years being celebrated rather than later. They received Charles Clifton Awards, named for the late Pierce-Arrow executive who long headed AMA. These were twenty-inch aluminum statues symbolizing "the genius of man, his mind and his work." They were designed by the sculptor Avard Fairbanks and donated by the Aluminum Company of America.

General Knudsen presented the awards and, in a surprise arranged by Romney, received a special one himself in recognition of his wartime and Jubilee service. It was a moving event and the only time the old-timers were ever assembled. Many of them were to die in the next two years.

A million persons, the biggest crowd in the history of Detroit, next day braved unseasonable fifty-degree weather to watch a four-hour parade. In the march were ten thousand persons, one thousand vehicles, eighty floats and thirty bands. Wearing a four-carat diamond once owned by Diamond Jim Brady, James Melton drove a White Steamer from his old car collection. Among the ancient machines that rolled under their own power were a 1904 Ford, a 1902 Pierce-Arrow, a 1909 Rambler and a 1907 Packard that had been driven from Chicago. George C. Green won a grand prize with a 1904 one-cylinder "curved dash" Oldsmobile in which he and his wife had driven from Lambertville, New Jersey, to Detroit.

Trygve Lie, Secretary General of the United Nations, asked understanding of the aims of the UN at a Briggs Stadium rally which concluded the Jubilee on June 9. Victor G. Reuther and Frank X. Martel, labor leaders; General Knudsen, George W. Mason, then president of the AMA, and Chairman Brown all pleaded that the community spirit aroused in the previous ten days be kept alive.

"If we work together," said Mason, "there is nothing this community cannot do." Knudsen asked that "we bury our differences and bigotry and work for the betterment of all our people." Martel urged that petty differences be laid aside in a worth-while program of civic betterment. "If Detroit cannot find within itself the resources for building full employment, abundance and freedom," said Reuther, "no law passed in Washington can save us, nor any slogan." Brown spoke last. "This great industrial Detroit," he said, "since the war has been writhing in invisible chains, eager but uncertain, angry, impatient. The greatest job of production is just ahead and Detroit's opportunity for sound growth and expanding prosperity is at hand. This is the hour to unite, close ranks and march."

Lauritz Melchior, a Danish-American friend of Knudsen, and Dorothy Maynor, the Negro soprano, sang at the event with a massed choir of three thousand voices assembled from Catholic, Jewish, Negro and other Detroit music organizations. In conclusion an American Legion color guard raised an American flag on a tall pole in front of the choir in center field. The flag hung limply as it was pulled up but at the top, as the crowd roared, unfurled and rippled spiritedly in a sudden breeze. With all hearts beating faster, everybody sang the national anthem.[4]

Chairman Brown that evening entertained at dinner some of the people who had worked hardest on the Jubilee. All of the men at one table had "George" for the first name and "W" for a middle initial. They were George W. Romney, George W. Mason, George W. Carter, a committee chairman; and George W. Stark of the Detroit *News,* who reported the coincidence in his newspaper.

Less elaborate celebrations, usually bringing together automobile, tire and gasoline dealers, were held in scores of other cities. These resulted in interindustry committees on highway safety which proved enduring. The Detroit celebration, which cost only $375,000 and was partly self-liquidating, earned world-wide notice and enough newspaper clippings to fill a mountain of scrapbooks that eventually were presented to the Detroit Public Library.[5] It also started a revival of civic spirit. "Real reforms never come through mass production or mob emotionalism," wrote Malcolm Bingay in the *Free Press*. "But it is a good thing to have the whole city stirred up. Gets us all out of the rut and gets us to thinking of better things."

As a result of the feeling engendered by the Jubilee a long-discussed program of waterfront rehabilitation and Civic Center development became a reality. In a revival of a community fund idea which the city had pioneered after World War I and gradually abandoned, Detroit in 1949 formed the United Foundation to raise funds for a score of national and state agencies as well as local private hospitals and charities. These had been collecting three to four million dollars a year in Detroit by their own efforts but, with all the forces of the community working together in one gigantic campaign, soon were sharing contributions of more than fifteen million dollars a year. The Red Cross and several other organizations which usually conducted their own campaigns cooperated. Romney had a leading part in this and explained the plan in addresses in Akron, Ohio, and elsewhere. Soon two thousand cities had similar campaigns and were exchanging information through the United Community Funds and Councils of America.[6]

Henry Ford, most famous of all the automobile pioneers, died at his home on April 7, 1947, in a room lit by oil lamps and candles, a flood of the River Rouge having cut off electric power. A hundred thousand mourners filed past his bier at Greenfield Village the next day. Though Ford had never been a member of AMA, his company had joined the Automotive Council for War Production, and Ford executives many times had George Romney represent them in dealing with the government or the press. Romney reported his part in the mourning of the creator of the Model T in a letter to his father:

What would you say if the United Press called you unexpectedly from a deep sleep at 2 in the morning and asked you to make a statement for the industry on his passing? Every time I'd start to say something, the words would stick in my mouth because they seemed so inadequate.

I went to the funeral—in fact, we handled special tickets for industry executives and selected those to attend. Also, the idea of a pause in all the automotive plants throughout the nation and of everyone in Detroit and Michigan was our idea. He gave our industry its soul. His concepts of producing things everyone can buy will never die.

The floral tribute was stupendous. The tribute to him was short and simple. The Dean made four points: 1. His simple habits were exemplary; 2. His family life was ideal; 3. His charities were numerous but unpublicized; 4. He had a conviction of immortality.

Former Brigadier General Albert J. Browning, a native of Utah who had handled War Department purchasing, at this time was vice president in charge of purchasing for the Ford Motor Company. As both were from the West, had spent their boyhoods in Idaho and had known each other at intervals, Romney and Browning and their families became friends. When Browning died of a heart ailment a few months later, his widow, though not of the Mormon faith, asked George Romney to conduct the funeral for his friend. He did so at a suburban church crowded with Ford executives.

In the summer of 1947, George made his father a present of a new Nash car and Maurice Romney, eldest of the brothers, picked it up and drove it to Salt Lake City. Gaskell Romney at this time, in addition to his usual church duties, was chaplain of the House of Representatives of the Utah legislature of which his son, Charles, was a member.

President Truman named George Romney as a United States employer delegate to the Metal Trades Industry conference of the International Labor Office at Toledo, Ohio, in 1946. The International Labor Office is one of the few surviving activities of the League of Nations. After the session in Toledo, the hundred delegates from abroad visited Detroit. Giving his wife only one day's notice, Romney invited all of them home for tea. She stayed up all night making sandwiches. All arrived by bus at the same time but remained late and were voluble in their thanks for a glimpse of American family life.

The 1947 meeting of the organization was September 3 to 12 in Stockholm, Sweden. The Romneys crossed on the *Queen Mary*, taking food packages to some of the friends of George's missionary days. After the conference, they took a vacation on the Continent and also visited the British Isles. There they retraced his missionary travels and Lenore photographed him in Hyde Park and other spots where he had preached two decades earlier.

In Edinburgh, they met two young missionaries starting for the Mound to conduct an evening service. They invited Romney to come along. "Sure, I'll go," he said. When they failed to attract an audience, he got up and began to talk. Soon the audience was sizable. Mrs. Romney, wearing one of her New York Saks Fifth Avenue dresses, watched and listened from the edge of the crowd.

A distinguished-looking gentleman stopped and noticed her. "My word," he demanded, "what's a woman like you doing here this time of night?" Lenore gestured to the speaker and said: "Well, that's my husband up there."

They returned on the *Queen Elizabeth*. Depressed and concerned with what he had seen during their six weeks in Europe—food was still inadequate in Britain and many other countries—Romney on November 14, at the invitation of Senator Arthur H. Vandenberg, of Michigan, appeared before the Senate Foreign Relations Committee then starting hearings from which evolved the Economic Cooperation Administration program, popularly known as the Marshall Plan. Romney urged that the new government agency be partially directed and largely staffed by people from existing national and international relief organizations.

"It may be necessary in the early stages," he said, "to move primarily through our government and through their governments. But, as a long-range program, I cannot overemphasize my belief that this method will not provide the economic assistance most needed to revitalize European economies. It will not place them on a self-sustaining basis.... At the conference I attended and throughout Europe, businessmen, as well as government and labor representatives, rejected the basic concepts of competitive co-operative capitalism which has supplied the human vigor and vision on which our technological and production accomplishments and our unparalleled standards of living have been based. Even before the war Western Europe relied primarily on private monopolistic cartels. The difference between such private cartels and governmentally nationalized industries is slight indeed. If European nations are to become self-supporting in terms of twentieth-century industrialism, they need the American concept of competitive co-operative capitalism more than they need American dollars, materials and machines."

He urged that Congress require the new agency to stimulate and encourage American business and financial institutions to carry the burden of economic assistance abroad. "If the assistance is rendered primarily by our government to their governments," he said, "the charge will be that their governments have become satellites of America. It is time for America to realize that, regardless of how we render the assistance needed, we will be subjected to vicious, violent and immediate attack. The attack will undertake to distort and twist our motives and our methods. . . . Europeans need more knowledge about America. We cannot afford to make a mistake made repeatedly at home as well as abroad, namely, to overestimate the people's information and underestimate their intelligence. . . .

"Our record during peace and war establishes incontrovertibly that free labor, free management, and free capital in co-operation with free government can outproduce slave labor, shackled managements, and governmentally confiscated capital. Freedom and voluntary co-operation are our most valuable assets in assisting a sick world."

In its technical assistance and other activities, the Economic Cooperation Administration as headed by Paul Hoffman, on leave from Studebaker, carried out many of Romney's suggestions.

XI

Packard or Nash?

The achievements of the Automotive Council for War Production had made Romney one of the best-known trade association executives. The Automotive Golden Jubilee had made his name even more widely known. In the course of it, for example, International News had even carried around the world a dispatch under his by-line. As he was known to be chafing a bit at not being able to pursue larger programs at AMA, he began to receive suggestions or offers of jobs in many fields. He was proposed as a possibility for the National Association of Manufacturers, where an executive vice president was retiring. Nothing came of this. He was little interested and had an ill-wisher in John L. Lovett, manager of the Michigan Manufacturers Association, an affiliate of NAM. They had served together on the Detroit Area Labor-Management Committee during the war but differed on so many things that Lovett informed NAM that Romney should be the last choice for it. A more definite offer from an automobile parts company was declined.

One day in February of 1948, Romney called on Alvan Macauley of Packard. They had worked together almost daily during the war but Macauley had resigned as president of AMA in 1946 so the two had not seen each other in some time and Romney wanted to say hello. Macauley suddenly asked if he would consider joining

Packard as an executive and a member of the board of directors. Romney replied that he was honored and would certainly consider it. The next day Macauley had him see George Christopher, the coal miner's son who was then president of Packard, and they worked out the terms of the contract.

Two days later Packard offered to employ Romney as executive vice president at fifty thousand a year, with the promise that within two years he would succeed Christopher, who was eager to retire to his farm near Tipp City, Ohio. The offer was in writing, in the clear prose of Henry E. Bodman in which important Detroit legal documents had been phrased for half a century. The contract was drawn up and Hugh J. Ferry, vice president and secretary, was informed that "we are hiring George Romney."

Macauley's successor as president of AMA and Romney's boss was George W. Mason, president of Nash-Kelvinator. He was then vacationing in Bermuda. Romney telephoned him he was resigning from AMA to go with Packard.

"Now look, George," Mason spluttered through the phone. "Wait until I get back. I'd like to talk with you. Promise me you won't make any decision until I get back."

Romney agreed to wait. There were some things to consider about Packard. Wartime cost-plus business had not improved Packard's management. There was labor trouble. There were rumors of dissension among its elderly officers. His friend Macauley was about to retire.

On the other hand, Packard was a glamorous name in the automobile industry and beyond it. Its engines had roared to fame on land and sea, and in the air. The first man to drive his family across the United States had done so in a Packard. Its legendary twelve-cylinder "Twin Six" had been the favorite car of President Franklin D. Roosevelt, Czar Nicholas of Russia, and thousands of other motorists of distinction. Songs and poetry had been written about Packard cars and engines. Its slogan, "Ask the man who owns one," was world-famous. Packard had made Liberty Motors in World War I and PT boat engines and the Rolls-Royce Merlins for World War II.

It had come out of the war well heeled. It was one of the two publicly listed automobile companies without bank loans or other funded indebtedness, and was enjoying in 1948 the greatest percentage share of automobile sales in its history. Its earnings were its best since 1929. It had come through the depression while its alliterative rivals, Peerless and Pierce-Arrow had disappeared, the first into the beer business[1] and the latter into bankruptcy. On an original cash investment of $525,000, Packard had earned profits of $192,000,000 and paid out $121,250,000 in dividends.

When Mason got back, he offered Romney a job at Nash-Kelvinator. It was neither as high nor as definite as the Packard offer. He would come to work as Mason's assistant at thirty thousand a year. He would spend a year or longer if necessary to learn everything about the company. After that, Mason would see what he could do about a top executive job for him. Since making Nash-Kelvinator a long-term twenty-million-dollar loan in 1946, executives of the Prudential Insurance Company of America concerned with getting back their money had been urging Mason to find and designate a younger man as his successor to assure continuity of management. It was one of the unpleasant things that he avoided, but when Romney telephoned him in Bermuda he at once thought of the AMA manager as a possibility. Mason had known his war work and had seen a lot of him during the Jubilee.

Outwardly the two men had little in common except the name George. Mason was a huge and happy man. He dined well. He chain-smoked fine cigars. Although mentally sharp and surprisingly fast on his feet, he always looked as if he were relaxing. Romney was tense, lean, athletic, didn't smoke and skipped even tea and coffee. But both were hard workers and men of high principles. Both played golf and often with each other. They also shared a love for the outdoors. Mason fished and shot ducks but could not kill a larger animal. At his summer place on the Au Sable River near Grayling, Michigan, he once took in a stray fawn, gave her milk from a bottle, named her "Bambi" and kept her as a pet for twenty-one years.

Romney liked the Nash-Kelvinator executive and was impressed by the research work Mason showed him. Nash-Kelvinator was looking forward. It had mock-ups of new appliances and experimental models of small cars, some of them three-wheeled with engines in the rear. Mason had grown up with the automobile industry, and he knew exactly the things Romney didn't know about it.

The opportunity to prepare appealed to Romney. He realized there were many phases of the manufacture of automobiles that he had not been able to learn at AMA. At Packard, he would have to learn everything in two years and then step up to the helm. What if it should take more than two years? Nash-Kelvinator was the second-best profit-earner in the industry. And Mason was interested in working out a merger with some other independent. The Nash company had made an offer to Packard in 1929 and Mason another in 1948. If it went through, Romney might be working with both organizations.

At Mason's suggestion, Romney took a month to decide. He prayed hard and talked to the heads of other automobile companies. One he missed was Charles E. Wilson, General Motors president, then away, who later remarked that if he had known Romney was leaving AMA he would have liked to have him at General Motors. Arrangements were made for William J. Cronin, one of Romney's aides, to succeed him as managing director at AMA.

"It was clear," Romney explained later, "the decision would probably determine my last employment and vocational opportunity. The answer was definite. I knew I should take the least flattering offer."

The Romneys sold the Cadillac they had been driving and bought a Nash.

Nash-Kelvinator, of course, bore the name of Charles W. Nash, one of the pioneers honored during the Jubilee. As a boy of six, Nash was "bound out" by his parents to a farmer near Flint, Michigan. The 1870 court order said that Charles was to work until he was twenty-one when he would get two suits of clothes and one hundred dollars. When he was twelve, he ran away and got a job with a farmer near Grand Blanc at eight dollars a month. Three months later, he was offered twelve dollars a month on a farm near Mount Morris—enough to buy clothes and schoolbooks and put something aside for the future. At thirteen, Charles was working as a carpenter, returning to the farm for haying. He invested twenty-five dollars he had saved in ten sheep, which he "put out to double" with a farmer for three years, the farmer to get the wool. Five years later, young Charles owned eighty sheep.

At eighteen, Nash was running a portable gasoline engine with a threshing machine crew. Soon he and a neighboring farmer were in the hay-pressing business. Nash was twenty and running a hay presser when he met vivacious Jessie Halleck of Flint.

The two were married in April, 1884. Charles Nash was devoted to his wife and was to remain so through their long and close marriage. He gave up traveling with the threshing crew to stay with her and took a job as a farm foreman at three hundred dollars a year and the use of a cottage and garden plot. When Mrs. Nash fell ill in 1891, he moved to Flint where she could get better medical care. The move put him on the road to the automobile business.

His first job in town was stuffing upholstery at a dollar a day for the Flint Road Cart Company, a carriage and wagon manufacturer employing 150 men and the talents of J. Dallas Dort and W. C.

Durant, future automobile builders. Stuffing was easy work for an ex-farm worker, and Nash found time to learn other phases of the manufacturing operation. Dort liked his energy and in six months made him superintendent of the plant.

The older hands resented the rapid promotion. Their attitude plainly said: "What the hell does that farmer know about building wagons?" But Dort had judged his man well. Nash was friendly but firm in his dealings. Resentment gave way to admiration and respect as production increased.

The company flourished, but 1906 was to be its peak, and Nash sensed why. As sales fell off he cut overhead and looked for an opening in the horseless carriage business. The chance came in 1910, when he was forty-six years old, and it came through his old boss, W. C. Durant, who had just acquired Oldsmobile, Cadillac, Oakland and several other small automobile companies and was trying to weld them together with his Buick in an enterprise hopefully called General Motors. Remembering Nash's success with the cart company, he offered him the presidency of Buick.

Automobile manufacture was new, and mass production a mere word. Buick was a leader in the industry but its organization was loose, its production low, and its costs high. Nash extracted a modest profit from Buick in 1911. He put automatic starters in Buicks and added electric lights when few cars had them. Hearing that a man named Walter P. Chrysler, then works manager for the American Locomotive Company, had taken apart a car and reassembled it, Nash looked him up in Pittsburgh and invited him to Flint. Though Chrysler was earning eight thousand dollars a year and American Locomotive offered him twelve thousand to stay, parsimonious Nash hired him as works manager for Buick at six thousand a year. In 1913, Buick made a profit of $4,500,000 and Nash became president of General Motors, assuming direction of all the divisions while retaining the presidency of Buick. Chrysler became general manager of Buick, demanding and obtaining first $25,000 and then $50,000 a year.[2]

In 1916, Nash and James J. Storrow, chairman of the board, left General Motors in disagreement with Durant, who had regained control of the company. They invited Chrysler to join them in starting or buying another automobile firm. Durant, however, gave him $500,000 a year to stay as president of Buick and he did so until 1921, when he went into business for himself. Nash and Storrow, who was head of Lee, Higginson & Company, thought they were buying Packard in 1916 but the deal fell through. At that time, Henry B. Joy, president and principal stockholder of Packard, became so angry with his associates that he resigned, sold his stock and drove up and down in front of the Packard plant in a Cadillac honking the horn.

Nash and his backers instead paid five million dollars for the Thomas B. Jeffery Company of Kenosha, Wisconsin, and renamed it the Nash Motors Company on July 29, 1916. Nash, then fifty-two years old, was joined in Kenosha by several of his former General Motors colleagues. These included W. H. "Judge" Alford, a brilliant hunchback, who had been comptroller of GM, C. B. Warren, and James T. Wilson.[3]

Thomas B. Jeffery was an English-born inventor whose vehicles had made early automobile history. The company was then in volume production of the renowned "Quad" four-wheeled drive trucks, famous World War I vehicles. The year before it had advertised its swank Jeffery "Chesterfield" phaeton in one of the magazines with a daring picture of a woman driver smoking cigarettes. Its advertising manager, Edward S. "Ned" Jordan, was responsible for this. In 1916, he went into business for himself in Cleveland making the Jordan "Playboy" car and for it later wrote an even more famous advertisement titled, "Somewhere West of Laramie," commanding, "Step into the Playboy when the hour grows dull with things gone dead and stale."

Between 1902 and 1914, the Jeffery Company had made the name "Rambler" stand for an increasingly dramatic series of pioneer automobiles. Thomas B. Jeffery's first Rambler was a bicycle he built earlier in Chicago, with the clincher tire he invented which revolutionized the two-wheeled transportation business in the 1880's. In 1900, he and his son Charles bought a small bicycle plant in Kenosha for $65,000 and started making automobiles. For the 1900 International Exhibition in Chicago Charles hand-built a car which was the basis of the first Rambler car. In 1902, they were ready for the Chicago Auto Show with two Ramblers, priced at $750 and $825. They made a hit. The Jefferys sold fifteen hundred the first year, making the Rambler the second mass-produced car after Oldsmobile. Early Ramblers may be seen at the Henry Ford Museum, the Chicago Historical Society and Horn's Cars of Yesterday, Sarasota, Florida.

Customers loved the open runabout, with tiller steering, developing twelve horsepower from a single-cylinder engine, and its higher-priced companion boasting the luxuries of headlamps and top. "It is truly a wonderful piece of mechanism," a Lima, Ohio, owner wrote the makers. "It starts immediately, runs like a jackrabbit and stops only at our will."

In 1904, the Jefferys followed up their success with a two-cylinder model featuring wicker picnic baskets on the sides at $1,350. In 1909 it was the first American car to come with a spare wheel complete with tire. In 1910, the Rambler had grown into a limousine carrying five passengers and commanding a price of $3,500. The interior was finished in Bedford cord. It was electrically lighted and had mahogany ceiling and sides, speaking tube, mirror, clock, cigar case and broom holder. President William Howard Taft was photographed riding in a Rambler. Luxury was in style in those days, and cars were for the luxury trade. They were also the object of derision. Farm folk around Kenosha enjoyed watching horses pull the Ramblers made during the winter through the deep Wisconsin snow to storage against spring sale.

In 1910, Thomas B. Jeffery died while abroad with his wife, and his heirs carried on the business. To honor the founder, they replaced the name Rambler with Jeffery. This proved a mistake. The plant was making 96 per cent of its parts but began to slip. Charles T. Jeffery, a son who was actively in charge, was aboard the *Lusitania* when she was torpedoed and was so shaken by the experience that he welcomed the chance to sell out to Nash.[4]

Charles Nash lost no time getting his own name on the Kenosha product. The first Nash made its bow in the fall of 1917 with a new six-cylinder valve-in-head engine. In 1918 his company built more trucks than any other firm. Car and truck production rose to a total of 31,000 units in 1919. Nash invested his earnings in a half-interest in the Seaman Body Corporation of Milwaukee, originally a fine furniture manufacturer dating back to 1846. William S. Seaman had developed a soundproof telephone booth in 1887 which adorned public places throughout the world. Since 1909 Seaman had made bodies for Rambler, Moline, Velie, Dorris, Kissel, F.A.L. (built in Chicago by Fauntleroy, Averill and Lowe), and winter tops for Ford and Cadillac, but had concentrated on Nash when production soared in 1917.

In 1920, Nash opened a second assembly plant in Milwaukee on the site of the present American Motors parts and service plant. In 1924, he bought the Racine plant of the old Mitchell Motor Car Company and acquired the name and equipment of the LaFayette Motors Corporation, which he had served as president for three years. He started building the Ajax car in the Racine plant in 1925, but the name was changed to the Nash "Light Six" in mid-1926. By that year, there were twenty-four Nash models on the market and 135,500 cars were sold. The high point was 1928, when Nash sold 138,000 cars. During its first years, Nash Motors carried through to net profit a bigger share of its sales dollar than any other automobile manufacturer.

Nash made a hundred million dollars for himself and his backers out of the enterprise in seven years. "There was nothing to the Jeffery outfit," Storrow once said. "Nash was everything."[5] Though E. H. McCarty became president and Nash chairman of the board in 1930, the latter retained an active hand in direction of the company. He had the temperament for depression management. He built only 17,600 cars in 1932. To boost sagging sales, he brought out the low-priced LaFayette line in 1934, with a five-passenger two-door sedan at $645 and later a racy two-passenger coupé at $580, but he held to the proud Nash motto, "Built up to a standard, not down to a price." At the same time he introduced a "bed" car in which the seats could fold flat for sleeping. This helped bring sales to 36,000 in 1936. A Federal Trade Commission study of Nash Motors' figures through this year credited it with a ratio of profit to sales unequaled by General Motors or any other company in the automobile field.[6]

By this time Nash was seventy-two years old and eager to retire to California. He consulted his old friend and former employee, Walter P. Chrysler, then head of Chrysler Corporation. Chrysler was not interested in more mergers or purchases and suggested that Nash consider as a successor George W. Mason, a former Chrysler works manager, then doing well as president of the Kelvinator Corporation in Detroit. Nash did so.

XII

Mason and Kelvinator

Nash, as did Romney a decade later, found Mason to be a manufacturing genius despite his 260-pound bulk and his few words—and these frequently mumbled through a cigar. When Nash approached him, Mason had behind him forty-five interesting years, most of them spent tinkering with motorcycles and automobiles.

Born in 1891 on a North Dakota farm, Mason was enthusiastic even as a boy about anything that ran on wheels. His first love was the motorcycle, and his early romance with it contributed to his adult passion for small vehicles. Through a series of shrewd trades beginning with a jackknife, young Mason acquired his first motorcycle. He raced it on dirt tracks near Valley City, North Dakota, and at sixteen was a distributor of motorcycles with a tire-vulcanizing business on the side. In his spare time, he helped the mechanic in the local Maxwell dealer's garage, earning principally experience. Eventually the dealer hired him to demonstrate cars and teach new owners to drive.

"I drove a car for the first time in 1906," he once recalled in an address to the Automobile Old Timers.[1] "It was a two-cylinder, ten-horsepower Maxwell. My first motorcycle was simply an E. R. Thomas engine mounted on a Columbia bicycle for which I paid fifteen dollars secondhand. The second motorcycle was a Holly made in Bradford, Pennsylvania. I bought this for twenty-five dollars from a jeweler who had taken it apart and couldn't put it together. My third was a Mitchell made in Racine, Wisconsin. I purchased it in 1907 from a farm hand who had come to Valley City and had been caught in a snowstorm and couldn't get back home with it."

In 1909, Mason entered the University of Michigan. He took three years of mechanical engineering and a year of business administration. During his college years he helped his father distribute the Briggs-Detroiter automobile in his home town, Valley City. Young Mason would sell enough cars during the summer sales season to make the quota for the year, and pay for his schooling.

When he was graduated in 1913, Mason went to work for Studebaker. The next year he was working on layout and production for Dodge Brothers. He moved around restlessly in the industry, getting new experience at each stop. He spent the year 1915 as purchasing agent for the American Auto Trimming Company in Detroit. Next year he was in Waukegan, Illinois, learning how to process leather seat trim with the Wilder Tanning Company, a Dodge affiliate. When World War I came, U.S. Ordnance assigned him to the Rock Island Arsenal as a civilian specialist. After the war, the Irving National Bank put him in charge of business extension services in New York.

In 1921, Walter P. Chrysler brought him back to the automobile industry as general works manager of the Maxwell-Chalmers Company, which in 1924 became the Chrysler Corporation. As chief of all Chrysler manufacturing, Mason had an important hand in producing the first Chrysler car, which put the company into the front ranks of automobile manufacturing. But in 1926 he left to help his old friend, William R. Wilson at Copeland Products, Inc., a little company trying to make mechanical refrigerators.

The home refrigerator was born in the automobile industry. The dream of mechanical refrigeration was attracting inventors in

Detroit even before World War I. In 1914, Edmund Copeland of Buick introduced Nathaniel B. Wales, a young inventor "with a potful of ideas," to Arnold H. Goss, a Buick man who had helped W. C. Durant organize General Motors. Goss was an inventor himself. He had developed an oil-refining process and held patents on automobile tire carriers and locks which give him a near monopoly in this field. He was also an enterpriser who owned a chain of Michigan drugstores and was on the lookout for investment opportunities. Goss, Copeland and Wales decided to try to build a refrigerator.

Copeland was one of several General Motors executives who looked for other activities when the cautious Storrow-Nash regime replaced Billy Durant's open-handed leadership. "I left Buick and GM," he later explained, "because there was no more excitement in the job."[2] Though Goss stayed on, he backed Copeland financially and continued to back him as he went through the long and costly search for improvements without which the mechanical refrigerator would not have been accepted in the home. Copeland is entitled to a great deal of credit for banishing the messy and often unhygienic icebox from the kitchen.

As the U.S. edged toward war, young Wales produced one experimental model after another, some of which were installed in Detroit residences. One went into the Murray W. Sales residence. When this prominent Detroit family suffered a widely-publicized food poisoning tragedy, the whole development was slowed, though deadly bacteria in ripe olives were responsible for the deaths. The early units were of the "remote" type, with the cooling unit installed in the purchaser's icebox, and the condensing mechanism in the basement. Goss formed the Electro-Automatic Refrigerating Company, Inc. in May, 1916 and on July 28 of that year renamed it the Kelvinator Company, in honor of Lord Kelvin.[3]

William Thomson, named by Queen Victoria as Baron Kelvin of Largs, Scotland, died there in 1907 leaving no heir to his title, but as the father of modern thermodynamics it is appropriate that his name lives on around the world through a refrigerator. Knighted and later raised to the peerage for his contributions to transatlantic telegraphy and his improvements to the mariner's compass, he was a universal nineteenth-century man of science who ranged easily from theoretical mathematics to practical invention. During his fifty-four years as professor of "natural philosophy" at Glasgow University he stated the second law of thermodynamics on the dissipation of energy in mathematical terms which make it the keystone of mechanical engineering. He also suggested the absolute temperature scale.

"When you can measure what you are speaking about, and express it in numbers, you know something about it," he once said, and the quotation is framed today on the wall of many a research laboratory. A philosopher who encouraged younger scientists, his name is a beacon to modern engineers. His statement, "I've thought of a better way," is cut in the archstone of the entrance to the American Motors headquarters building on Plymouth Road in Detroit.

The Kelvinator crew had to find a better way to seal the compressor shaft so that the refrigerant wouldn't leak, and to regulate temperature. They found both in 1918, the year engineers in the Delco battery and farm-lighting division of General Motors christened the refrigerator they were developing the Frigidaire. Grave problems of installation and service had to be overcome but by 1920, ten thousand electrical refrigerators were operating in American kitchens, most of them installed in the iceboxes householders already had on hand. Kelvinator had 80 per cent of the growing young market, but everyone wanted to get into it. Copeland stepped out to form the company for which George Mason deserted Chrysler.

With sheet steel becoming cheap and abundant in 1923, the infant industry developed rapidly. In 1927, General Electric threw its hat in the ring with the "Monitor Top" hermetically sealed unit. As so often happens, the pioneers were shaken out, and mergers were the order of the day. Late in 1925, Kelvinator acquired the Leonard Refrigerator Company of Grand Rapids, Michigan, oldest and largest builder of iceboxes and refrigerator cabinets, founded in 1881 when H. Leonard and Son launched the "cleanable" icebox. In 1926, Kelvinator bought the Nizer Corporation, a pioneer ice cream cabinet manufacturer, and built a new plant for the enlarged company on Plymouth Road in Detroit. But Goss had overreached himself financially.

For all its leadership of the infant industry, Kelvinator was in bad shape when Mason went to Copeland. In 1928, it owed $4,200,000, working capital had evaporated to $230,000 and it was staggering under a 1927 loss of $2,467,000. The new acquisitions didn't fit together. Production pipelines were clogged. When Walter P. Chrysler looked the company over, possibly with an eye to acquiring it, he advised them to hire George Mason away from Copeland to untangle the production jam. Mason took over Kelvinator as president.

He was a natural for the job. He improved tooling and gauging, cut scrap losses. He showed Kelvinator engineers how to solder tubes of refrigerants to a plate under the ice-cube tray, which produced ice in less than an hour. He improved design and styling as he went along. "That handle is too long," he would sputter, or "This damned vegetable box is too narrow; it won't hold enough to feed a bird." These obviously were observations of a man who liked to eat and drink.

With product flowing, Kelvinator moved ahead. The depression may have slowed acceptance of the mechanical refrigerator but industry sales rose every year, proving that consumers can always find money for an undeniable benefit. Mason showed off the obvious advantages of the mechanical icebox with imaginative advertising. He once hired a meteorologist to forecast a hot spell far enough ahead to time an advertising campaign just before the thermometer shot up into the nineties. Competitors fumed that "that man Mason can even plan the weather."

No one was sure, at first, who should sell electric refrigerators or how the big ticket products should be financed. Kelvinator built quick volume early by selling through the electric light companies, who welcomed the new current users as load builders and were in a position to collect installments from customers on the monthly light bill. Metered pay-as-you-use plans, under which a housewife inserted a quarter a day to keep her refrigerator going, were inaugurated.

When refrigerator brands multiplied, however, utility companies could no longer undertake to distribute them. General Electric and Westinghouse had a distribution system to which refrigerators could be added. Frigidaire had the Delco distributing system. Kelvinator had to build its own through independent electrical supply houses. Since the refrigerators cost a lot of money, Kelvinator formed the Refrigeration Discount Corporation to finance dealer displays and stock. Redisco, Inc. soon expanded into the financing of customer installment paper, an innovation which widened the market and provided Kelvinator with an additional source of income which has steadied its profits ever since. Kelvinator was the first appliance manufacturer to own its own consumer financing company, providing special credit facilities for promotional sales plans.

The fame of the box that kept food cold spread beyond American borders. In 1925, Kelvinator shipped cabinets and condensers for twelve refrigerators to Shanghai, where John Stevens, son of a builder of the Great Northern Railway and the Panama Canal, assembled them for sale presumably to the old China hands. In 1926, a British Kelvinator company was formed to assemble refrigerators for the English market from parts made in Detroit, and in 1928 an Australian distributor was licensed to assemble Kelvinators.

Licensees were operating in Australia, New Zealand and Argentina before World War II and the currency restrictions which made license of local manufacturers a popular way for American manufacturers to do business overseas. The plan saved freight and allowed local dealers to vary the boxes to suit local taste, but it also won lasting good will for Kelvinator among foreign governments and businessmen.

In 1936, Kelvinator was selling 250,000 refrigerators, four times as many as in 1927. During his eight years as president, Mason had turned a million-dollar loss into a million-dollar profit and wiped out the debt. Both Mason and Kelvinator impressed seventy-two-year-old talent-hunting Charles Nash, but he really wanted only the man. Mason refused to leave Kelvinator but was not averse to a merger with thrifty Nash, having $22,774,000 in cash reserves to offer despite the depression. After long negotiations the companies were merged on January 4, 1937 as the Nash-Kelvinator Corporation. It was a marriage of strength, combining $55,000,000 of assets. Both refrigerators and cars were in the black at a time when many companies were faltering. Detroiters predicted Nash cars with ice-cube trays and Kelvinators with four-wheel brakes and George Mason, who was president of the new company, gleefully repeated the jokes. Harold G. Perkins, Kelvinator vice president, and Howard A. Lewis, Kelvinator treasurer, had the same titles with Nash-Kelvinator, and the latter later became a vice president.[4]

Nash was chairman of the board but, except for appearances such as at the Golden Jubilee, spent most of his time in Beverly Hills, California, where he long had maintained a winter home. His wife died there in 1947 and Nash a year later on June 6, 1948. He was eighty-four and left an estate that was first appraised at $43,183,624, including 62,900 shares of Nash-Kelvinator common stock. State and federal taxes, however, cut the estate to about $9,000,000.

The Nash operation Mason took over was putting out far fewer cars than in its 1928 heyday, but it was lean and sound. Mason put his designers to work on a new low-priced car that would compete in the Big Three volume market. They worked four years and spent $7,500,000 in tools and dies. In 1940 it was ready—the Nash "600," forerunner of today's compact Rambler. Although standard-sized, the new car was hundreds of pounds lighter than competitive cars and was designed to go six hundred miles on a twenty-gallon tank of gasoline. But the unique feature was its single-unit body construction. This is a single, all-welded unit that is stronger, lighter and more durable than the conventional bolted-together body and chassis. It is the *monocoque* principle used in aircraft design and in lightweight, streamlined trains. Nash collaborated with the Budd Company in adapting the construction principle to passenger cars. The "600" drove sales up to 89,574 in 1941 and Nash rolled from fourth place among the "independents" to second place behind Studebaker.

Meanwhile, there was trouble in the refrigerator business. In 1938, sales dropped sharply and Kelvinator's share of the market fell to 8 per cent. Competition was keener, and Frigidaire and General Electric were putting more money into their distribution setups. Mail-order houses like Sears-Roebuck were able to cut prices.

Mason moved fast to meet the challenge. In 1938, for instance, he personally rang doorbells in Lincoln, Nebraska, test town for a "National Salesmen's Crusade," letting newsmen pick the addresses. In six days he and his flying squadron sold 71 units and compiled a list of 234 hot prospects. Mason cut the sprawling Kelvinator line to six models and the two most popular sizes, six and eight cubic feet, and was able to announce retail price reductions of thirty to sixty dollars in 1940, removing the "price umbrella" over Sears Roebuck and Montgomery Ward. He streamlined distribution by weeding out dealers and organizing factory-owned "zones" to wholesale in the key markets. In 1940, Kelvinator was selling

149

11.3 per cent of the market, and in 1941, 16.7 per cent, their best slice since 1924.

Mason knew good men and could get them. One of Romney's reasons for choosing Nash-Kelvinator was the caliber of Mason's associates. He hired several men from Frigidaire. Two of these, W. F. Armstrong and Frank Pierce, returned to General Motors as vice presidents and the latter, before his death in a plane crash, also headed Ford's Dearborn Motors. Charles T. Lawson, previously in the same post with Frigidaire, became Kelvinator's household sales manager in 1939, a vice president in 1943 and, before retiring fourteen years later, headed the company's appliance business.

In 1941, Mason also hired a trio of Ford men forced out there when Harry Bennett and Henry Ford took over as Ford's son, Edsel, died of cancer. One was Albert M. Wibel, who had purchased more material for private industry than any other man. Wibel cannily kept Nash-Kelvinator supplied with steel during shortages and bargained so shrewdly for North American Aircraft's El Segundo plant in California that the company made a $2,500,000 profit when it was sold less than ten years later. Henry Clay Doss, Ford sales manager, became Nash sales vice president and Fred Black, Ford advertising manager, became Nash-Kelvinator public relations director.[5]

War froze Kelvinator's comeback, putting the industry to work on equipment for preserving whole blood and penicillin, and even the cold treatment of metals. The Kenosha automobile plant made Pratt & Whitney two-stage supercharged aircraft engines for Corsairs and Hellcats and other Nash-Kelvinator facilities were turning out parts for jeeps, tanks, trucks, ships, submarines and hydromatic propellers for twenty-three types of aircraft, including Flying Fortresses and Lancaster bombers. Nash-Kelvinator mass-produced R-6 Sikorsky helicopters.

Wartime sales soared, but profits dropped. In 1944, Nash-Kelvinator reported only $3,000,000 profits on $274,436,000 sales, reflecting, as Mason put it, "the obligation to make profit on war work subordinate to quality, volume and cost to the Government." Stockholders didn't worry. And he had $35,000,000 working capital to reconvert. He figured he could sell 250,000 cars a year and a million Kelvinators.[6]

Mason got civilian automobiles rolling faster than any other company. Kenosha was turning them out in October, 1945, and by the end of 1946, more than 100,000 had been eagerly bought. He acquired two hundred acres of rolling land near Burlington to prove out the new postwar cars. The next year George Mason personally piloted a Nash Ambassador as the pace car in the five-hundred-mile Memorial Day Race at Indianapolis.

Mason used a private plane to keep up with his crowded life. He flew frequently between Detroit, Kenosha, and Milwaukee and also to fishing spots. He was an ardent sportsman, a duck hunter and a founder and director of Ducks, Unlimited, a group of business leaders interested in conservation, and a skillful fly caster in spite of his unathletic appearance. In his later years he mellowed considerably.

One factor in this was his growing friendship with George Romney. Another was an article titled "It Is Later Than You Think," published by *Reader's Digest* in November, 1946. In this the late Dr. Frederic Morris Loomis urged busy people to take time to enjoy themselves and to perform kindnesses. Mason was so moved by the article that he gave away hundreds of autographed copies of the book, *In a Chinese Garden,* from which it had been extracted. He worked with the Boy Scouts, served as director of Detroit's United Foundation and Path-Finding Guide Dogs, Inc. and sponsored a "coffee lift" for Lutheran Churches in Germany. He was devoted to the University of Michigan and helped launch its multimillion-dollar Phoenix Project for the peacetime uses of atomic power. He recorded the reminiscenses of his father-in-law, Donald A. Johnston, one of the four men who founded Kiwanis International in 1915 in Detroit.

Mason had two weaknesses. He was inarticulate and he avoided anything unpleasant as long as possible. "He wasn't articulate and he didn't try to be," Romney once analyzed Mason. "I don't think he quite understood the importance of having everybody understand the basic concepts we were trying to sell. There was a certain reluctance to spell out our product advantages in terms that might detract from the product concepts of our competitors. He was reluctant to hurt anybody. He could let people do more things to him unjustly and still love them more than any man I ever knew. He avoided a dispute. He couldn't go to a funeral. He couldn't go to a wedding. He was easily moved to tears."

George Mason, for example, did not hear General Douglas MacArthur's "old soldiers never die" address to Congress but burst into tears when Romney told him about it later.

XIII

Educating an Executive

George Romney reported for work at Nash-Kelvinator on April Fool's Day, 1948, at eight o'clock sharp and was given a third-floor office formerly occupied by a public relations man. Nobody was certain why he was there but to Fred Black, the former Ford advertising man, it was apparent that Mason had chosen his successor. For one thing, Romney was getting a rug. As it was unrolled, Black said: "This is the man." But the newcomer was not aloof. Starting with his next-door neighbor, he introduced himself with a smile and a friendly "What do they call you?"

He certainly didn't act like an heir apparent. His first job was to put on overalls and take the training course for service men in the Milwaukee plant. He took cars apart to see how they were put together. He came to work in work clothes with the men, used their washroom, and sat down with each foreman in turn to learn what he was doing. At night he studied books on automobile engineering and design and styling.

One day he noticed workers tacking upholstery to the seat frame and holding the tacks in their mouths to spit out as needed. Reminded of his shingling and lathing days, Romney took a mouthful of nails and amazed the workmen by spitting them out like a practiced expert. Upholstering has since been improved to eliminate this process.

Romney studied his way through every square foot of the company's domestic floor space. "I now have a pretty good working knowledge of how refrigerators, electric ranges, home freezers, water coolers, ice cream cabinets are designed, engineered, and built," he wrote in the "Dear Folks" family newsletter of December 20, 1948. "After spending a little time at one of our local steel mills to become well acquainted with the processes of steel production, I am going to dig into Nash engineering and research. I will then have covered all the operating phases and will be ready to get the policy and administrative picture."

The "policy and administrative picture" proved tough going. Romney was discovering all sorts of things that he thought should be changed, but he had no authority to change them. Mason was running a one-man show, just as Henry Ford had done. "Mason could do it because he had grown up with it," Romney later recalled. "It had built around him. But it created quite a few problems."

Men up and down the line seized the opportunity to tell George Romney what was on their minds. Department heads told him how they were handicapped because they didn't know what related departments were doing. A man who had been a foreman for twelve years told him how he met his plant manager for the first time at an outside function. Plant labor relations directors didn't know whether there was a labor relations policy or not. Foremen beefed that requests on drinking fountains and toilets they had been denied were granted when the union asked for them. New employees weren't being told anything about the company. Some foremen didn't even ask their names.

The lax labor standards were hurting. Romney discovered that Kelvinator warranty payments for defective parts had risen sharply. At the last minute the interior color of the cars had to be changed because of lack of co-ordination between styling, production and sales people. No one was exactly sure how to get approval on a new car model. Sales and advertising people complained that Nash-Kelvinator wasn't doing anything to establish itself with consumers as a company with a personality.

Romney used his talents of persuasion. He would talk a problem through with the man on the spot and tell him what he thought was wrong before he told Mason. It was almost a year before Mason gave him decisions to make, and then he might not pass down word that Romney was supposed to settle the matter. One of the first was the paint colors for the 1950 model. Another was a new ornament for the Nash hood. President Mason asked Romney to have George Petty, creator of the famous *Esquire* girl, design a new female figure for this purpose. Petty's first efforts were entirely too voluptuous for Mason's tastes but after several shrinkings of the metal maiden's attractions a new ornament was evolved. She adorned the cars for three years.

When he could wait no longer, Romney turned his talent for persuasion on Mason. On February 8, 1949, before he had been with the company a year, he submitted a well-documented series of recommendations for improving the organization with specific action steps for each suggestion. Most of the suggestions were intended to improve communications: weekly exchanges of information among executives, a plan for industrial relations, weekly Kelvinator quality meetings, a procedure for new model decisions, a public relations plan.

He also pointed out that Kelvinator's competitors in the compressor business were back to prewar labor efficiency and the company couldn't afford to lag behind.

Nothing much happened, but Mason began tossing odd jobs to Romney. In the fall, Romney was invited to serve as employer delegate at the Metal Trades Committee meetings of the International Labor Organization in Geneva, the meetings he had attended when he was with AMA. In New York to get his plane for Europe he met Mason who was returning from a trip abroad.

"The most beautiful cars at the Paris automobile show were designed by an Italian named Farina," Mason told him. "I don't know which one. There are two brothers. Go down to Turin and get that man to design cars for us."

Farina designed cars for Fiat (the name is derived from the initials of Fabbrica Italiana Automobili Torino, Italy's biggest industrial enterprise). Romney had helped show Vittorio Valletta, president of Fiat, around Nash-Kelvinator's Wisconsin plants when he visited America in 1948, and he wired Valletta for help in locating the designer who had impressed Mason. Valletta had helped turn the Italian tide against Communism by giving Fiat workers model social benefits and staunchly resisting Red-led strikes and he admired America. He knew at once that Mason meant Pinin Farina, the dean of the imaginative Italian *carrozzerias,* or coach designers, and builders of one-of-a-kind fine cars. Cars designed by Pininfarina, his brand name, carry instant prestige among automobile aesthetes.

Romney rushed down to Turin to sign up the independent Italian maestro, son of a coach builder and heir to a long artistic tradition. With the help of Enrico Minola, Fiat sales manager, Romney tried to explain how cars were built at Nash. Square-faced Pinin Farina looks like a sturdy Italian peasant. American cars, he once said, are built to ride in, not to drive. He said he would think about designing for Nash. Romney pushed for an agreement. His schedule gave him only two days to make the deal. Farina wanted to think it over.

"They don't do it this way in America," Minola explained to his countryman. "They make up their minds."

Farina wondered if Nash would give him a car to drive when he came to America. Assured that he would have a Nash for his personal use on every visit, he signed. Romney got back to Detroit just in time for Thanksgiving dinner, with Farina's signed agreement to help build prototypes and to advise Nash on an exclusive basis. The Italian eased Nash out of building dependable conservative-styled cars. One of his suggestions, since standard design for all American cars, was to widen the cowl opening for the heater by leaving a vent all across the front of the car under the windshield instead of a narrow raised section. Farina continued to advise American Motors and, released from his exclusive agreement, other companies as well.

The 1949 trip gave Romney a chance to see how European businessmen club together to hold up prices. At the conference it was a real battle to persuade the employer delegates to agree to a statement of principles containing the concepts of economic freedom as we understand them in this country. He single-handedly talked them into such a statement, however, and handed out reprints of a *Reader's Digest* article by Frank Taylor, "Competition Is So Vulgar," attacking British cartel methods.[1]

As he worked more closely with Mason, Romney caught the engineer's product philosophy. For twenty years, Mason had dreamed of a small, lightweight passenger car that would provide minimum-cost transportation both in original investment and cents-per-mile operating costs. It was the logical extension of Henry Ford's vision of transportation for all, but Mason was not able to explain it to others, and the industry was moving toward bigger and flashier vehicles.

An engineer, Mason expressed his dream in metal instead of words. The experimental three-wheelers he had shown Romney in 1948 had been built up to a four-wheel automobile without raising the calculated retail price over a thousand dollars. Mason hoped to keep the price down by buying transmissions and components from veteran small-car makers in Italy, Britain or France. The economical, functional small car fitted Romney's heritage of unostentatious service. But Romney, Jack Timpy and Meade Moore, a Nash engineer, were the only ones in the company who shared Mason's enthusiasm. When Mason decided to test his idea on the public by showing them a prototype, he put Romney, the man with the words, in charge of the unprecedented presentation.

In 1950, the Nash Experimental International, known as the N.X.I., was unveiled to special audiences in cities from New York to San Francisco.[2] At the same time, a quarter-million other Americans were asked to study pictures of the car and answer a questionnaire about it. They saw a well-proportioned car weighing 1,350 pounds or two-thirds a standard-weight car, with an 84-inch wheel base which seated two passengers comfortably and had adequate luggage space. Its 36-horsepower engine could drive it 60 to 70 miles an hour and yielded 35 to 50 miles per gallon of gas. One of the things the preview jury liked was the designer's sparing hand with "brightwork" trim.

In spite of favorable response, the little N.X.I. was a casualty of galloping inflation. When new taxes, shipping costs, dealer markups and other costs were brought up to date, it was obvious that the N.X.I. couldn't be sold for the price Mason had intended. Its best features were saved, however, for the Metropolitan, an 85-inch wheel-base car later built in England for American Motors. A top Nash executive unsympathetically called the Metropolitan a "puddle jumper." But Mason persisted in seeing the advantages of compact construction.

Not all product ideas generated by Mason's high-voltage mind were successful. A unique model in the 1949 Nash line featured individual "chairs" in the rear-passenger compartment. Also, Mason thought, a wide armrest between the seats would be ideal for gin rummy fans on long trips. The public thought less of this idea than did Mason. It was dropped after one year. Likewise, the "closed-in" front wheels of Nash cars in the early fifties were viewed with dim enthusiasm by owners. They made wheel changing difficult and restricted the turning radius. Mason held doggedly to his theory that the enclosed wheels were essential to the car's basic styling.

Economical air conditioning for cars was a Mason ambition that fitted in neatly with Nash-Kelvinator's product spread. The portly Mason was miserable in hot-weather driving, and saw no reason why the comforts of air-conditioned cars could not be provided motorists at lower price. Units offered by other manufacturers were huge, bulky contrivances that filled virtually all trunk space in the car. Price was upward of six hundred dollars, far beyond the means of average buyers. Mason reasoned the air-conditioning unit could be combined with the car heater and placed up front for greater efficiency. His engineers were assigned the project. The result was an all-season air-conditioning unit that cools in summer and heats in winter. The price with heater was $395, well within the range of hundreds of Nash buyers. The same combination in a Rambler cost $345.

Romney was Mason's right-hand man in launching the smaller 1950 Nash which was to be the turning point of the company. Mason had spent more than twenty million dollars developing it. Its single-unit construction, pioneered in the 1941 Nash "600," saved several feet of length without sacrificing passenger capacity. It ran more than thirty miles to a gallon of gas, leading the industry in operating economy. The convertible carried a factory-delivered price of eighteen hundred dollars, with such extras as heater, radio, directional signals, clock, foam cushions, and an electrically operated top thrown in.

So radical a departure deserved a special name. Romney proposed "Diplomat" in keeping with the sister Ambassador but his public relations people urged "Rambler," from the company's early history, and a poll of executives overwhelmingly favored the old name. "Rambler" was resurrected and proved a happy one even for customers too young to remember the splash created by the sturdy Rambler the Jefferys, father and son, produced between 1902 and 1914.

But emphasis continued on bigger automobiles. Nash sold a

record 190,000 cars in 1950 but only 15,577 Ramblers were registered. But Rambler sales rose to 52,851 next year, though total car sales of the company dropped to 162,000. In 1951, Mason brought out the Nash-Healey, a sleek two-passenger speedster with foreign body which was the first American sports car in thirty years. "Our business is terrific," Romney wrote his father. "We can't keep up with demand. Our new Rambler is creating a sensation within the industry and you mark my word, before too many years have passed, General Motors, Ford or Chrysler, if not all three, will be producing cars about the same size."[3]

Always optimistic and appreciative of his associates, Romney said little in his family letters about the internal organization of Nash-Kelvinator or his own ambiguous role. "I am just beginning to reach the point where I have enough background on the company's policy, program, production, plants and personnel so that I feel as much at home as I did over at the A.M.A.," he wrote in the spring of 1950. "Breaking away from old activities, organizations and associates is always a real undertaking, as our family should know as a result of all the moving we did after we left Mexico. It's probably a good thing I had that experience because it has made the jumps from Washington to Detroit and from one job to another a lot easier." Mason was leaning on Romney more openly and regularized his role with the title of vice president.

The promotion only increased Romney's determination to do something about the appalling internal disorganization of Nash-Kelvinator at upper as well as lower levels. There was no company publication, no systematic channel for company news. New vice presidents were announced to a handful of top men through a one-line memo from Mason and the rest allowed to learn of the change in the newspapers. After much persuasion, Mason agreed to authorize a Policy Committee of key executives which would meet regularly, but without authority to act. Mason named Romney chairman of it and stayed away to give the younger man a free hand.

His ideas were rebuffed by many. He suggested that an elaborate presentation to dealers of the new 1950 automobiles in Chicago be repeated in Kenosha and Milwaukee for the employees who were making the cars. "My idea," answered an industrial relations executive, "has always been to tell those fellows as little as possible and get as much out of them as possible." The presentation was not made but Romney's plans for informing foreman and supervisors proceeded.

Middle managers were handicapped by this policy of silence. When several of them wrote to Mason suggesting that something should be done to acquaint supervisors and newcomers with the company, Mason referred them to Romney and let him form a committee to plan an employee information program. An old hand at organizing events, Romney helped his committee set up a series of "Town Hall" monthly dinner meetings for all salaried Nash-Kelvinator men. To carry out the theme, John A. Conde, assistant public relations director, became the "Town Crier," ringing a huge bell to open the meetings and announcing news.

Although social in providing an opportunity for men in different parts of the company to know each other, each meeting was devoted to an explanation of the functions of one department. Jack Timpy, the financial vice president, for example, used cartoons of female figures to enliven his accounts of the numerical kind. Response was resounding. About two-thirds of the six hundred men eligible turned out, paying $1.50 apiece towards the cost of the evening. In 1952, Romney created a new post, Director of Communications, and hired his former associate at AMA, William H. McGaughey, to fill it.

A basic and, as it later turned out, an irreconcilable difference of opinion barred talking to hourly workers. Don C. Rulo, a former salesman who had become director of industrial relations for Nash-Kelvinator, insisted that management should communicate with hourly workers only through the union. Rulo was supported by his superior, R. A. De Vlieg, vice president in charge of manufacturing, a veteran automobile man who helped design the first Dodge. Flagrant violations of normal work discipline went uncorrected in the Kelvinator plant on Plymouth Road adjoining the Nash-Kelvinator general offices. Romney knew the incredible details firsthand because he had spent time on the factory floor.

There was a men's barbershop in the men's rest room, operated by company employees on company time, with company pay. Workers had taken company parts and made electric ranges and refrigerators for the rest rooms. One woman was cooking breakfast for five men every morning after they got to work as a small-scale restaurant business. Some women were cooking evening meals on company time in the rest rooms and taking them home so they wouldn't have to cook after they got home. One employee bagged a bear during the hunting season and roasted cuts of it in the big ovens used to bake moisture out of the compressors. Poker games and numbers bets flourished. If foremen tried to interfere, they were barred from the rest rooms by employee-appointed "lookouts." A law school student on the afternoon shift typed his briefs in an unused women's washroom.

The men were literally working only half the time they were paid, and had come to regard the situation as legitimate. One day a worker was hurt in a plant accident at 10 A.M. The rules provided that any worker who had to go home before noon because of injury should get a halfday's pay. The man, however, demanded and received a full day's pay because between 7 and 10 A.M. he had already done a day's work by plant standards.

Romney could get no action. Rulo believed that workers should take their grievances to the union, while Romney contended that a grievance didn't exist until after management had been given a chance to act on a complaint. Foremen and plant guards belonged to the union.

The union was Matthew Smith's Mechanics Educational Society of America, known as MESA. Matt Smith was old-school and an old-world individualist. Born in Manchester, England, he came to the United States in 1928 but never became a citizen because he was "too much of an Englishman to go into Federal Court and pretend I could ever become an American." Described by Jack Strohm of the Detroit *Free Press* as "an acid-tongued Englishman who delights in non-conformity," he once campaigned for office in MESA as an "alien, athiest and Socialist." He did not want a checkoff of union dues because he believed it undermined union morale, and he had the same purist objection to the rival UAW's demand for a share of company profits.[4]

Smith readily admitted that the workers were having "a picnic," but he maintained that the same conditions prevailed from the front office down. Mason once confessed that he couldn't sit down with the union because it made him "too nervous" and the rest followed suit. Cost-plus contracts during the war, when labor was hard to get, had left management with little incentive to enforce discipline. Instead of writing a comprehensive contract, industrial relations officers patched up difficulties with "supplementary agreements." When Edward Cushman took over as director of industrial relations for American Motors Corporation on May 1, 1954, he inherited a stack of confused memos and agreements dating back to 1937 which filled a suitcase.

Management let the high labor costs at Kelvinator slide during the sellers' market after the war, but when Romney came in it was already apparent that Kelvinator had been left behind. Competitors had jacked up the loose wartime work stride and were able to offer compressors at a price below Kelvinator's costs, with the result that Kelvinator "missed the boat." The custom compressor market expanded fifty times its prewar size as newcomers rushed in to supply the postwar demand for appliances, while Kelvinator's sales only tripled.

The appliance industry's postwar spree was soon over. Too many inexperienced new manufacturers, too much new productive capacity and too many dealers without sales experience soon led to the collapse of orderly distribution. Instead of redoubling sales efforts, most distributors resorted to covert and finally to overt price cutting.

As usual, Mason had good product innovations. Kelvinator introduced an automatic defroster and the full-length refrigerator with usable space from top to bottom, but the latter advance was lost on the sellers' market of 1948. As pent-up demand for refrigerators was satisfied, Kelvinator's dependence on the home refrigerator market made it vulnerable. Mason moved to broaden the line. In 1952, he acquired Altorfer Bros. Company, makers of the ABC home washer. The Altorfer brothers had put a four-fingered dolly run by a gasoline motor in a wooden washtub in 1909 and sold enough of the laborsavers to move production out of an abandoned schoolhouse in 1911. Mechanical washing machines were on the market ahead of mechanical refrigerators, but they did not grow as fast. People bought a refrigerator first. But perfection of the automatic washing machine and perhaps the postwar baby boom made the home washer the growth appliance after World War II.

The foreign market, in which Kelvinator was well established, helped maintain appliances sales. In 1946, production was resumed in Crewe, England, from where refrigerators could be supplied to countries which at that time had British pounds but no dollars. Crewe was able to supply low-cost precision parts for Kelvinator of Canada, Ltd. and to ship compressors to Detroit at less than the home plant could make them.

While the market for appliances was shifting to Kelvinator's disadvantage, little was being done to make the home plant on

Plymouth Road competitive. De Vlieg, a kindly, immaculately dressed gentleman, on the basis of the reports of his subordinates could not believe that conditions were as bad as Romney reported and would not walk into the factory to see for himself on the ground that it would show lack of confidence in the manager. When the red ink became apparent, he and others proposed closing the plant as too inefficient.

Romney respected and admired De Vlieg but the younger man believed the people who worked in the plant should be given the facts and an opportunity to help save their jobs. Though he regretted it, a clash became inevitable as he pushed ahead with an employee communications program. Romney had worked out a plan for giving gold pins to men with twenty-five years' service and watches or clocks to men who had worked thirty years. In January, 1953, a public relations man brought De Vlieg a memorandum announcing the project.

"Tell George Romney that he has nothing to do with manufacturing!" said De Vlieg. The crisis came later when Romney at a meeting of executives urged a new industrial relations policy. The usually quiet De Vlieg exploded.

"George," he said, "this is child's stuff. We tried all these things. If you think you are so smart, you take it—go ahead and handle it."

That afternoon Mason, who had not been at the meeting, made Romney executive vice president.

His authority as second man in Nash-Kelvinator confirmed, Romney girded for the housecleaning. It was high time. Kelvinator lost $750,000 the first quarter of 1953. The dismissal of a union steward for hitting a foreman in the face when reprimanded for returning from lunch late and drunk touched off a series of disputes. Matt Smith ridiculed Romney's efforts as "Romneyism" and called him "Romeo Romney" and "Lochinvar Romney." The plant continued inefficient.

Romney met with union leaders at the Dearborn Inn in July and put the facts before them. Cocky Matt Smith denied nothing.

"Look, Romney," he said, looking him straight in the eye, "I have your workers, your foremen, your plant protection people. What are you going to do?"

Both men were fighters. Both were crusaders for principles. In the series of strikes that ensued, the two took each other's measure. Romney called a mass meeting of all hourly workers, morning and afternoon shifts, and told them that the plant would have to be moved if they didn't raise productivity 20 per cent. He asked them candidly to think in their hearts whether any plant could continue in business under the conditions they knew existed. He did not blame them. He frankly admitted that management had fallen down on its responsibility to manage. He stated the facts over a loudspeaker, with visual aids. The men stood for more than an hour to hear him.

Matt Smith struck the plant in protest. Romney wrote the workers at their homes. Smith replied in kind, setting off a letter-writing exchange during which Romney composed sixty-two personal letters to workers. Smith sneered at Romney's "drooling into a microphone." Romney met Smith's sarcasm with patience and persistence.

"I am no college man," he said. "I've laid floors, I've done lathing, I've been in beet fields. I know what it is to do physical work." At one point during the bargaining, the works manager called for a recess.

"What did you do that for?" Romney asked as they walked out together.

"To get you off the hook!" the man replied.

"Look here," Romney exploded. "You'll never need to get me off the hook."

During the thick of one crisis, Lenore was in the hospital. She had been given a transfusion of the wrong kind of blood and her life was in danger. In a Woodward Avenue hotel Romney was interviewing foremen one at a time, ten minutes each, from eight in the morning to ten-thirty at night, asking each one individually what he thought should be done. Whenever he had a moment he would call the hospital or run over to be with his wife. Nothing changed his lifelong priorities: family first, church second, work third.

In the next year and a half, the plant was out on strike 160 days.

Romney and Smith wound up respecting each other for all the hard words. The foremen left the union and affirmed their loyalty to the company. Productivity rose and the union agreed to time studies on individual jobs that lagged. But the operation of the plant still was so costly as to place the company at a disadvantage in the highly competitive appliance industry. Romney was known and respected by workers as no previous Nash executive had been.

Dave Bevan, a twenty-four-year veteran of Nash-Kelvinator who was then chief timekeeper, attributed Romney's success to an indefatigable optimism, and a respect for moral law which put cynics at all levels off balance. In his view, Romney gave Nash-Kelvinator something it badly needed—character.

XIV

In Search of Mergers

One of George Mason's post-World War II dreams was a three-way merger of Nash-Kelvinator with Packard and the Hudson Motor Car Company. Past mergers had been profitable to General Motors, Chrysler and his own company. Mason saw many advantages in bringing together Packard, Hudson and Nash-Kelvinator. He also considered the Studebaker Corporation but dropped it from his thinking for two reasons. Its labor costs were the highest in the industry and it was so rooted in South Bend, Indiana, that it would be difficult or impossible to remove production from there, as might be necessary to realize the full economies of such a merger.

All of these companies prospered immediately after the war. The government favored them slightly in allocating steel and other controlled materials. There was a great backlog of demand for any kind of car. With some attractive new models like the Raymond Loewy-designed 1947 Studebaker and with Kaiser entering the field, the independents increased their share of the industry's business. Only 9.7 per cent in 1941, the figure grew to 14.4 in 1946, 15.3 in 1947 and 19.09 per cent in 1948.[1]

Costs were advancing, largely because of higher taxes and wages, and Mason foresaw difficulties for the independents when the sellers' market ended and the Big Three returned to unrestricted competition. He believed the independents could continue to compete with the big companies only by getting together, through merger or reciprocal agreements, to cut their costs and make the best use of their facilities. He approached both Hudson and Packard in 1946. He made Packard a proposal in 1948 which was rejected by the directors of that company.

"We might have been agreeable to a 55 to 45 per cent arrangement," said Hugh Ferry of Packard later, "but this would have been 66⅔ to 33⅓ in favor of Nash." Mason insisted this was just his first offer. He continued his efforts but with little response as long as the independents continued to sell their cars profitably.

Romney included a section titled "Some Observations on Merger" in his important 1949 report to Mason, already mentioned. "If future merger on any scale is going to be necessary," wrote Romney, "merger now while companies are financially strong would be the soundest course. Waiting until others are weakened may find all too weak financially to survive in the competitive car market where volume sales and production are an absolute necessity. Even under the most favorable circumstances, successfully merging organizations is a slow process requiring several years." He observed that the independents could effect economies "if the will to seek them exists" by buying parts from each other.

Merger talks were resumed after James J. Nance became president of Packard with considerable fanfare in 1952. In his previous post as president of General Electric's Hotpoint, Inc., Nance had been a competitor of Mason in the appliance field. He now became his rival for leadership of any merger of Packard and Nash-Kelvinator. As the sellers' market suddenly changed to a buyers' market in the summer of 1953, the interest in mergers quickened. After heavy losses, Kaiser Motors already had merged in May with Willys.

A. E. Barit, president of Hudson, asked Mason for an appointment and they met June 16, 1953 in Room 2607 of the then Book-

Cadillac Hotel in Detroit. After a two-hour lunch, they shook hands on the essential points of a plan to merge Hudson and Nash-Kelvinator into a new company. In an August 31 letter to Barit, Mason wrote this would have a divisional system such as General Motors, with separate Nash, Hudson and Kelvinator divisions. These would use common tooling wherever possible to cut expenses.[2] Mason personally decided it should be called American Motors. As the two companies used different accounting systems and had different fiscal years, it was six months before comparable valuations could be worked out for their assets. While proceeding with the legal steps involved, Mason renewed his efforts to bring Packard into the project.

Before the merger with Hudson was concluded, Mason proposed that Packard join American Motors in a "combined product program." Romney's assistant, John Brown, Jr., who had joined Nash after running propeller and helicopter production for Pratt & Whitney during the war, calculated the advantages of this. In his home in suburban Birmingham, Brown, Howard Hallas and John Conde worked long hours in secrecy preparing and hand-lettering an easel presentation.

Mason and Romney showed this to Nance and other Packard executives in another closed-door session at the Book-Cadillac in February of 1954. It reminded that Ford produced seven series of cars from two basic body shells and that from four basic body shells General Motors made fourteen series of cars and Chrysler eleven series. But Packard, Nash and Hudson required five basic bodies to make only eight series of cars.

"American Motors," said Mason, "could produce seven series of cars with only two body shells. Body A could be for a basic-volume car. Body B would be used for the Hudson Wasp and Hornet, Packard Patrician and Clipper and also for the Nash Ambassador and Statesman. Packard V-8 engines, axles and Ultramatic transmissions would be used on most cars."

The basic-volume car, which Mason planned as a fourth low-priced car, would give Packard dealers an additional market and strengthen marginal outlets. The companies together could afford more research. The public, the government, the national economy would benefit from a bigger, stronger company.

"American Motors offers Packard," the proposal concluded, "new opportunities for greater volume, earnings, security, prestige and public service." Packard expressed misgivings over the Hudson part of the merger and declined again to join in it. Nance soon was working out a merger of his own with Studebaker.

As Barit was sixty-four years old and ready to relinquish authority, no conflict of personalities interfered with the Hudson and Nash-Kelvinator merger. He bargained sharply, however, for adequate valuation of the five Hudson plants in Detroit and a four-year employment contract for himself as a consultant. George Mason became chief executive officer with the titles of president, chairman of the board and general manager. George Romney continued with his title of executive vice president. As both companies made cars of single-unit, *monocoque* body construction the merger promised speedy production economies.

Boards of directors of both companies on January 14, 1954, approved the merger proposal. Legally this provided for the merger of Hudson into Nash-Kelvinator and changing the name of the latter to American Motors. Nash-Kelvinator stockholders kept their shares and Hudson stockholders exchanged three of their shares for two of the surviving company. The proposal listed its book value as $197,793,366 or $34.85 a share for the 5,675,710 shares to be outstanding.

It was the largest merger in the history of the automobile industry. The companies had produced over six million automobiles and more than ten million household appliances and other products. Directly concerned were more than 30,000 employees, 58,000 stockholders and 10,000 dealers and distributors in one hundred countries. The Detroit afternoon newspapers bannered the news of the directors' approval. In other newspapers it shared headlines with another merger, the marriage of Joe DiMaggio, the ball player, and Marilyn Monroe, the actress. Hudson and Nash stockholders, though not without some criticism, approved the merger. Dissatisfied with the $9.80 cash value put on their shares, a few Hudson stockholders demanded a court appraisal. After much expense and nearly three years, they received $9.8125. American Motors came into being on May 1, 1954.

While Hudson sales had dropped steadily in the years before the merger and the company lost ten million dollars on its 1953 operations, it was an enterprise that in its forty-five years of life had contributed many engineering improvements to the automobile. Associated with it had been some of the best-known pioneers of the industry.

Roy Dikeman Chapin was one of these. He was so much more interested in the four-wheeled toys that moved themselves than in becoming a lawyer that he left the University of Michigan during mid-term examinations in 1901 and persuaded skeptical Ransom E. Olds to let him file rough gear castings at thirty-five dollars a month in the Olds Motor Works. A fire burned down the plant, destroying everything—cars and blueprints—except a little runabout that happened to be standing near the doorway. Although it would not start, the little runabout was pushed to safety.

Undaunted, Olds and his crew went to work readying the curved-dash little car for the New York automobile show in November. To make a splash with it, daredevil twenty-one-year-old Chapin undertook to drive it the 860 miles of dirt roads and towpaths from Detroit to New York. Nobody had driven the route before. In fact, the farthest anybody had then driven was the two hundred-miles-shorter distance from Cleveland to New York.

Chapin left Detroit on October 27, 1901, at the tiller of the little open bug which looked like a glorified bicycle on four wheels. He took along enough spare parts to put together a new car and used most of them, and he wore a high starched collar and a leather motoring coat. At Syracuse, heavy rains left only the old Erie Canal towpath dry, and Chapin competed for it with mule drivers. Seven days after the start, he drew up in front of the plush Waldorf-Astoria Hotel after dealing with a broken axle, punctures, broken springs, ignition trouble, a broken feed line. Chapin and the curved-dash Oldsmobile were so muddy and greasy that the doorman at the Waldorf wouldn't let him in. He had to enter by a side door and up a service elevator to report to Olds.[3]

The exploit was a sensation and saved the company. It also convinced young Chapin that the horseless carriage needed new roads. Next year, Olds turned out three thousand cars, the first quantity production in the automobile industry. Chapin became its advertising manager, snapping pictures of the cars in production with a "pin hole" camera he had made himself for the mail-order catalogue through which Olds sold direct from the factory.

Until then, cars had been toys. Olds had once considered franchising A. G. Spalding and Company, the sporting goods firm, to sell them. Quantity production meant serious selling, and young Chapin went to work to persuade dealers to handle the cars at a time when the retailing of automobiles was regarded as a poor risk and bankers discouraged depositors from withdrawing money to buy them. Chapin pitched in and demonstrated cars to prospects in order to encourage dealers. In 1905, when 6,500 Oldsmobiles were sold, Gus Edwards and Vincent Bryan gave the company a free ride by creating the song hit, "In My Merry Oldsmobile," the only song naming an automobile which has become a classic.

Olds was a millionaire virtually overnight. His success stimulated young men in his shop to go into the automobile business themselves. In 1906, Roy Chapin's lawyer father drew up partnership papers putting his son, Howard E. Coffin, an Olds engineer, Roscoe B. Jackson, a college chum of Roy, and Frederick O. Bezner of the

Olds purchasing department into business manufacturing automobiles with a capital of six thousand dollars. The others prudently
kept their jobs, but Roy Chapin quit to find more money. In San
Francisco, he made a deal with E. R. Thomas to supply a lower-
priced car for Thomas Company dealers to distribute along with
the heavy, high-priced Thomas Flyer. Thomas advanced the partnership $150,000 against deliveries of five hundred cars in a year
and they formed the Thomas-Detroit Company.

The four youngsters rented a building from the Modern Match
Company in Detroit and started assembling the car Coffin had
designed with parts Bezner bought from suppliers to Coffin's specifications. By June, 1907, the five hundred cars were delivered and
the partners were chafing at the limits imposed by their dependence
on the Thomas-Buffalo Company for distribution. Next year, they
persuaded Hugh Chalmers, former sales vice president of the pre-
cociously promotional National Cash Register Company to help
them buy part of Thomas' interest and develop sales outlets for
them. In the reorganization, Chalmers became president of what
now was called the Chalmers-Detroit Company. The Chalmers car
sold well, but two-thirds of the profits went to Thomas and
Chalmers.

With the help of Jackson and George W. Dunham, another Olds
graduate, Coffin and Chapin again planned to develop a car of their
own while remaining on the Chalmers-Detroit payroll. Jackson—
whose name lives today in the Roscoe B. Jackson Memorial Laboratory for cancer research at Bar Harbor, Maine—had married a niece
of J. L. Hudson, owner of Detroit's largest department store. On
February 20, 1909, the Hudson Motor Car Company was organized
with J. L. Hudson the biggest subscriber to its capital stock of
$100,000, followed by Chalmers, Jackson, Coffin, Bezner, Chapin,
James J. Brady, an experienced production man, and Dunham.

Their first car, the Hudson "Twenty," so-called because of its
horsepower, was announced in a full-page advertisement in the

Saturday Evening Post of June 19, 1909. The car had a hundred-inch wheel base, the same as a modern Rambler American, and was a four-cylinder roadster guaranteed to do fifty miles an hour. At nine hundred dollars, it was the first low-cost automobile with a selective sliding gear transmission with three forward speeds and reverse. Inquiries poured in, and down payments totaling $100,000 helped get production under way. The next year, Hudson had enough money to build a plant of its own with 172,000 square feet of floor space at Jefferson and Conner avenues on Detroit's east side. It was designed by Albert Kahn, the architect who later planned the Plymouth Road plant inherited by American Motors, the River Rouge works and the Willow Run bomber plant for Ford, the General Motors building in Detroit and even factories in Stalingrad.

Always restless, Chapin visited every automobile plant in Europe and came back loaded with information on the manufacture of closed cars for all-weather motoring. In December, 1909, Chapin, Coffin and Bezner sold their interests in the Chalmers-Detroit Company to Chalmers and bought his interest in Hudson. They now had a successful automobile company all to themselves. J. L. Hudson retained his financial interest. Coffin and Bezner remained key operating officers. But corporate policies were shaped by Roy Chapin. The young man who had quit college at twenty-one became a millionaire at thirty.

In 1914, Hudson produced the first medium-priced enclosed car or "sedan," and the first medium-weight six-cylinder car. In 1915, Hudson engineers solved the problem of engine vibration with a fully balanced crankshaft, introduced in the 1916 Hudson "Super Six," which made 102 miles an hour at Daytona Beach and traveled from San Francisco to New York in a record-breaking five days, three hours and thirty-one minutes. Hudson became known as an automobile man's automobile company, producing cars that won races even when they did not look glamorous.

Roy Chapin's greatest contribution to the industry was the popularizing of the enclosed car. He organized Essex Motors, a subsidiary of Hudson, to make the Essex coach in 1918. Hudson engineers and the body-building Fisher Brothers, who later merged their business with GM, collaborated on its design. When first offered it sold for only $100 more than the traditional open touring car of comparable value. It was made and sold at a loss for a year because of Chapin's faith. The price was then cut to the touring car price.

Edsel Ford termed this car one of the most significant of its time. More than any other vehicle it was responsible for the turnabout in motoring preference which changed 90 per cent open models in 1919 to 90 per cent closed models by 1929. The automobile became a year-around necessity rather than just a fair-weather luxury. Hudson, which made the Essex cars in its factories, meanwhile absorbed its subsidiary.[4]

When Hudson merged with Nash in 1954, it brought the new company claims to seventy-five American automotive firsts: first crankshaft balanced in motion, cutting engine weight, increasing horsepower and improving gasoline mileage (1916); adjustable front seat (1921); starter located on the instrument panel (1926); unit engineered body integrated with chassis (1932); luggage compartment and enclosed tire in the rear (1934); vacuum power shift located at the steering wheel (1935); selective automatic shift (1937); airfoam seat cushions (1939); "step down" design with low center of gravity (1947).

When not in Europe scouting new engineering ideas, Roy Chapin was apt to be out promoting roads. Unlike some of his competitors, he favored taxes on gas and cars to support the roads they would use, and he was an early advocate of the Lincoln Highway, the first paved coast-to-coast automobile road. In World War I, he headed the Highways Transport Committee of the Council of National Defense. In 1924 he helped organize the Pan American Highway Commission, helped found the Highways Education Board, and represented the United States in foreign conferences on transport. Youthful but scholarly-looking enough for the role, Chapin became President Hoover's Secretary of Commerce on August 8, 1932, in the darkest trough of the depression. With the inaugural of President Roosevelt in 1933 he went back to Detroit to fight the depression in his own back yard.

Roscoe B. Jackson, one of the founders, was president of the company from 1923 until his death in 1929. He was succeeded by W. J. McAneeny. He became chairman of the board when Chapin returned and took charge as president on May 20, 1933.

In 1929, Hudson ranked third in industry sales as it produced 300,962 cars, its peak year. More than two-thirds of them were the Essex. But the crash plummeted Hudson stock from 93.5 to 38 and only 114,000 cars moved in 1930. In 1931, the company lost nearly $2,000,000; in 1932, $5,500,000.

The Terraplane, a 108-inch wheelbase, low-priced car with partly unitized body and "airplane ratio of power to weight," was christened by Amelia Earhart, the aviatrix, in impressive ceremonies on July 21, 1932, and the first Terraplane off the line went to Orville Wright, survivor of the brothers who flew the first heavier-than-air machine. The Terraplane broke performance, endurance and speed records, some of which were still standing in 1959, but it did not bring sales and income back to profitable levels.

Luckily, Hudson had been conservatively financed, largely out of its own earnings. When creditors pressed and repossessions brought unredeemed notes back to the company, Chapin's old friend Lewis Strauss of Kuhn, Loeb and Company helped him work out a six-million-dollar loan and Commercial Investment Trust, Inc. offered to finance Hudson sales to the amount of fifty million dollars a year for the next five years.

Hudson had profits of $600,000, the first in five years, in 1935 and had turned the corner when Roy Chapin died of pneumonia on February 16, 1936, a week before his fifty-sixth birthday. He was succeeded by A. E. Barit, a shy, reserved man of a different type. He had started with Hudson as a stenographer in the purchasing department in January, 1910, and had risen through purchasing to treasurer, vice president and general manager.

During World War II, Hudson made wings for Lockheed P-38s, armored cabins for the Bell King Cobra fighter plane, wings for Curtiss-Wright Helldivers, fuselage sections for Martin B-26 Marauders, outer fuselage sections for B-29s, mine anchors, engines for landing craft and other military hardware. Hudson emerged from the war with plants worth fifty million dollars, but postwar sales were disappointing.

While Hudsons outsold Nash cars in both 1948 and 1949, the Hudson postwar models seemed either ahead of or behind popular taste. Neither the Hornet, Hudson's senior car, the Wasp, its medium-price entry, nor the Jet, its small car, won wide acceptance. In a nostalgic stunt, two women drove a Jet over the route of the record 1916 run of the Hudson Super Six, cutting that record by two days to cover the 3,373 miles in 80.25 hours. This won publicity but not sales and the Jet was dropped after the merger.

With the merger, four Hudson men became officers of American Motors. Barit and Roy D. Chapin, Jr., son of the Hudson founder, were elected directors. Other directors then were Mason, Romney, Harold G. Perkins, a vice president of Nash-Kelvinator and American Motors; Dean George Granger Brown of the University of Michigan College of Engineering; Percy J. Ebbott, president, Chase National Bank; Harlan T. Pierpont of the Worcester Mechanics Savings Bank, Worcester, Massachusetts; Eustace Seligman, a member of Sullivan & Cromwell, New York law firm; and James T. Wilson, chairman of the board of the First National Bank, Kenosha, Wisconsin. Wilson had been an associate of Charles W. Nash both at General Motors and Nash Motors.

American Motors began operations in the toughest year for independents up until that time in the history of the automobile business. A rejuvenated Ford company waged a slugging battle to dislodge Chevrolet as the sales leader in the low-priced field and for the first part of 1954 led in registrations. With Chevrolet and Ford dealers being pressed to sell at all costs, new cars were bootlegged as secondhand, and prices were cut. Sales of Hudson and Nash cars declined further. Nash operations, which had been profitable until shortly before the merger, began to show losses along with those of Hudson.

As much as Barit and some others would have liked to do so, there was no chance for American Motors to operate a divisional automobile manufacturing organization along the General Motors line. After talks with the UAW, it was announced on May 29 that Hudson manufacturing would be transferred from Detroit to Kenosha at the end of the 1954 model run and consolidated with Nash and Rambler production. Several hundred Hudson workers who eventually moved from Detroit to Kenosha had their seniority rights preserved.

With high horsepower still the vogue, American Motors desperately needed a V-8 engine. While both had once made eight-cylinder engines, neither Hudson nor Nash had one at the time of the merger. Mason and Romney tried to buy a V-8 from all of the Big Three companies and almost obtained one from Pontiac but General Motors executives decided they didn't have capacity to meet more than their own needs. A new V-8 made by Packard, with long experience in making eight- and even twelve-cylinder engines, appeared to be the answer.

After President Nance of Packard began negotiating a merger with Studebaker, Mason gave up on his idea of inducing Packard to come into American Motors but redoubled his efforts to obtain a reciprocity understanding on components. Many of the almost idle Hudson stamping facilities in Detroit could make components of the sort used by Packard. After several discussions, American Motors contracted on August 22, 1954, to buy V-8 engines from Packard for its 1955 cars.

"Insofar as it is possible to do so on a competitive and advantageous basis of price, quality and style," said a clause in the contract, "Packard will endeavor to purchase from American Motors products suitable for use by Packard. . . . To the extent possible Packard will endeavor to make such purchases in dollar amounts at least approximately equal to dollar volume to purchases from Packard by American Motors."

But another paragraph, in the legal prose of Bodman, Longley, Bogle, Armstrong & Dahling, made it plain that failure of Packard to do this would not excuse American Motors from paying for the Packard engines and said: "Packard shall be the sole judge of whether products offered to it by AMC can be purchased by Packard . . . on a competitive and advantageous basis."

On the basis of this and what had been said at the meetings, Mason and Romney believed they had a contractual reciprocity commitment from Packard and turned to other problems. One was liquidation of contracts which Hudson had made with 150 firms, including Murray Body, to supply components for the discontinued small Jet cars. This cost around eleven million dollars and occupied Albert Wibel and others for months.

Despite a great improvement in productivity, the Detroit Kelvinator plant continued to be less efficient than the one at Grand Rapids. At the end of July, manufacture of ice cream cabinets, home freezers and beverage coolers was shifted from Detroit to Grand Rapids. Matt Smith's union members walked out on August 2. They stayed out sixty-five days, in the course of which the union sued the company for $2,538,000 in wages and union dues and the company asked damages of $888,135 from the union in federal court.

The suits were dismissed as part of a settlement reached October 6 with the aid of government mediators. This recognized the right of the company to determine the location of its production and provided for prior discussion with the union of similar moves if made in the future. In a joint statement, Ed Cushman and Matt Smith said: "Both the company and the union believe that a sound foundation has now been laid for constructive relationships. We are determined to make the Detroit Kelvinator plant an outstanding example of union-management cooperation." This was framed on the wall of the plant personnel office. Before his death in 1958, Matt Smith, previously so critical, changed his mind and praised Romney's sincerity and integrity. When compressor production was shifted at that time from Detroit to Grand Rapids it was not due to any lack of productivity. General Electric's Hotpoint Division, previously the principal customer, then was required to use compressors from a big new GE factory in Louisville, Kentucky.

Sixty-three-year-old President Mason took a fishing vacation in Wyoming and flew back to Detroit on Sunday, October 3, 1954. He had an October 8 plane reservation to Europe to discuss the Metropolitan program with the Austin people. He arrived in Detroit feeling fine but was stricken Sunday night and taken to Harper Hospital. He was well enough to talk to Romney about hiring a new sales executive for Nash. But on Friday, instead of taking a plane for Europe, he died at 11:45 A.M. His pancreas had ceased to function and he had developed pneumonia.

News of Mason's death stilled conversation at the Detroit Athletic Club and other haunts of automobile men. Henry Ford II requested prayers at a lunch of United Foundation officers. His hunting and fishing friends on the Au Sable River mourned Mason. A small mountain of messages included condolences from Jack Beni, president of Local 72, UAW-CIO, at Kenosha, and from Pinin Farina in Turin, Italy. For the funeral on the following Monday Henry Ford II, Defense Secretary Charles E. Wilson, K. T. Keller and other leaders of the automobile world crowded into Christ Church in suburban Cranbrook.

They listened in hushed surprise as George Romney, at the family's request, rose in the pulpit and eulogized his friend as "a great man with human frailties overbalanced by his good and noble qualities." Romney described Mason as a deeply religious man who kept a Bible at his bedside and read it regularly. "George Mason did not seek the motes in the eyes of his friends," said Romney. "He constantly sought the good and the true. . . . He never lost the common touch. . . . Redcaps, bellhops, waitresses, janitors adored him. . . . George Mason's alms and charities were legion. . . .

"His great capacity for love included nature in all of its aspects. His preferred environment was on the streams and lakes among the trees and flowers. The animals sensed his friendliness. . . . One of his dearest relationships was with a beautiful doe named Bambi. Found as an orphaned fawn, with his affectionate care she lived twenty-one years."

Romney also presented a moving tribute to Mason at the anniversary dinner of the Detroit Round Table of Catholics, Jews and Protestants at the Masonic Temple on November 18. By tape recordings, Mason's kindnesses were recalled by Lester Royce, his fishing guide; Alexander Ruthven, president emeritus of the University of Michigan; George Griffith, a member of the Michigan Conservation Commission; Bob Jenson, an Au Sable River neighbor for whom Mason obtained a college scholarship; and others. Jenson later became an American Motors engineer.

Money which friends contributed in lieu of flowers for the funeral was used to establish a Mason Phoenix Memorial Library at his alma mater, the University of Michigan, which had given him an honorary Doctor of Laws degree three years earlier. An awards program for achievements in conservation set up by Mason was continued by American Motors as a tribute to him.

In an unusual will drawn by Richard E. Cross, Mason bequeathed fourteen miles of land valued at one million dollars along the Au Sable River to the people of Michigan on condition that its natural beauty be maintained. With it he left twenty-five thousand dollars to be used at the rate of one thousand dollars a year "to replace the trout I took out." His memory is recalled by a small Norwegian log sportsman's chapel in Hartwick Pines State Park. With the permission of the Michigan Conservation Commission he built this at a cost of twenty-five thousand dollars before his death and personally wrote a prayer for it. Titled "Nature's Prayer," this occupies the altar location in the chapel beneath a plate-glass cross. The words are:

Our heavenly Father, creator of all that is nature, we humbly come to you in the midst of nature's splendor to thank you that as Americans we are free to worship as we please, work as we please, and move about as we please to enjoy all that is nature—its mountains, its hills, its valleys, its lakes, its streams, and the living things that dwell therein; we pray unto you that some day the world may be at peace and all men be free to enjoy nature's abundance. We ask you in the name of our Lord Jesus Christ that we be guided to protect this priceless heritage which we, in America, are privileged to enjoy. Amen.

XV

Building American Motors

George Romney was named chief executive officer of American Motors on October 12, 1954, the day after George Mason's funeral. To show that they had complete confidence in him, the board of directors gave him all of Mason's titles—chairman, president and general manager. With them Romney inherited a world of problems, which he attacked simultaneously with a breakneck schedule of speeches, press conferences and meetings that would have crushed a man of lesser stamina. To keep on time, he wore a wrist watch with an alarm.

Externally, he had to convince the public and especially the creditors of American Motors that it had worth-while products and would stay in business. Soon after assuming office, for example, he had to spend two days explaining to representatives of the Prudential Life Insurance Company, the principal backer of American Motors, that it could survive without joining the Studebaker-Packard merger which had come into existence on October 1.

On the appliance side, he had to cope with the competition of General Electric, Frigidaire and Westinghouse, then at the fiercest in the history of the industry. On the automotive side, he had to deal with the idea that only the Big Three could build good cars and the fear that American Motors makes were likely to be orphans. The Ford-Chevrolet battle for first in sales grew hotter toward the end of the year, with many dealers actually registering cars which were not sold until the following year.

Internally, the first job was to build a management team to which he could delegate some of the authority that Mason had wielded single-handedly. He had to finish fitting the Nash and Hudson organizations together. There were still two men for many jobs. He had to cut costs, especially labor costs. He had to make critical production and design decisions. He had to find work or purchasers for several surplus plants. Finally, and most important, he had to find for several important posts executives in sympathy with his concepts.

His first move was to hire a sales executive who believed in small cars. On the Wednesday before his death, Mason had talked to Romney about hiring Roy Abernethy, a former Packard man who was then sales vice president for Kaiser-Willys, makers of jeeps and other small vehicles. Kaiser-Willys was then moving away from passenger cars and Abernethy was not interested in selling anything else. After telephoning Edgar Kaiser, Romney offered Abernethy the job of sales manager of the Nash Division and he accepted it. Henry Clay Doss, who had no enthusiasm for the small-car development, retired as vice president of Nash sales exactly a week after Romney became head of the company. Abernethy brought two associates, John W. Raisbeck and Fred W. Adams, to American Motors as administrator of sales operations and director of automotive advertising.

Abernethy was a 235-pound, cigar-smoking man with thirty years' experience in the automobile business. The youngest of six children of a coal mine foreman, he began life on a farm outside West Monterey, Pennsylvania. As a boy, he took care of mine mules and in summers laid track for the Pennsylvania Railroad. At the East Brady, Pennsylvania, High School he played fullback, pitched on the baseball team and also tossed the shot and discus. He moved on to Pittsburgh and studied engineering in night classes at Carnegie Tech with the idea of becoming a bridge builder.

At the same time, he entered the automobile business as an eighteen-cents-an-hour apprentice mechanic for a Packard dealer in Pittsburgh. He switched to automotive engineering at Tech but soon left for a full-time job with a Packard distributor. He rose through district, zone and regional sales posts to assistant general sales manager for the company. For some years while out of the company, he was a Packard dealer in Hartford, Connecticut, one year doing a business of more than a million dollars. He had had experience in every phase of automobile selling and knew dealer problems as only a dealer could know them.

Romney put into practice many of the recommendations he had made to Mason in 1949. He was determined to manage as leader of a team. He created a new, eleven-man Policy Committee, six of them younger than himself, to consult on all major decisions. Before Mason's death Romney had asked his assistant, John L. Brown, Jr., and John Staiger to make a study of the organization structures of all automobile and appliance companies. A streamlined staff and line chart was set up which, unlike Mason's practice, delegated responsibility for earnings to lower-level "profit centers." Scores of executives had reported to Mason; eventually only a half-dozen operating chiefs reported to Romney.

Two days after he became president, Romney met the Detroit press to tell them what he intended to do. He introduced his key men one by one and pointed out that they were both young and experienced. To dispel the many rumors afloat, he announced no merger negotiations were under way. He eloquently underlined the strengths of the company. Ten days later he took on the hard-boiled New York financial press at the Waldorf-Astoria, and went on to do the same in Washington.

Romney mentioned product reciprocity with Packard at both his Detroit and New York press conferences and the *Wall Street*

Journal carried the headline: "Studebaker-Packard, American Motors Are Agreed on Reciprocity."[1] He was chagrined to learn that the Packard people did not interpret the V-8 engine contract signed in August as he did. Packard asked American Motors to bid on the making of a few small parts, "five and ten-cent items" as engineers term them, but there was no important bodywork forthcoming for the big Hudson equipment.

Romney became concerned when Chapman and Bernitt returned one day from Packard with word that the Packard vice presidents in charge of manufacturing and procurement didn't recognize any obligation to buy from American Motors. Late on October 22, a few days later, the news ticker at American Motors carried an item saying Packard had taken an option on the Murray body plant. Unable to reach President Nance of Studebaker-Packard on the telephone, Romney sent a telegram to his home:

"Believe consummation of deal with Murray as it is reported to us would be contrary to the spirit, contractual and moral obligations of your current understandings with us. . . . Believe you and I should meet and discuss this entire situation."

Nance replied by letter. He denied any breach of faith. He maintained that Packard was doing American Motors a favor in selling them its V-8 engines, and that Packard was free to buy wherever it pleased. "In view of this," he concluded, "we regret that our company name was used in a discussion with the press of a reciprocity policy." Romney felt that this letter was a repudiation of the written agreement and ordered Meade Moore to proceed with a V-8 engine program for American Motors. This cost more than ten million dollars but produced a more suitable engine at two hundred dollars a unit less cost to American Motors. The engine contract with Packard was canceled and its fine new twenty-million-dollar engine line at Utica, Michigan, eventually was sold for scrap metal.

Romney and Abernethy at this time needed an additional incentive for dealers to sell American Motors cars. The answer was the

Dealer Volume Investment Fund. As worked out by Jack Timpy, this credited all dealers with a bonus on every domestic car sold. For Ramblers this was $30 a car for the first 25,000, $40 for the next and $55 for those after 50,000. This helped sell 73,807 Ramblers the next year. The bonus began at $50 on Nash and Hudson cars. At a time when the company was short of money, it paid out seven million dollars in this way in two years but the outlay was an important factor in preserving the dealer organization.[2]

Romney was unhappy with the company's past advertising. The fact that a talking dog chased a Nash didn't seem a very logical argument for a human buying one. He had many sessions with copywriters of the Geyer agency, which had handled Nash advertising since 1937, before he made himself understood. A new advertising policy statement for the company was worked out at a Saturday morning meeting in November of 1954. In part it said:

1. American Motors copy must be as simple, informational and factual as possible. Banish the superlatives . . . kill the tired clichés . . . rule out "conventional" advertising language . . . use "news" language to the greatest possible extent.

2. Every advertisement must be centered on a dominant idea that is validated by a quality or feature in the product. This dominant idea must be used consistently to secure universal recognition and maximum acceptance.

3. Whether we use a news lead or one stressing consumer benefit, there has to be validation of the headline statement in sub-headline secondary illustrations, main copy and picture caption.

4. Traditional ways of saying things and picturing things are out. Let's not be afraid of any copy or picture idea . . . no matter how different or unconventional. Don't worry about it's being too crazy; you never can be sure until you get it down on paper and look at it.

5. We can screen out the completely crazy ideas . . . but we can't screen out no ideas. So, let the ideas come . . . and forget all the traditional "can'ts" and "mustn'ts."

As the agency men absorbed Romney's ideas, the advertising became more persuasive and he credited them with making important contributions. Sam Ballard,[3] who joined the agency two years earlier, developed the "Love Letters to Rambler." The agency produced the X-ray booklets.

Despite his worries, Romney managed to get to Salt Lake City for a 1954 Thanksgiving dinner at his father's home. For the first time in thirty years he and his sister and three brothers and their families sat down together on the holiday. There were thirty-eight present. He immediately flew back to Detroit for an intense campaign to make American Motors better known.

To dramatize the resources of American Motors, Romney had an exhibit of the company's products assembled along with panel charts, pictures of its facilities and maps showing Kelvinator's world-wide operations. Plans were made for Romney to show it to stockholders, community leaders, editors and other influence groups all over the country. The important unveiling of the exhibit at Detroit was set for 5 P.M., of December 7, 1954, the same day he was to address a luncheon meeting in Manhattan of the New York Society of Security Analysts.

This was his critical first appearance before the New York financial community after becoming president. Anticipating sophisticated and pointed questions, he frankly and persuasively outlined his plans for the company. "I have not one idea of uncertainty in my mind or heart about this company," he concluded. The skeptical analysts must have agreed, because the stock, which had dropped below ten dollars in November rose to twelve and hovered there for two months.

As soon as the luncheon at the Downtown Athletic Club was over, Romney rushed to the New York Police Heliport at the foot of West Thirtieth Street. There his assistant, John L. Brown, Jr., had arranged with his Sikorsky friends to have a helicopter waiting. This landed Romney at La Guardia Airport alongside an airliner ready to take off for Detroit. At Willow Run, Ernie Wirth, the company driver, picked him up and, escorted by state police, delivered him to the Masonic Temple in downtown Detroit where the exhibit and its distinguished audience were waiting.

Everyone who heard Romney talk hoped he would succeed, but problems mounted. In addition to failure of the reciprocity program with Packard, there were other disappointments. Expected military contracts failed to materialize. The company's automobile sales rose only slightly in 1955, the year in which the industry sold a record seven million cars, and the total sales for all independents dropped to 4.8 per cent, the lowest in history. Romney and his key executives had been given options on 150,000 shares of American Motors at $9.56 on November 18, 1954, but a steady downward drift made the incentive academic in the fall of 1955.

The merger had not envisaged combining the Nash and Hudson sales organizations. Hudson dealers, however, proved less strong than expected. After a year of selling the Rambler with different name plates as the Nash Rambler and the Hudson Rambler, integration of the sales and dealer organizations became inevitable when the company concentrated on the compact car. This involved costly liquidation of many long-term leases and other commitments.

To cut overhead costs and to infuse a sense of urgency in the organization, Romney launched a company-wide economy drive under the slogan, "Let's Be Competitive!" Employees coming to work one morning had their curiosity whetted by "L.B.C." tags hanging everywhere and some thought that the initials stood for "Let's Beat Chevrolet." Through cost-reduction committees already set up, this campaign reached all departments. Every employee was asked to make suggestions for improving the efficiency of his own job.

Romney and twenty-four other executives voluntarily cut their own salaries by as much as 35 per cent. He insisted that zone managers book a simple single room instead of the flower-decorated suites they had been providing for his visits to their territories in the past. Vice President Jack Timpy, who guided some of the larger savings, sold the company's two executive planes to Chrysler in the course of a golf game with an executive of that company. Romney had been using the pilots so early and so late that they departed with no regrets.

All expenses were reviewed. The company's advertising agency, which for years had been given space in the Plymouth Road plant as a matter of convenience, was required to pay rent. A less costly agreement was negotiated with Pinin Farina and he was allowed to work for Cadillac and others. The company resigned from the National Association of Manufacturers and many other organizations. Contributions of many kinds were cancelled or postponed.

Economies filtered down to middle managers. The company garage stopped giving free gas and service to executive cars. It didn't save much money, but it impressed people down the line who did not enjoy these privileges that the top brass meant business. At one point, offices were cleaned only every other day for a saving of forty thousand dollars a year. Another forty thousand dollars a year was deferred by delaying the customary gifts of watches or clocks to employees with thirty years of service. Lunch scraps deposited in unemptied wastepaper baskets attracted rodents and a bat which wreaked havoc among the stenographers. Offices went unpainted, and sheet toilet paper replaced rolls.

Important economies, as well as clearer thinking, resulted from a review of the company's paperwork, co-ordinated by John L. Brown, Jr. and Charles L. Epker. They eliminated 112 of the 1,257 regular written reports, saving not only many man-hours of clerical time but the valuable time of the managers who wrote and read them. Others were condensed, combined, cut in frequency, or limited in distribution. For some intercompany correspondence, a "speedimemo" form was adopted. This allowed one man to write another in his own handwriting and to receive a reply on the same letter with a carbon for each. It all added up to savings in millions.

A pleasant accolade came to Romney in the fall of 1956 with his election as president of the Automobile Manufacturers Association, succeeding James Nance, who resigned this post as well as the presidency of Studebaker-Packard. Romney's first action as head of the Association was to welcome to membership the Ford Motor Company, a hold-out for forty-three years. The work of Romney during the war had impressed Ford executives. After the death of Henry Ford, membership had been only a matter of time. As he took office, Romney posed for a memorable all-smiling photograph with Henry Ford II, Harlow H. Curtice of General Motors and L. L. Colbert of Chrysler. The Automobile Old Timers on December 11, 1956, gave Romney one of their awards.[4]

During the years American Motors was finding itself in the automobile business, the appliance division provided about one-third of its sales and, except for the rash of strikes at the Detroit Kelvinator plant, a reliable profit that helped to stabilize income when there were losses on cars. Kelvinator had stood fourth in the U.S. appliance industry after Frigidaire, General Electric and Westinghouse and second in appliance sales to the rest of the world. Yet Kelvinator did not regain the share of the domestic market it held when the industry shut down for World War II.

Its principal consumer appliance, the refrigerator, faced a saturated market. Its major competitors had resources for expensive advertising which American Motors could not match during its time of automotive troubles. New companies had entered the field and existing ones had increased their productive capacity.

B. A. Chapman, executive vice president and general manager of the Appliance Division, moved energetically to broaden markets. A number of additional fast-growing products were added to give dealers a full line. American Motors now manufactures electric refrigerators, electric ranges, home freezers, automatic and wringer-type washers and clothes driers, under the Kelvinator, Leonard and A.B.C. names. Room air conditioners, electric water heaters, water coolers, dehumidifiers, garbage disposers, dishwashers and kitchen cabinets are bought and distributed under the Kelvinator name. The commercial department makes ice cream cabinets, beverage coolers, and merchandising display cabinets for frozen foods.

At the same time, new products were developed to tempt consumers to replace outworn appliances. In 1955, Kelvinator brought out the Foodarama, a luxurious two-door unit with an upright freezer and a refrigerator compartment in the same cabinet. In 1956, styling was separated from the engineering department and set up in its own right. Meanwhile, investment of twenty million dollars in new production facilities since World War II, principally at Grand Rapids, Michigan, helped offset the high and inflexible labor costs squeezing appliance profits. By 1959, laundry equipment production, previously in Peoria, Illinois, and compressor manufacture, previously in Detroit, had been moved to Grand Rapids. A new $2,000,000 warehouse was completed there in 1960.

The world market, entered almost by accident in the 1920's, has proved the brightest spot in the American Motors appliance picture. In 1954, American Motors sold 20 per cent of the stock in its Canadian subsidiary to the Simpson-Sears retail organization in Canada, which provided distribution for its major appliances in that growing market. In 1957, a new appliance plant in Bromborough, England, doubled English production to supply overseas markets better served through England than the United States. The same year, foreign manufacturing and distributing operations were organized as Kelvinator International Corporation. In 1958, the company sold more refrigerators outside the United States than in it. In one year, the company sold a thousand refrigerators to Iceland and did a brisk business in air conditioners in India.

Kelvinator enjoyed a historical advantage in penetrating the exploding postwar market for refrigerators in Europe and South

America. Kelvinator International works with licensee plants on a fee determined by billings. It provides product plans and specifications, tooling information, assistance in plant layouts and in purchasing equipment, and controls quality, while leaving the operation of the business to native businessmen close to their markets. Partnership with local capitalists has earned Kelvinator a warm reception in countries where American imports would be resented.

In 1959, there were Kelvinator licensee plants in France, Australia, New Zealand, Argentina, Brazil, Colombia, Mexico, the Philippines, India, Greece, Spain, Germany, Finland, Norway, Sweden and Italy, and others under negotiation. One licensee in Italy, the Necchi sewing machine company, makes compressors for S.A.F.T., the Italian firm licensed to produce finished refrigerators as well as for other manufacturers of refrigeration equipment in that country and elsewhere. Along with Rambler automobiles, four Kelvinator appliances were chosen to illustrate American life at the U.S. Exhibition in Moscow in 1959.

Romney opened a personal campaign for Kelvinator in 1959 with an advertisement in major newspapers and magazines inquiring, "Do you want more complicated or more useful appliances?" In inspirational speeches to dealers, Romney warned that intelligent homemakers would not replace satisfactory appliances unless they demonstrably saved time, money or space. In display space, Romney was pictured in front of a Foodarama urging housewives to shop for real benefits under a headline, "I wish more appliance customers would say 'Show Me' *before* they buy!" He followed up with a booklet, *How to Select a New Electrical Appliance,* which showed homemakers how to pick their way through a welter of conflicting advertising claims.

As a result he received letters from some Kelvinator users saying they did not need to be shown. A woman in the Philippine Islands reported a refrigerator in use fifteen years without attention. A Houston, Texas, woman told of one that had survived a flood, and

Mrs. B. F. Schwarm of East Hartford, Conn., sent a picture of one that had been in use thirty-three years.

The first five years of American Motors saw many executive changes but able men were so numerous in the organization that only Vice Presidents Cushman and Abernethy came from outside. Joseph W. Eskridge, who had been in charge of Hudson manufacturing, became vice president and general manager of the special products division when Stuart G. Baits retired. Homer L. Travis became vice president in charge of Kelvinator sales and G. T. Etheridge vice president of Kelvinator International Corp. Herschel F. Powell became director of appliance engineering and research when Dr. Lawrence A. Philipp, a vice president, retired.

Richard T. Purdy succeeded Roy D. Chapin, Jr., as treasurer when the latter was promoted to executive vice president. Donald P. Else, a veteran of Kelvinator accounting, became comptroller soon after the merger. John L. Brown, Jr., assistant to the president, succeeded Andrew Hood as secretary on the latter's retirement. V. E. Boyd became automotive field sales manager, and Wallace S. Berry director of automotive research. Edmund E. Anderson was named director of automotive styling and William F. Reddig director of appliance styling.

Dr. William E. Stirton, vice president of the University of Michigan and earlier associated with Romney in many civic activities, was elected to the board of directors in 1958. J. Willard Marriott of Washington, D. C., president of Hot Shoppes, Inc., restaurant and motor hotel chain, was added in 1959.

XVI

The Case for the Compact Car

In the practical eye of the industrial designer, the merit of an automobile or any other article depends not on its size but on the ease,
efficiency and economy with which it performs the function for
which it is designed. Henry Dreyfuss, one of the pioneers of industrial design, has said: "Mere common sense dictates that cars should
be just big enough to hold three packages comfortably—power,
people, luggage—and not an inch bigger."[1]

Back in 1938, Delmar G. Roos, who helped develop the jeep and
many other small vehicles, said: "The object of an automobile is to
transport a given number of people with reasonable comfort, with
the least consumption of gasoline, oil and rubber, and for the
slightest operating cost and prime price." In a 1945 book,[2] Christy
Borth added that such an appraisal was not infrequently topped off
with a fillip about the folly of "using two tons of automobile to
transport a 105-pound blonde."

George Romney's great achievement was in first convincing his
associates in American Motors and then the car-buying public that
the compact Rambler answered the needs of many thousands of
motorists better than either the bigger cars of the Big Three or the
tiny and cramped small cars imported from Europe. In doing so he
led a revolution in the automobile industry. That there was a com-

pact car, of course, was due to George Mason and many years of experiment at Nash.

"When I came into the company," Romney once recalled, "there were only three men in the management at that point who really believed in the Rambler smaller-car program. Other officers endeavored to enlist my help in killing the whole thing." That Romney had the discernment to recognize its value and become its apostle when others thought it would be fatal to the company was the result of earlier independent experience of his own.

Soon after he joined the Automobile Manufacturers Association, the organization analyzed the first nationally compiled car-use figures. In order to determine highway needs, the Public Roads Administration with the help of state highway departments had collected a great mass of statistics on automobile use and automobile travel. The government had money enough only to analyze them partially so the AMA took over and made a detailed tabulation.

The biggest single fact that came out of the study was that 85 per cent of all car trips were thirteen miles or less in length and that the bulk of the trips were for essential purposes. When John Gibbons, then head of the AMA public relations department, gave these figures to Romney, both predicted that they would revolutionize the country's highway program and also the design of automobiles.

People were beginning to rely on the automobile, the figures showed, not so much as a means of travel between cities but as a means of going from home to work, home to school, home to church, home to stores and other short essential trips predominantly within urban areas. Much of the rural driving was of exactly the same sort. The war intervened, however, and the reports were forgotten by everybody except Romney. Automobile manufacturers continued to make bigger and bigger cars and millions of people who had little or no choice continued to buy them.

In his earlier aluminum apprenticeship, Romney had learned the advantages of lightness in the construction of anything that had to be propelled and also the possibilities of weight-saving by the use of light metals. As a stunt, the Aluminum Company of America had made some aluminum automobiles on a Pierce-Arrow chassis as early as 1926. One is preserved in Detroit's Henry Ford Museum. Nobody rushed to make a car of aluminum but use of the metal increased in cars and spread from airplanes to buses and streamlined trains. Airplane construction methods were adopted along with the airplane metal.

Charles Nash had been interested in small cars in the twenties. "The great advantage of the smaller car is its easy handling and ability to turn in comparatively small space," he told a writer[3] in 1926. "I believe that the old type of extra luxurious long wheel-base car will be virtually eliminated. The time is soon coming, I believe, when we will see on the roads scarcely any cars exceeding a chassis wheel base of 125 inches, and the majority of cars in use, I predict, will be 110 inches or less."

Ford, Chevrolet and Plymouth all achieved their greatest market penetration with cars of no more than 107-inch wheel bases. For Ford this was in 1924, when the 1,414,293 Model T's, with a wheel base of only 100 inches, were 50 per cent of the cars registered. Chevrolet achieved 39.9 per cent of registrations in 1927 with a 103-inch wheel-base car. In 1933, Plymouth had 16.7 per cent of the market with a 107-inch wheel-base model. These manufacturers, however, moved to bigger models and a score of newcomers went broke trying to introduce new small cars.

As it is easier to make a clock than a watch, it is technically easier to make a big automobile than a small one. Materials, of course, are less but labor costs may be almost the same. The big savings on small cars are for their owners. Registration fees usually are based on weight or horsepower, and the annual registration of a small car may cost only half that of a big one. As small cars use less, sometimes much less, gasoline than big cars, small-car owners pay less for gasoline and less in federal and state taxes on gasoline. The last have been rising steadily since Oregon imposed the first levy in 1919, and with an increase of the federal tax from three to four in 1959 there is an average tax of about ten cents a gallon on gasoline.

George Mason, of course, was a motorcycle and small-car enthusiast. When the Edward G. Budd Manufacturing Company, which had pioneered the all-steel automobile body, began to work on unit construction, Mason was interested. His engineering vice president, Eric Wahlberg, and the latter's assistant and successor, Meade Moore, began to experiment with it. Moore had been to Europe in 1929 and later to study the French Citroën and German Porsche, which employed unit construction. Ted Ulrich, who had helped Budd develop streamlined trains, was hired as body engineer.

They had to overcome many difficulties. The early single-unit construction was troublesome. The cars were stiff, the noise level was high and the ride was not so good. The project resulted in the Nash "600," a car of conventional size which weighed only 2,600 pounds in comparison with an average of 3,100 pounds for similar cars as World War II stopped car production.

Moore conceived the smaller car project during the war. He was loaned then to United Aircraft at Hartford. As he commuted there daily by train from Westport, Connecticut, he noticed many lone men driving to the stations in big cars and leaving them there all day. As the war ended, Mason authorized Moore to develop a small car.

Engines of all types and small cars of every kind were studied. Moore broke his arm falling out of one of them. Among the many cars tested were the Panhard, Austin, Vedette, Volkswagen, Opel, Fiat, Alfa-Romeo, Peugeot and Cisitalia. The aim of the program was not a miniaturized big car but a new type of car providing full American-type passenger space while reducing sharply over-all size and weight, thus adding European economy and ease of handling while meeting American comfort and style standards. In 1949, the American Automobile Association protested the trend to impractical styling, termed higher horsepower dangerous and pleaded for cars economical to operate. Only Nash engineers paid any attention.

Moore and his colleagues developed three basic cars. These were the small Metropolitan, the 100-inch wheel-base Rambler and the 108-inch wheel-base Rambler. The first was a two-seated small car made for the company in England, beginning in 1954. With an engine and parts available, tooling for it cost only $800,000 at the Austin plant. The 100-inch Rambler was a five-passenger two-door car introduced in 1950 and the 108-incher a six-passenger four-door car with full interior space but a foot and a half shorter than comparable cars offered in 1954.

The three cars saved money, space and gasoline. Because of the single-unit construction, they also were safer than bigger cars but sales were slow at first. The big-car idea had been sold to the public so thoroughly that ownership of a small car then connoted poverty, eccentricity or bad judgment. Dealers were not eager for them and it was not until Romney became president that American Motors concentrated on them. As resources were limited Romney put his advertising behind the Ramblers.

The 85-inch wheel-base, four-cylinder Metropolitan received modest but clever promotion. James W. Watson, the sales manager, made every purchaser a member of the Metropolitan Club. This had a "Motores Prudentiores" coat of arms, a membership certificate, car insignia and a magazine. The club's arms showed a bankbook, an oil well, an ore boat and a tree representing its platform:

1. The conservation of vital natural resources, such as iron, oil and rubber.
2. The reduction of personal motoring costs—both capital and operating—thus making additional funds available to car owners to be used for whatever purpose they may desire—including savings.
3. The encouragement of the use of the proper car for the need at hand.

4. The dissemination of the basic philosophy that waste in any form is unwise and unintelligent.
5. The belief that many American cars today are almost vulgar in their wasteful ostentatious monstrosity.
6. The reduction in the present inexcusable number of highway fatalities.
7. The conviction that high speed is one of the greatest enemies of motoring safety and economy.

Metropolitan owners eagerly reported their "prudent motoring" adventures in their magazine. A Phoenix, Arizona, woman bought one a month after her sixty-ninth birthday. A Kansas couple sent in a picture of their two Metropolitans with the doors marked "His" and "Hers." An Alabama woman, who weighed 375 pounds, forwarded a photograph proving that there was room in one for herself and her 209-pound husband. A Wichita, Kansas, family reported they operated three Metropolitans. A Cleveland owner reported he saved enough on gasoline to buy an additional ten-thousand-dollar life insurance policy. A California couple, the man a six foot two inch welder, drove 8,328 miles at a cost of only $121.55. A Rocky Mount, North Carolina, man drove 7,758 miles at a total gas cost of $86.82, antifreeze, grease and oil $16.45, and repairs $7.25. He calculated the rate per mile: gas, .011; grease and oil, .0021; and repairs, .0001.

In Miami, a man used a Metropolitan to deliver Western Union messages and in San Fernando, California, the police used a right-hand drive Metropolitan to tag cars parked overtime. Ann Sothern, motion picture and television actress, drove one. The *Ledger-Enquirer* of Columbus, Georgia, bought a fleet of twenty-five for its circulation department. The Metropolitan began to be sold overseas as well as in the U.S. and Canada and the club publication blossomed with pictures from Alaska, Okinawa and Germany.

Romney advertised similar testimonials for the Rambler in magazines. A New York grape grower told how he averaged 25.5

miles per gallon of gasoline "at fast thruway speeds" to California. A Kansas cattle buyer reported 27.6 miles per gallon for 37,238 miles over rough range country in five months. A Mercedes, Texas, mail carrier averaged 29.8 miles to the gallon on his daily Star route from Harlingen to Mission. A Wisconsin osteopath "relaxed" in Ramblers better than bigger cars and found the bed seats valuable for taking patients to or from the hospital.

When the 108-inch four-door Rambler sold better than the 100-inch two-door, the latter was discontinued for a time but was brought back successfully as the Rambler American in 1957. American Motors engineers later discovered that they could design a four-door car with the shorter wheel base.

Sales of both Ramblers and Metropolitans were helped by a rising tide of resentment against big cars. In their efforts to effect production economies the Big Three at that time standardized on their larger rather than their smaller basic body shells. They were led to this by their past sales and a considerable mass of motivational research which suggested that many people with frustrated lives could be happy only with big cars.

Suddenly big cars were being treated with ridicule rather than reverence. Romney's crusade for the small car inspired a large part of the criticism but much also developed spontaneously. A resolution "suggesting respectfully" that big cars were "wasteful" was adopted in 1957 by the board of evangelism and social service of the United Church of Canada. Doctor James R. Mutchmor explained people complained they could not get their new cars into their garages and that parking was more difficult. He deplored the tail fins. "Now if they increased the size of the trunk that would be something," he said. "But those large tail fins—what do they do?" Religious News Service carried the item and the *New York Times* and many other newspapers published it.

Dr. S. I. Hayakawa, an authority on semantics who happened to own a 1952 Nash Ambassador and a 1954 Hillman convertible, in

1958 stirred a controversy in marketing and advertising circles with an entertaining but scathing attack on the idea that motorists yearned for big cars for Freudian reasons. Dr. Hayakawa said the automobile industry had overlooked what Freud called "the reality principle" and had been led astray by motivational researchers who, he said, believed appeals to human irrationality were likely to be more profitable than appeals to rationality.

Different people have different needs, both with respect to transportation and self-expression. Hence there should be, in a rich economy like that of the United States, variety in automobiles no less than in other facets of life. Hence, I believe that manufacturers should build *some* cars of very high horsepower for those who need such cars, whether for practical or psychological reasons. . . . *Some* cars should be little and unpretentious, because there are many modest, unassuming people in the U.S., hard as that may be to believe on the basis of our car ads.

My quarrel with the American automobile industry in 1957 was not that it produced overpriced, overpowered and overelaborated cars, but that it produced them almost to the exclusion of all other kinds. Except for some interesting experiments at the fringes of the market by American Motors and Studebaker, the dominating forces in the industry—General Motors, Ford and Chrysler—are still carrying on (in 1958) their assault on consumer intelligence. The Big Three are producing no cars that are not expensive, hideous and (except for a few sizes) costly to operate and powered far beyond any ordinary needs.[4]

Columnists turned critical (Inez Robb asked for "something smaller than a Mark IV tank and slightly less unwieldy in traffic"). There were jokes (the lady parking her new car couldn't figure which meter to put the nickel in). There was a complaint from *The National Underwriter* against attempts to "lure drivers into taking dangerous chances with speed" and advertising that "seduce[s] the typical American into laying out money in monthly payments that he should be using for building up a decent insurance and retirement program." A survey by the Federation of Women's Clubs also turned up some sharp criticism of the automobile industry. In the interest of public relations for the medical profession, the Los Angeles County Medical Association asked its members to keep medical insignia out of sight if they drove Cadillacs.

But side by side with all this went something more serious in tone. It was to the effect that the continuing trend toward bigger and bigger cars was imposing an unbearable strain on parking space and traffic in general. Columbia University's C. Lowell Harriss wrote in the *American Economic Review*:[5] "If the average new auto were only a foot shorter, and if 4 million cars a year were destined for city use, about 800 square miles of street space equivalent would be released." He advocated a graduated system of licensing fees to discourage the hogging of parking space and of traffic areas generally by extra large autos, starting, perhaps, with a dollar per inch of length for each inch between 180 and 185, and running up to ten dollars for each inch in excess of 190.

Several aldermen in Chicago supported a legislative move to abolish the horsepower rating systems for auto license fees and substitute one based on the length of the car. Jack Bruce, city traffic engineer for Denver, bemoaned the fact that because of the increasing car lengths drivers were having more and more difficulty maneuvering their way into the city's twenty-foot metered parking areas.

Romney and his alert public relations staff watched the United Press International news ticker in the American Motors office for opportunities to relate their story to news of the day.

When President Eisenhower remarked that business should stimulate buying by giving the public what it wants, Romney was promptly on the wires with a statement agreeing with the President: "I think we're again witnessing the fact consumers in this country are still king. Consumers are rebelling against the size, the large horsepower and the excessive styling changes made each year by many auto manufacturers."

When Mayor Robert Wagner of New York appealed to the industry to help relieve traffic congestion by making shorter and narrower cars, Romney not only endorsed the idea but gave the Mayor figures on what he would save by substituting Ramblers for his Cadillacs and offered to send him three Ramblers for test driving. Mayor Wagner did not accept but later banned big luxury cars as official automobiles for commissioners and deputy commissioners. This resulted in a well-publicized auction of twenty-four Cadillac sedans and two Chrysler limousines by the city in 1959.

On the other side of the country, Mayor Norris Poulson of Los Angeles, then president of the U.S. Conference of Mayors, canceled his order for a Cadillac and bought a Rambler as his official city automobile. As mayor of the city with the largest per capita number of cars of any in the world, Poulson denounced big cars not only for the traffic and parking problems that they caused but for their exhaust fumes. These contributed to the Los Angeles smog, which he feared was a factor in lung cancer.

"I recommend we get little cars," he said. "If a car uses one-third as much gas there will be one-third as much exhaust fumes in the air." He termed big cars the No. 1 air pollution problem in Los Angeles and on the subject of bigness in cars said, "The bigger the car, the bigger the problem."

While Romney and American Motors were named in only a few lines, mostly in footnotes, John Keats' 1958 book, *The Insolent Chariots*[6] with its Robert Osborn cartoons of big cars helped Romney's cause. "American auto design is steadily proceeding away from reality with the speed of light," Keats said. And after a look at the current Big Three models he was moved to raise a question posed by Milton in *Paradise Lost:* "Whence, and what art Thou, Execrable Shape?" Keats attacked automobile styling, advertising and distribution. The automobile, he pointed out, is a machine and not "a love-object" and the industry ought to produce "better made, longer lasting, more dependable and economical automobiles."

Tin Pan Alley also gave the Rambler a free boost with a 1958 song, "Beep Beep," which many stations banned as an outright commercial:

> While riding in my Cadillac,
> What, to my surprise;
> A little Nash Rambler was following me,
> About one-third my size. . . .
> Now we're doing a hundred and twenty,
> As fast as I could go;
> The Rambler pulled alongside of me,
> As if I were going slow. . . .
> My fellow rolled down his window
> And yelled for me to hear,
> "Hey, buddy, how can I get this car
> Out of second gear?"

As in the case of "In My Merry Oldsmobile," the company had nothing to do with the song. Donald Claps and Carl Cicchetti wrote it and first sang it in night clubs. The Patricia Music Publishing Corporation issued it in sheet form and Roulette Records sold a million discs to make it fourth in popularity for some weeks. It reminded old-timers of a 1914 song, "The Little Ford Rambled Right Along." While Hudson once had something musical titled "This Time It's Hudson," neither Nash nor Hudson in their long history ever had anything like "Beep Beep." It also was published and recorded in England but the Rambler was replaced by the Bubble Car in the British version.

The Rambler American was the "only current U. S. contribution to economical motoring," according to the 1958 automobile issue of *Consumer Reports,* a no-advertising magazine with 800,000 devoted readers. Its consultants also chose the Rambler Ambassador as the foundation for an ideal hypothetical automobile to be assembled from the best features available. On the basis of road tests the magazine rated the Rambler the "best buy" among six-cylinder 1959 cars. A Rambler American driven by Woody Bell, a toolmaker of Sunland, California, won the 1959 Mobilgas Economy Run of 1,898 miles from Los Angeles to Kansas City with an average of 25.29 miles per gallon. A deluxe Rambler driven by Les Viland of Livonia, Michigan, was second with 22.96 miles per gallon. These were cars with automatic transmissions, carrying loads of 750 pounds during the event. *Popular Science* in August, 1959, found a Rambler American could be driven at a total cost of 10.87 cents a mile as compared with 13.46 cents for a Ford Fairlane V-8.

The Allstate Insurance Company, a subsidiary of Sears, Roebuck and Company, on November 1, 1959, reduced insurance premiums on compact cars by approximately 10 per cent in several states. "Our experience in insuring compact-type cars," Judson R. Branch, Allstate president, said, "indicates that due to lower acceleration, smaller size and weight, better maneuverability and related factors, these cars cause less damage in an accident than the standard-size cars."

If a compact car could effect important gasoline savings for the operator of one or two cars, it naturally could save thousands in fleet operations, especially as increased taxes sent the price of gasoline higher and higher. Since 1941 nearly every state has increased gasoline taxes. With the federal tax counted, motorists were paying upward of seventy cents in taxes on every eight gallons of gasoline bought in 1959.

The Texas legislature in that year, for example, in a highway department appropriation stipulated that the department could not use the money to buy big eight-cylinder automobiles. The advantages of Ramblers over competitors were spelled out in Delta Airlines advertising, which offered to rent new Ramblers at airports for thirty-five dollars a week and eight cents a mile as compared with Fords and Chevrolets at sixty dollars a week and eleven cents a mile.

A fleet of 1,748 Ramblers was ordered by the Ordnance Tank Automotive Command in 1959 for use at Army, Navy, Marine and Air Force installations in the United States and abroad. Swift & Company, Quaker Oats and General Mills had Rambler fleets in Chicago. Western Electric and many other Bell Telephone System divisions, Commonwealth Edison of Chicago and Consolidated Edison of New York also were using Ramblers. Though many car rental companies had long-term commitments with the Big Three, Ramblers also began to appear in the fleets of Olin's, Inc., Avis and the Hertz Corporation.

The compact car, a term which American Motors attempted to copyright, made the company profitable in the closing months of 1957. With a handkerchief labeled "Business is Good," in his pocket, Romney announced the news at a press conference. It was the only success story of the American automobile industry in 1958, a year which saw more cars imported than exported for the first time in the century. In 1959, it was so thoroughly accepted that American Motors profits set new records and all companies began to work on compact models.

Romney was confident this would broaden the market. If the national economy continued to prosper, there would be more and more multi-car families. These reached six million in 1957 and were forecast to pass seven million in 1960. If business declined, the Rambler would have great appeal as a first car for reasons of pure economy and dependability, also for its high resale value.

Romney is no longer an unsung prophet. His dogged stumping of the country has been crowned with financial success. He has had the satisfaction of being right all along—right on the compact car and right on the Rambler. But these do not exhaust his missionary zeal. He has deep personal convictions on a variety of public issues.

XVII

Of Power and Competition

"All that is necessary for evil to triumph," said Edmund Burke, famous eighteenth-century English statesman and orator, "is for good people to do nothing." George Romney is deeply in accord with this belief and has expounded it to countless audiences of all sorts. He believes it is the duty of a good citizen not only to take the proper stand on an issue but to speak out about it regardless of whether or not it is popular at the moment to do so. In fact, the less popular the stand, the greater the duty to talk about it, in his opinion.

"He is going to say what he pleases," says a friend of Romney, "and he is not just going to keep quiet like some people of integrity. They just don't go out of their way to hit somebody on the nose, yet they won't say what they don't believe. But George has a form of integrity that requires him to believe everything he says and, in addition, requires him to say everything he believes. This is an even greater degree of integrity and it causes many people to get a little upset at George when he flails out at things which seem removed from the problem at hand and whose success can only be in the distant future."

He has devoted a great deal of thought and words to two subjects. These are voluntary co-operation, which he favors, and excessive concentration of power, which he strongly opposes whether in government, industry or labor.

He learned the value of voluntary co-operation as a boy in Mexico and the West, where every drop of irrigation water that made parched ground fertile was the result of voluntary co-operation.[1] His concern with excessive concentration of power has been a gradual development. As one of its young employees in Washington, Romney thought nothing wrong with the Aluminum Company of America having all of the aluminum ingot business. The experience of his later years caused him to change his mind on this point.

As one of his recommendations to President Mason of Nash, Romney urged that the company institute a program of cash awards for achievements in voluntary co-operation. "Our country," Romney wrote, "is distinguished by two basic characteristics—individualism and teamwork. In no other country have individuals worked more successfully as individuals or more effectively as teams. . . Americans have established more private, voluntary organizations to aid them in serving the common good through teamwork than any other people. The important part they play is not widely understood or acknowledged. Focusing the public spotlight on the most notable annual achievements by community agencies would be a public service of the highest order. . . . People engaged in such work are hungry for encouragement and recognition. In nearly every case, they operate on small budgets and badly need additional funds."

There was no action, but as Romney drafted his recommendations late in 1948 Raphael Malsin of the Lane Bryant stores began giving annual awards for achievements of individuals and organizations in community service. The Sears-Roebuck Foundation also launched a community service contest through the National Grange, and in 1949 the Kroger Stores sponsored a "Build a Better Community" contest through the General Federation of Women's

Clubs. When he was president of the Automobile Manufacturers Association in 1956, Romney urged that organization, which had achieved so much by voluntary efforts, to establish a national foundation for voluntary co-operation, but there was no action. In 1958, he had American Motors join the U.S. Junior Chamber of Commerce in sponsoring cash and silver cup awards to Jaycee chapters achieving the most in community improvements. In 1959 cash awards of $3,000 and silver cups went to Jaycee chapters in Canton, Ohio; Centerville, Iowa; and Stinnett, Texas.

"The importance of voluntary co-operation as a mechanism for meeting our most difficult community problems deserves wider recognition," said Romney, "and we believe that the Jaycee program will help foster such co-operation on a broad scale. The philosophy and approach are in concert with President Eisenhower's memorable statement that 'to blend, without coercion, the individual good with the public good is the essence of citizenship in a free society.'"

When Romney is convinced of something, he then becomes the missionary. His jaws become firm and compromise is then difficult, but if it can be shown that the facts are different from what he believes them to be, or if conditions have changed, he is not so stubborn but that he will change his mind. If he has done anybody an injustice in the course of the controversy, he will apologize handsomely.

Romney never carries a dispute over from one day to the next. "He never starts the day mad at anybody," says a colleague. He does, however, frequently wind up the day with somebody mad at him, for despite the pressures exerted on him as top man in a highly competitive automobile and appliance business, plus his responsibilities as a leader in the Mormon Church, he stumps the country constantly in an effort to get some highly controversial messages across to the American people. In this sense he is no less a missionary now than during his tour of duty in England.

Although he can accept only a small fraction of the speaking invitations that pour into his office, Romney turns up before a wide variety of organizations, large and small—at Junior Chambers of Commerce, automobile groups, economic associations, women's societies and university commencement exercises, to mention a few. His messages, which most frequently tee off with brief quotations from a wide scattering of authorities from Isaiah to George Santayana and, at times, his own chief competitors, vary in approach, but almost invariably come earnestly to grips with the small assortment of public issues that concern him most—anti-trust law, labor law, the need for voluntary co-operation and the need to rid both politics and thought of the dominant and rigid influence of powerful economic groups.

For most people this would be a thankless task. To many people George Romney seems in the position of a man who is trying to sell cars and appliances, yet is rubbing the biggest interests in this country the wrong way by attacking simultaneously Big Business, Big Labor and the Republican and Democratic parties.[2]

And some will find curious inconsistencies in his insistence at one and the same time that: General Motors is a good competitor; General Motors should be split up; citizens must think and act for themselves, not as members of economic groups; citizens can only act effectively in co-operation with other citizens; this economy is so dominated by the consumer it should be called "consumeristic" rather than "capitalistic"; in the automobile industry the consumer has been led around by a "chromium ring in his nose"; and so on.

But these contradictions are only contradictions when measured in terms of the cliché form of expression to which Americans have become so accustomed—e.g., that if you're a Republican you're anti-Democrat; if you're a big business official you want labor curbed; or if you're a labor leader you want the most stringent antitrust laws clamped on big business. George Romney does not subscribe to any of these clichés. He is hewing his own path, and to date this path has followed a clear line of logic, whether he is trying to help straighten out Michigan's tangled fiscal affairs, warning Mormon students of the responsibilities that weigh upon them, or arguing before a Congressional committee for the break-up of General Motors. Moreover, he is not actually attacking anybody. He has something more serious in his mind.

From the numerous speeches he has made and from his statements to legislative groups, Romney has made it clear he looks upon the American economy and its future with mixed feelings. He recognizes its massive accomplishments, and lays these in good part to the soundness of four basic principles—competition, voluntary co-operation, rewards based upon contribution and the wide distribution of the fruits of progress among consumers, workers and owners.

As against this, however, he sees some dangerous internal weaknesses developing at a critical time—namely, while the country is engaged "in the greatest struggle for survival that has ever occurred in the history of the world." And because there appears to be a military stalemate, he sees this struggle centering in the fields of subversion, propaganda and economics.

What, on the economic front, do these internal weaknesses constitute? Among other things the periodic repetition of the wage-price spiral since the war; a continuing increase in industrial prices, in more and more business mergers; the excessive reliance on monetary controls to halt inflation and the wage-price spiral; mounting public attacks on the profit-and-loss system "resulting from a lack of public understanding"; excessive use of union power to squeeze profits down to a dangerous level; a trend toward the further concentration of union power as exemplified by the merger of the CIO and AFL, and a resulting rush toward concentration of industry's economic and political power which threatens a dangerous division of America into two contending self-interest groups.

The economy of the United States he views as "unique and distinct." It is not so much "capitalistic"—a European development which amounts, in the dictionary sense, to a system under which a few benefit from the labors of many—but "consumeristic."[3]

The consumer's power as the ultimate arbiter in the economy has been built up partly because of the relentless pressure of competition and partly because, as Romney puts it, "through the antitrust and labor laws we have distributed and divided power in this country." Thus far, he says, this system has operated in such a way as to make consumers the "principal beneficiaries and bosses of our economy."

But while he favors in principle both the laws to break up business monopoly and those protecting the rights of labor, including collective bargaining, in practice he feels the antitrust laws are outmoded and misdirected while the labor laws have gone far beyond their originally commendable goal of creating a counterbalance to the influence of big business. Both in terms of economics and politics, he says, the power of big unions has grown to the point "where it is dangerous to our future and where it is blocking our future economic progress and development."

"I happen to believe," he has said, "that the labor laws passed to promote collective bargaining were very necessary. I think they broke up an excessive concentration of industry power of an economic and political character."

But today—with many unions in a position to shut down industries absolutely vital to the nation, and with one in a position to starve the whole country in a matter of a few days—a serious imbalance has been created. Romney sees it as worse than a mere imbalance, in fact. It amounts, he says, to "a fundamental, fatal conflict between the labor laws, which are premised on the principle of monopoly, and the antitrust laws, which are premised on the principle of competition."

It is to this conflict, and to the means of solving it, that Romney has been devoting a large part of his missionary efforts.

Competition is much touted as the real sparkplug of the American economy. If so, American Motors ought to know because, as Romney told the Senate group,[4] "few other companies face as many large competitors." In the automobile industry it is up against General Motors, Ford, Chrysler and Studebaker-Packard, not to mention the foreign cars that have been entering the American market in ever-increasing numbers. But that is not all: in the appliance field it competes with General Electric, Frigidaire, Whirlpool with its RCA and Sears-Roebuck partners and customers, Westinghouse, Philco, Admiral, Norge (Borg-Warner) and others. Yet he feels that a good deal of this necessary competitive urge is being lost.

Since his longest continuous experience has been in the automobile industry, Romney uses it more often than any other to prove his point. Over the past sixty years nearly fifteen hundred different manufacturers have offered more than 2,400 different makes of car on the American market. Only five are left today— General Motors, Ford, Chrysler, American Motors and Studebaker-Packard.

There hasn't been a successful new birth in the auto industry in thirty-five years that was not, as Romney puts it, "the result of a merger or of reinvigoration of an old company (as with Walter Chrysler's use of Maxwell as the nucleus of the Chrysler Corporation)." Kaiser-Frazer did, it is true, enter the market in the "lushest" period the industry has ever known, but it failed to make the grade. Nor are any new ones likely. Romney figures the cost of setting up a new company would run about $250,000,000 each for plant and dealer organizations plus another half-billion for product promotion and acceptance, the lack of service business, uncertain resale value and other competitive conditions—the total initial investment required being about one billion dollars.

Romney thinks that five companies constitute just about the minimum required in such an industry to protect the consumer and command consumer confidence and to nourish the "competitive principle of discipline." In view of the fact that hundreds of auto companies have perished in the competitive struggle thus far, what assurance is there that today's five won't be reduced to tomorrow's three, two or one?

There are five theoretical ways of assuring a minimum number of companies, Romney has said on several occasions.

1. Acquisition of the capacity for "economic immortality." He doesn't think any automobile manufacturers have acquired that capacity.

2. Restraint of competitive effort on the part of the more successful companies, to keep all competitors in business. "I don't think we can afford that sort of restraint in view of the all-out competition we face all around the world," he says.

3. Government regulation of competition to protect marginal firms. "I think it is perfectly obvious that this is undesirable, because again it would deny us the economic growth and vitality we need to cope with a rival system that is going all out."

4. Federal subsidization. The government has already done that in one case (i.e., via the arrangement under which Curtiss-Wright was given large defense contracts as a part of a deal to take over Studebaker-Packard). Romney thinks that is wrong "because it leads to statism."

5. The fifth alternative is Romney's own. It is the alternative he has been preaching up and down the country for some years. He views further "deaths" in industry as inevitable. What he wants is a drastic revision in the antitrust laws—actually a whole new approach to them—to ensure that "as we have further deaths we would have births to replace them."

In general terms, he puts it this way:

"I do not know of any way by which our most successful companies can grow without limit under our present antitrust concepts, unless they divide and create more than one company through the process of fission voluntarily, on whatever basis is in their best interest. That is the only way I know of by which the most successful enterprises in America can grow without limit. We need to maintain the vigor of the competitive principle and to benefit from its full and effective expression."[5]

There are two aspects of antitrust procedure under the Sherman Act that Romney doesn't like.

The first is that it is too slow. He points out that it took twenty years in the courts to conclude proceedings against the Aluminum Company of America, fourteen to wind up the case against General Motors Acceptance Corporation and more than ten to settle the problems of monopoly in the moving picture industry, in the course of which, as he notes wryly, "the advent of television completely changed industry patterns."

The second difficulty, expressed in his own words, is that the proceedings are conducted in the atmosphere of a criminal trial. Questions of morality and ethics rather than economic and social policy have often determined court decisions in this field. With very few exceptions, the Government has been unsuccessful in curbing economic monopoly unless it could show that the defendant has been motivated by evil or predatory intent. Even the most advanced definition of a monopoly requires proof not only that the defendant has the power to exclude his competitors from the industry but also that he has the desire or intent to use this power. And this intent is provable only by demonstrating that he has, in fact, used exclusionary practices to obtain and maintain his position.

What Romney wants for American industry in general and for the automobile industry in particular is the maintenance of competitive vigor and an assured means of having a minimum number of competing companies in our huge basic industries—the number to be determined by a specified percentage of total industry sales over a specified period of time. Reaching and passing this ceiling, a large company would face not prosecution by the Justice Department, but the need to come forward with an acceptable plan for splitting off some of its operations and the consequent "birth" of a new company. The only compulsion upon it would be a plan of divestiture that promised to bring its percentage of sales below the specified level.

There would, of course, be some complications. One would arise when the firm concerned was engaged in more than one basic industry. In that case, Romney feels the maximum percentage should be set lower because such a corporation is in a position to dominate a single market through its ability to concentrate all its resources on a single industry or product at any time, and to expand its position by relying on earnings from other activities.

Where would the ceiling be set? In computing this, Romney took as a rule-of-thumb the government's indications that the aluminum and automobile industries require five or six companies to provide adequate competition. To insure this, he feels, the maximum should be set at 35 per cent for a company not engaged in more than one basic industry and about 25 per cent where its operations are more diverse. Equated in terms of the automobile industry, this formula would mean that General Motors and Ford would "each become the source of new companies; General Motors as a result of its outstanding success in the automobile and several other basic industries, and Ford because of its success in the automobile and agricultural implement industries."

Offhand, this might look like nothing more than a scheme through which American Motors might get some of its toughest competition off its back. But not according to George Romney. Privately he quotes a Ford executive as saying: "Don't you know the competition for AM would be tougher if we were split up?" Romney cheerfully admits this would be the case.

Bigness per se, he maintained, does not make a company competitive. Appearing before a Senate monopoly inquiry in 1955,

GM's president, Harlow H. Curtice, repeatedly stressed the same thought, namely that "size has nothing to do with the ability of a company to compete successfully in industry." And Romney is able to use his own company as an example. It can "break even" on 120,000 cars a year out of a total industry production of five million, which, as he said, "should be a good indication that you don't have to have the volume of the Big Three manufacturers to be efficient." It can "make a very good profit and not take a back seat to anyone in the industry in production efficiency" in a production range of 180,000 to 220,000 cars a year, and on a one-shift basis. By going over to two shifts and producing 360,000 to 400,000 cars a year it could achieve additional small economies, but beyond that, Romney says, "only theoretical and insignificant reduction in manufacturing costs is possible." To this he added—as his 1958 record demonstrated—"It is possible to be one of the best without being the biggest."

If mere bigness is no guarantee of efficiency or competitive strength—and both Romney and Curtice appear to agree on this—why is AM's president so insistent that it be curbed?

One part of the answer is to be found in his argument that in the postwar automobile industry the few surviving smaller companies have contributed relatively more basic product pioneering than their bigger competitors. For example, Studebaker-Packard pioneered torsion bar suspension, separate rear wheel traction, greater driving vision, front and rear, as well as other functional and styling advances. American Motors pioneered modern car heating and ventilating, low-cost air conditioning, improved body painting and rust prevention including full body dip, smaller and more economical cars and, "most fundamental of all, the application to automobile design of the latest engineering principles developed in aircraft construction."

Romney also acknowledges the unsung contribution made by parts suppliers to technological development. Theirs has been the "greatest," he said in Detroit in December, 1958, although "the largest credit has gone to vehicle companies." He credits them with leadership in the field, for the engineering and research knowledge they represent simply "dwarfs anything of the vehicle companies."

When he mentions "vehicle companies," naturally enough, he includes his own. So far as the Big Three go, he grants they introduced the modern V-8 engine, automatic transmissions, wraparound windshields "that do not significantly improve vision," and power brakes and steering, both of them made necessary "by the constant increase in car length, weight and speed." But their primary emphasis, he says, has been on greater car size, horsepower and annual styling obsolescence—all of them attributes of General Motors' prestige philosophy, which was ultimately, though perhaps reluctantly, adopted by Ford as well as Chrysler.

Romney does not maintain that a big corporation is necessarily a "bad" corporation. On the contrary, he has gone out of his way on many occasions to pay tribute to GM's astuteness as a market leader, and in its recognition that the "cheap but dependable" car formula on which Ford thrived for some years had to give way to a more complex formula involving more prestige, more horsepower, more room, more chromium and more money. He has also paid tribute to GM's moderation as the dominant car producer in the country.

His main point is that: "Where competition is shrinking below adequate minimum levels, even the most efficient company will ultimately lose its competitive drive. Like boxing champions who lack suitable opponents, companies will become soft and flabby. Furthermore, artificial and undesirable restraints on competition develop more easily and even unintentionally."

And what is true of a single company, or of a group of companies in a single industry, can apply in time to the whole American economy. It is the possibility of a gradual erosion of the nation's competitive strength in all fields—political and military as well as economic—that prompts Romney to keep pounding away on this theme week after week, and to plead for his own solution as the happiest way out.

He points out that the country (as well as the shareholders) has benefited greatly from the division of Standard Oil into what ultimately became thirty-four vigorously competing companies.

"It is time," he said on one occasion, "to remove any stigma from those who manage successfully. Instead the public should hail enterprises that can give birth to new companies in the interest of maintaining adequate competition and furthering the vigor of our economic progress. The men who built the Big Three companies have rendered a great public service."

He insists they would be neither penalized nor stigmatized under his plan, for the size of the economic reward should be "related to the degree of economic success achieved." (He proposed, for example, that where divestiture becomes necessary, the capital gains tax payment should be postponed. Payment would be made when stock is sold by the holder, so the government would not lose any revenue, either.)

This is the nub of Romney's proposal to revise the antitrust laws. And, interestingly enough, its approach appears to have received some legal sanction in the agreement recently under which, at the direction of the courts, the United Fruit Company has been given ten years to launch a new company that will ultimately compete with it. However, as he points out, this kind of settlement takes a long time. His own would work much more rapidly.

As his Mead Committee testimony in 1945 evidenced, Romney has long been even more concerned over the monopoly drive fostered by the labor laws. His motivation is the same, but his choice of words is stronger on this subject.

"The present nature of collective bargaining in this country must change," he declares, "or the United States is going to lose its

221

present world economic position. We are in the process, as a result of excess power, of putting American industry on the same sort of economic stilts that we have put under American agriculture as a result of agricultural subsidization. This has lost for us much of our previously large world agricultural market."

In his view the damaging effects of the labor laws fall into eight categories: (1) the "fatal conflict" with the antitrust laws previously mentioned; (2) their premise that collective bargaining must be based on class conflict; (3) the extent to which they have overemphasized areas of labor-management disagreement at the expense of areas in which mutual interest is clearly established; (4) their creation of an "almost total absence of union-management co-operation"; (5) the premise that it is desirable that wages alone should absorb the full national rate of improved productivity; (6) their unsettling influence on buying occasioned by heavy inventory accumulation at times in anticipation of major strikes; (7) their buildup of labor power to the degree that unions are able to saddle industry with excessive costs, and (8) also able to channel this union power into so much political activity that the whole economic system is being perverted "into a primarily political system, and stimulating a dangerous war among economic organizations for political power."

So far as the automobile industry is concerned, Romney argues it has been forced in recent years to raise wages exceeding productivity gains by the relentless pressure of Walter Reuther's United Automobile Workers, "whip-sawing" now against one and now against another of the Big Three. As a result of this pressure of a united union backed by the combined forces of the AFL-CIO, the industry has been compelled again and again to raise prices. Automobile employment has dropped; so has the national purchasing power; so have auto exports, though imports have been rising spectacularly during recent years. Consequently, "there is evidence today that we could experience a decline in America's position as the leading producer of automobiles. This is more apparent today than was the danger in 1955 of our being surpassed in missiles and satellites."

The five automobile producers bargain with UAW individually, four generally going along in most respects with whatever contract the fifth finds it necessary to accept. The steel industry (like the glass and coal industries) comes to grips with the United Steel Workers as a monolithic unit in which the twelve largest companies have ultimately been able to reduce their representation at the active bargaining sessions to one man. Two men—one representing USW—thus work out the agreement. Romney doesn't like this either.

"As a result of the monolithic power on each side," he said in a 1959 address, "each is in a position to shut down an industry that is absolutely vital to the economy of this country. . . . I think our situation would be quite different if we did not have collective bargaining power organized on an industry-wide basis. When you get the collective bargaining power of either employers or unions or both organized on an industry-wide basis in a big basic industry, you have power of such magnitude that it gravely threatens the public interest."

The steel industry concentration, he maintained, is in direct conflict with the nation's fundamental concept of keeping power divided. "The process is destroying the competitive principle, because wages constitute 85 per cent of the ultimate cost of product. And when you permit wages to be dealt with on the basis of monopoly, then you are nullifying the competitive principle in the antitrust laws to the extent of 85 per cent. The wage-price spiral is creating economic imbalance in our country, the chief beneficiaries of which are the organized employees. The unorganized are left in a less favorable position, and this contributes to the decline on a broad basis of economic growth in the United States."

The limitations, faltering and misdirected though they may be, on business concentration, plus the uninhibited, unhindered concentration of union power are combining to create a sort of crumbling indiscipline in the economy. Romney has cited this often, adding (just as often): "There are only two ways of disciplining an economy. One is competition—the competition of the market place and the vote of the consumer—and the other is absolute authority, either public or private." By "public," of course, he means by government; by "private" he means by cartels, which are barred by law. Neither system is working at the moment.

What does Romney want? Does he want repeal of that section of the antitrust laws exempting unions from prosecution as monopolies in restraint of trade? He has denied this from the beginning. He told the Senate Judiciary Subcommittee that he subscribed "fully" to the exemption given unions from antitrust prosecution.

"The one sound and adequate solution is the elimination of conflict in our national economic policy, with adequate division of union and industry power," he said a little over a year later. His actual proposals to the committee for labor law revision were four in number:

1. The combining of national unions for the establishment of common bargaining demands or use of economic power should be prohibited.

2. In basic industries, affiliated unions of a national union representing employees of a single large company should be permitted to combine their collective bargaining demands and joint use of bargaining power.

3. Affiliated unions should be free to combine in bargaining with employers having less than ten thousand employees, but only within prescribed geographical limits. However, those representing more than about ten thousand employees of a single employer should be prohibited from combining to establish collective bargaining demands or exercising joint economic power against more than one company.

4. Nothing in the law should prohibit union co-operation aside from the above limitations.

He explained that in the mature basic industries, where national unions now combine the bargaining demands of hundreds of thousands of workers, collective bargaining problems are distinctly different from those of unions representing workers in smaller industries and in many of the crafts and trades.

His concern is with the unions, some of them international in scope, that enjoy an overwhelming power that not only threatens the competitive strength of the U.S. economy, but could detonate a national calamity.

He sees this concentration of power as an immense force not only in economics but in politics. In the tendency of business to influence the Republican party and of the unions to dominate the Democratic (in some areas anyway) he sees the seeds of much potential and possibly damaging strife.

Commenting on this last point, Romney says: "I am not talking about individual citizens, whether they are businessmen or union leaders, engaging in politics as individuals. I am talking about unions as economic organizations and corporations as economic organizations. When they get into politics they begin to pervert themselves into political instrumentalities, to the detriment of the country."

Politically, Romney can see little difference in principle between the present excessive political influence of unions and the earlier excessive political influence of business denounced by both Roosevelts. "One excess is as bad as the other," he has said. "Both are obstacles to political freedom and economic justice. Both are morally and socially wrong." He adds: "I believe we must prohibit economic organizations from direct or indirect political activity and expenditures."

As strongly as his negative feelings run on these points, however, Romney is not only a believer, but a fervent believer, in "the need for enlisting the voluntary, co-operative effort of more and more informed men of good will to do the many things that must be done, not only for the gradual betterment of the human race as such, but urgently for national survival."

Sometimes recalling the co-operative efforts to irrigate farms in the parched lands of the West, he says: "We have carried the art of voluntary co-operation to its highest levels. As a social tool, it possesses remarkable qualities. It is sufficiently flexible to embrace a variety of different problems, large and small, simple and complex; it is adaptable to shifting needs and conditions; it can be utilized for short-range purposes or can be continued over an indefinite period of time. The more actively one participates in voluntary co-operative attitudes, the greater his personal satisfaction. Even when the particular mechanism is brand-new, it can produce results more promptly and efficiently than the older social forms, provided sufficient energy, vision, faith and determination are applied."

This is what Romney offers to "the many union members who are defaulting on their political citizenship" and to the business executives and white-collar employees who have become politically inactive and who have "substituted corporate citizenship and the hope of economic advancement for their priceless heritage of independent political action."

"We must bring back to life the feeling that each can participate with effectiveness," he says. "We are confronted today not only with lassitude but with a sense of helplessness."

At the Rutgers University School of Business Administration, in 1959, Romney singled out two broad issues which, he said, must be faced, met and corrected. One was the concentration of power groups. The other was the failure to develop the competitive principle.

Through the proper resolution of these issues, he said, "we can unleash more fully the innate capacities of individuals to make a contribution to our future economic development. I believe that what we need in this country more desperately than anything else from a political and economic standpoint is men who will insist on facing the issues and facing the problems. I think we need a political party dedicated to the principles of Americanism and more interested in the preservation of these principles than in winning the next election."[6]

XVIII

Help for Detroit Schools

A notable example of voluntary co-operation in Romney's career was the Citizens Advisory Committee on School Needs. He agreed to head this, as recorded earlier, in December, 1956, when he already was carrying heavy responsibilities. He accepted with only two questions for President Merrifield of the Board of Education, who was a Chrysler personnel executive.

"I am going to ask you a very blunt question," said Romney. "Your point of view is strictly a management point of view and I suppose mine is too. Is labor going to be given a real voice in this?" Merrifield assured him that it would. In view of his other tasks, Romney asked that Vice President Cushman of American Motors be named vice chairman of the committee. A resident of Dearborn Hills, Cushman like Romney lived outside Detroit.

The committee was charged ". . . to help the Board of Education in the development of plans for an educational program that will meet the needs and desires of the Detroit citizens in the decade following 1959." The committee was free to determine the scope of its studies and procedures. It was to be composed of one city-wide committee and eight regional committees, with the latter making separate reports for their areas.

Members were to represent only themselves, but the forty persons in the City-Wide Committee were a careful cross-section of Detroit.

Among them were Charles J. Wartman, editor of the *Michigan Chronicle,* local Negro newspaper; Brendan Sexton, educational director of the UAW-CIO; Mrs. Mildred Jeffrey, UAW-CIO director of community relations; Kenneth A. Meade, director of General Motors educational relations; George T. Higgins, secretary of Chrysler; and others. A number of school people served on committees not as representatives of the schools but as citizens.[1]

Romney began at once to take the lead in the project. The Board agreed to supply quarters and an executive secretary to be approved by the chairman. The first two candidates were Dr. Robert E. LeAnderson, in charge of audio-visual work in the schools, and Dr. Norman Drachler, a school principal. After checking their references and interviewing them, Romney and Cushman asked for and obtained the services of both. Dr. LeAnderson became executive secretary and Dr. Drachler co-ordinator of research. The committee established headquarters at Chadsey High School and met for the first time there on February 28, 1957.

Full information and free access to all school records, buildings and personnel were given the committee. Meeting every other Thursday at 4 P.M., with some sessions extending into the night, the City-Wide Committee began its work, naming subcommittees to study school curriculum, personnel, community relations, physical plant and finance and also choosing chairmen and the members of the eight regional committees.

At breakfast meetings in school cafeterias, Romney explained aims of the study to each regional committee as it was formed. He assured each group that the report it would write would go direct to the Board of Education. It would not be funneled through the top committee for approval. He promised everybody a hearing.

Romney was hopeful of finding ways to cut school expenses by increasing efficiency in various areas. To this end he had the committee incorporated and at a meeting of civic leaders and by mail raised largely by his personal efforts $42,000 for the employment of outside consultants. Of this, $1,500 came from the United Automobile, Aircraft & Agricultural Implement Workers of America. All Detroit automobile companies contributed.

The accounting and management consulting firm of Touche, Niven, Bailey & Smart was employed to make a survey of business practices of the school system. They reported to the subcommittee on finance, of which Roy L. Stephens, Jr. was chairman. Lawrence Perkins of the Perkins-Will architectural firm, Chicago, was a consultant to the school plant subcommittee, of which Mrs. Lola Jeffries Hanavan was chairman.[2] Several educational consultants were employed.[3]

The committee had just started its work when a stop-gap tax proposal to provide $33,000,000 for school buildings for the next two years was crushingly defeated by Detroit voters on April 1, 1957. The measure had the support of all the Detroit dailies but was formally opposed by a downtown business group and several neighborhood taxpayers' organizations.

Romney crowded his work with the committee into a busy schedule. "I am flying to Los Angeles," he telephoned the committee office one day. "Have you something I can read on the way?" He did this regularly and later would ask questions about what he had read. He spoke about the project to all sorts of audiences.

As a speaker George Romney is earnest rather than polished. His platform manner has a certain awkward quality of innocent, unsophisticated sincerity that strikes a friendly chord with listeners. "He leaves you feeling," a lawyer says, "that he is not a smooth speaker, maybe not even a trained speaker, but that he is in the right and, if you know what is good for you, you will go out and vote for bonds, or buy a small car, or whatever he is asking you to do."

"George just oozes integrity," a school associate on the committee said, "and, nicely enough, it rubs off on the people who work with him."

He was at his best in an address to Detroit principals and supervisors on November 6, 1957. With a new Superintendent of Schools and a committee headed by an industrialist studying them, many of the school people were apprehensive and worried. Romney explained that the Citizens Advisory Committee on School Needs was not starting with "answers." He asked the principals and supervisors to help in the study. He spoke with humility, mentioning that he had not finished college. "We are going to start fact-finding," he promised, "before we start fault-finding."

Romney concluded with a paraphrase of Lord Henry Brougham's famous lines in an 1828 address to Parliament.[4] "I believe public education," said Romney, "is one of the major and indispensable reasons for America's rapid rise to world leadership and responsibility. I believe only the educated can be free—that education makes a people easier to be led constructively but difficult to drive; easy to govern, but impossible to enslave. I believe education should have as its objectives the formation of character and citizenship and the development of individual intellects and talents. I believe ignorance is the obstacle to progress, and knowledge is essential to human happiness." The audience was visibly moved and gave him the first standing ovation in the history of the organization. Excerpts from the talk were published in the Detroit school publication.

As originally projected, the committees planned to make minority reports. Romney opposed this. "The job of this committee," he asserted, "is not to divide the community but to unite it." He won the others to this viewpoint largely by sheer force of personality. The fewer than half a dozen subjects on which the committee was hopelessly divided were tabled for a possible later study. These included the possibility of school financing on a metropolitan area basis, twelve-month use of school facilities and merit pay for teachers. Romney advocated the last but the local teachers' organization, the Detroit Education Association, the largest local teacher group in the world, opposed it.

Committees held 212 meetings. The subcommittee on school plant, for example, with Anthony Adinolfi as consultant, had citizens inspect each school building with a "Citizens' Workbook for Evaluating School Buildings." Each school site and each of more than three hundred school buildings was evaluated as to adequacy, suitability, safety, healthfulness, accessibility, flexibility, efficiency, economy, expansibility and appearance. To keep all concerned informed, a newsletter titled *CAC Highlights* was published and circulated to all committee members.

George Romney had a hand in nearly everything. "His judgment all the way along and his handling of the problems that arose and his work with the committee were of a very high order," said Superintendent Brownell. To the final report, Dr. Drachler recalled later, Romney contributed more than anybody else. "He was the one person who spoke of Detroit not in terms of the past but in terms of the future," said the educator. "Without realizing it he became the spokesman for a better Detroit." The foreword of the six-volume report of more than a thousand pages as it was finally assembled expressed this in these words:

Detroit's primary role today lies in the research, development, organization and management of production across the nation and in a large part of the world. Our children must have far greater skill and training to maintain Detroit's supremacy in the more complex and specialized age that we are already entering. Individual freedom and the voluntary blending of the private good with the public good will require human, social, civic and spiritual research, development and organization that can catch up and keep pace with scientific, technological and economic change. Our children need our help now in securing the fundamental and highly specialized training needed for the new age. It cannot be deferred. We either train them now or they will lack the skill and character their destiny demands.

The report,[5] the largest compendium of facts ever assembled on Detroit schools, was presented formally on November 25, 1958 to the Board of Education, of which its first Negro member, Dr. Remus G. Robinson, a surgeon who graduated from the University of Michigan, had just become president. It contained 182 recommendations for economy or efficiency; some were: a cumulative record system which would follow a child from kindergarten through his school career; a reduction of all classes to an average of thirty pupils; increased attention to reading, writing and mathematics; a division of "school relations" to improve communications with the daily press and other media as "basic to improving understanding and awareness of school needs on the part of the general public."

The most immediate recommendations had to do, however, with the urgent need for money to pay teachers adequately and to finance the construction of badly needed additions and new buildings. Some structures were eighty-five years old. A few were firetraps. Some 22,000 high school students had only an average of four and a half hours' instruction a day and five thousand elementary school pupils were on half-day sessions. While Detroit families had an average after-tax income of $7,649 in 1956, the highest per-family income of the five largest cities in the country, Detroit's daily per-pupil expenditure was only $1.87 as compared to $1.91 for Los Angeles, $1.99 for Chicago and $2.17 for New York.

Newspapers were so interested in the project that the Detroit *Free Press* published a draft version of the finance subcommittee's report. Released as a series of six reports, the final versions were printed almost in full by the *Free Press, Times* and *News.* The Detroit *News* received an award from the Education Writers Association for the coverage of the reports by Marjorie E. Porter and others.

Romney gave a summary of the report to the Economic Club of Detroit. As some members of this important organization had been responsible for defeat of the 1957 school proposal, he prepared with care, enlisted the help of Dr. Drachler and others, had charts drawn, and dictated several versions before he was satisfied with it.

Introduced by Don Valley, president of the National Bank of Detroit, which had been one of American Motors' creditors, Romney recalled a story about a minister, a lawyer and a banker who went to a restaurant. By a remarkable coincidence each found a fly in his soup. The minister ate his soup, fly and all, with no comment. The lawyer took his spoon and ladled out the fly.

"But the banker picked up the fly," said Romney, "squeezed it over the soup and said, 'Come on, spit it out, you little rascal, spit it out. Let's get back every drop of it.'" The crowd roared and Romney explained Valley wasn't that sort of banker.

Romney presented the charts, vividly described antiquated and hazardous school buildings and teachers leaving Detroit for higher salaries in the suburbs. He reported that in the last five years a baby had been born to a Detroit mother every twelve minutes and schools had to be built for all these children.

"Detroit must invest in its schools or see them deteriorate at the time of their greatest importance to our future. Personally, I have reluctantly reached the conclusion that we must pay more for the education of our children. The cost of delaying an adequate tax program will be paid by our children because they must be educated now—it cannot be postponed." Money, he said, is to education what water is to agriculture.

Anticipating questions about "frills," Romney said: "English, social studies, business education, mathematics, health, science, industrial education and foreign language education constitute 87.6 per cent of the total teaching time. Of the remaining 12.4 per cent, 9.01 per cent is used for music, home economics and art. Only 3.13 per cent covers such subjects as Reserve Officers Training Corps, vocational guidance and driver training. This dissipates the idea of savings through elimination of fringe or frill subjects."

As expected, somebody asked a question about frills in school construction.

"You are a successful businessman, recognized nationally," said a voice. "You are a success in America, yet you didn't have a school with a swimming pool and all these fine things. You went to a little red schoolhouse and you did very well."

Romney arose red-faced and waving his arms.

"This question," he retorted, "was raised just to confuse the people of Detroit. Sure, there are one or two schools that have this or that. I can tell you dozens of others that don't have what they need. Don't ask me about that little red schoolhouse in my state.

"When my people went out into that desert, first we built a church. Then we built schools. And only after this did we think of our homes. When I was a boy I went to as fine a school as we have in Detroit today!"

The report was summarized for editors of high school newspapers at a breakfast at the local Statler Hilton Hotel. A young Negro girl, Lola Irby, editor of the Sherrard Junior High School *Sun,* had never been in a hotel before but found herself seated next to a graying man who gallantly hung up her coat, inquired as to her pencils and encouraged her to eat. Not until the speaker was announced, she wrote later in her newspaper, did she know that she was sitting next to George Romney.

With presentation of its report, the Citizens Advisory Committee on School Needs went out of existence, returning part of the $42,000 collected for expenses. The 270 members of the committee signed a book and presented it and a Bible to Romney as a tribute to "a spokesman for a better Detroit," in a surprise ceremony in the new building of his Church of Jesus Christ of Latter-day Saints in Bloomfield Hills. This had been completed just two months before and opened with a program by the Mormon Tabernacle Choir from Salt Lake City.

The Board of Education adopted some of the committee's recommendations at once and asked Detroiters to vote $90,000,000 for school buildings, $60,000,000 in bonds and $30,000,000 additional as part of an increased tax which replaced a $4.50 tax per $1,000 valuation expiring in 1959 with one of $7.50 for the next five years. It was the largest amount ever sought for schools in Detroit or Michigan. Federal Judge Arthur F. Lederle headed a new "Citizens for Schools" committee organized to back the two proposals.

It was not a propitious time to ask voters to approve higher taxes for themselves. In the spring of 1959, Michigan had serious fiscal troubles. In Detroit, 13.9 of the labor force was idle. Influential national magazines had been assailing extravagance in school building. Bond issues in suburban Royal Oak and many other communities had been voted down. As much more modest propositions had been rejected just two years before, politicians saw little chance for the proposals.

George Romney was the main speaker at a rally launching the campaign. "No automobile company can compare with the Detroit schools in efficiency or in the low ratio of administrators to productive workers," he told the crowd in a review of his committee's report. He addressed the Rotary Club, the League of Women Voters and many other organizations.

"You are building a new Civic Center," he told business groups. "What is this to be used for, if we don't have good schools? If Detroit is to have a future it will be dependent upon people wanting to come to live here. The first thing that a family asks is: 'Do they have a good school system?'"

Though organized opposition was limited to a single neighborhood property owners' association that eventually reversed its stand, the outlook for the proposals continued dubious. A suburban editor, Paul Chandler of *The Livonian,* wrote: "Romney is doomed. He's dead right, and his plan doesn't have a chance." A few weeks before the election a newspaper check of ten Smith families in the Detroit telephone directory found only one Smith in favor of voting more money for schools.

But half of the Smiths questioned were willing to listen if somebody cared to call and explain the proposals. Thus encouraged, the Citizens Committee for Schools enlisted eight thousand volunteers in a door-to-door campaign. Led by the Detroit High School Student Activities Council, local teen-agers tacked up posters and offered to baby-sit for voters on election day. Some three hundred organizations backed the proposals. Governor G. Mennen Williams and Mayor Louis C. Mirani approved them. They had the support of all Detroit dailies and also radio stations like WJR, which broadcast "editorials."

George Romney, Walter Reuther, head of the UAW, and Father Celestin John Steiner, Jesuit president of the University of Detroit, joined in an appeal over Station WJBK-TV on the Sunday before the election. Two days later, on April 6, nearly 60 per cent of the voters approved the bond issue and 64 per cent, almost two to one, voted for the tax increase. The Board of Education began to implement more recommendations of Romney's committee, including the suggestion for citizen committees to make more studies and suggestions.

"Inestimable credit," said the Detroit *News* in commenting on the election results, "belongs to the Citizens Advisory Committee on School Needs, which George Romney headed." Others hailed the committee as one of the great unifying influences in Detroit's history, something that was badly needed and that will be helpful for years to come. Wayne State University gave Romney and Dr. Brownell honorary Doctor of Laws degrees and the Detroit teachers' organization presented Romney with its annual civic award.

"There was in this two-year program," said Dr. Brownell, "a number of things that can be useful to other large cities. One of the things that the Board wanted, and I was anxious to do, was to see whether it would be possible in one of our great cities to show that the schools are still the people's schools, and that you can get citizens to take the same kind of interest in schools that has caused many to move from the city to the suburbs, and to pitch in to get the schools they want."

Dr. Brownell, who earlier organized the White House Conference on Education, said he had never worked with "a person more stimulating and at the same time more comfortable to work with than George Romney."

XIX

Citizens for Michigan

The economic troubles of the Michigan state government gave George Romney his next opportunity for public service. He and Ed Cushman talked about the possibility of applying the school advisory committee approach to this problem as they rode on a train to Boston where Romney addressed the New England Council on November 20, 1958. It was not until the next spring, however, that they joined others deeply concerned over what was happening in the state capital in seeking a solution. "We met to pool our frustrations," as one of them remarked later.

They had good reason. For while the fiscal crisis had been long in developing and while its gravity had been obvious for months, nothing had been done about it. Moreover, it appeared that the state government lacked either the capacity, the will or both to do anything about it—despite the fact that the problems involved were by no means unsurmountable.

Michigan is one of the wealthiest states in the Union. Between 1950 and 1959 its population increased by 1,494,000. Only California and Florida had done better. Its treasury, which took in slightly more than half a billion dollars annually ten years earlier, was drawing in more than a billion in 1959. True, it had lost some industries, but it had gained more. For example, it lost 25 in 1957 and gained 27, for a net job increase of 275.

This isn't to say the state didn't have its troubles. The 1958 recession had hit its automobile industry hard. This aggravated a trend toward unemployment already set in motion by such factors as the disappearance of Packard, Hudson and Kaiser-Frazer from the automobile industry as independent producers; the shift of national defense spending away from tanks, aircraft and mobile guns (a Michigan specialty) into missiles; the centralization of auto parts production combined with the decentralization of assemblies and a gain in the momentum of automation.

All these factors combined to push Michigan's unemployment rolls up to the highest levels in the nation (11.6 per cent throughout the state and 13.9 per cent in Detroit as against a national average of 4.64 per cent, as recently as March, 1959), despite the general business pickup then in effect.

Still, this does not explain the financial disaster that benumbed Lansing at that time. Automobile production was running ahead of the same month in 1958 by half a million units. March sales tax collections were among the highest ever recorded for that month, and $71,000,000 ahead of those for March, 1958. Things should have been better, but they weren't.

One trouble lay in the structure of the state government. It was fettered by a constitution which, though revised somewhat in 1909, was in large measure drawn up in 1850, when the population was sparse and almost wholly rural. One consequence of the failure to streamline the whole governing process was that a substantial proportion of Michigan's tax revenues was assigned by statute to specific purposes, such as road-building, and could not be utilized for any other.

Another was that Governor G. Mennen Williams, a Democrat, and the Republican-controlled legislature did not seem able to get together to break the stalemate. By late April, the state's General Fund had fallen to the point that 325 state employees, including 144 legislators, went payless. By the end of the first week in May,

26,000 state workers were unable to collect their pay. By then there
was no longer any doubt that Lansing was in real trouble. Nor was
there much room for confidence that it could surmount these difficulties by itself, for throughout the critical months during which
the approach of that crisis had become obvious to almost everyone,
the Governor and the legislature continued to wrangle over what
kind of new taxes to impose, neither having either the strength to
prevail or the willingness to compromise.

It was against this cheerless background that the little group of
admittedly frustrated citizens discussed the alternatives and reached
the conclusion that nothing short of a grass-roots, nonpartisan
citizens' movement of the type that had just dealt successfully with
the Detroit school crisis could fill the bill. In late April Romney met
with "seven other concerned individuals" at a dinner in Detroit
at the Sheraton-Cadillac. At a second meeting the following month
at the Student Union Building in Ann Arbor fifteen individuals
met with Romney and decided to form "Citizens for Michigan."
During the second week in June, Romney rather hurriedly called a
press conference in Detroit.[1]

The moment was dramatic. By then the impasse at Lansing had
become a matter of statewide vexation and embarrassment. Romney's reputation as the man who had put American Motors on its
feet and as the guiding light of the Detroit school rescue squad
virtually assured that when he spoke his voice would be heard. And
it was.

He described the situation in Lansing briefly, laid the blame for
it at the door of both parties, and stressed that it was more the
product of a "deterioration in public responsibility" that he had
noted for at least thirty years, though he granted that it may have
begun earlier, in the years when Michigan was being gradually
transformed from a predominantly rural to an urban-industrial
state. About a hundred individuals were being asked to join as
citizens only, not as representatives of any "party or other group or

institution." They would be asked to agree "to place the needs of the state above and apart from personal, political, economic or social affiliations."

Romney also listed eight individuals who were associated with him at the outset. These included Dr. Brownell, Detroit Superintendent of Schools; Vice President Cushman of American Motors; Ronald W. Haughton, co-director of Wayne State University's Institute of Industrial Relations; Mrs. Berrien C. Ketchum, former president of the League of Women Voters of Michigan; Dr. Charles Killingsworth, professor of economics at Michigan State University; Leonard Simons, president of Simons-Michelson Company; Dr. William E. Stirton, vice president of the University of Michigan; and Circuit Judge Wade H. McCree.

The announcement was greeted with general approbation in the press. Stating that some sort of grass-roots revolution "has become practically inevitable," the Detroit *Free Press* said: "It is fortunate, we believe, that someone of Mr. Romney's stature has recognized the need and assumed leadership. . . . No one would accuse [him] of being a wild-eyed, radical social reformer. On the contrary, he is a man of great acumen and broad experience in human relations."[2] The Detroit *News* said: "If anyone can shape and lead a citizens' organization to the rescue of Michigan from its political wilderness, it is George Romney. . . . The kind of 'third force' Romney's committee can become is more than a need: It has become a dire necessity."[3]

Reactions from political leaders were mixed. Several Democratic leaders voiced cautious approval of the project, but most were silent. A prominent Republican leader publicly called upon Romney to abandon his nonpartisan posture and work from within the party. Another was quoted in the Detroit *News* as saying he would support any study of state needs, but adding that he had reservations. "It's impossible to forget political affiliations when you sit down and discuss state problems," he said. "Our government has long been based on partisanship. Are we going to forget it now?"

That was precisely what Romney and his associates hoped that members of their committee would do: forget it. The fact was, as Romney himself admitted, despite his statement that political leaders would be welcome, he was cool toward their admission to membership in Citizens for Michigan, at least in its initial phases. Although he stressed the point that there would be a place on the committee for anyone who would sacrifice time and effort and check his group affiliations at the outer door, he wanted the committee to get off on the right foot. He had valid reasons for politely discouraging advances from both Republican and Democratic leaders who came around to the belief they ought to be represented on the committee.

One was that both parties, as previously noted, were responsible for the state's grave difficulties. Another, perhaps more important, was his conviction that neither party represented the will of the state's citizens generally, but of the "political organizations" he had been bucking in the business world. He felt that the Republican party in Michigan was dominated by Ford and General Motors, and that the Democratic party was dominated by Walter Reuther's United Automobile Workers. Where, in such a stalemate between two such massive sources of power, was a citizen to turn whose primary interest was in the welfare of the state itself?

These considerations prompted Romney and his associates to organize the committee along rather unusual lines. Not only were members accepted for themselves alone; financing was entirely by individual contribution. No contributor was permitted to donate more than a hundred dollars in any one year. This prohibition was imposed not solely for the purpose of forestalling combinations among the same (or similar) "economic groups" that had contributed so mightily to the deadlock in Lansing, but for the constructive one of maintaining that individual spirit of "voluntary co-operation" among all members that had proved so important in overcoming the school crisis in Detroit. Nor would the committee sponsor any candidate for public office.

"It is not the intention of this group," Romney said, "to grind any political ax, or to become in any way a sort of new political party. By making the necessary sacrifice of time and effort to isolate specific state problems and determine the facts about them, it is the intention of the group to develop recommendations that will command public support and attention by sheer force of logic and common sense. By shaking out public apathy and focusing attention on what must be done it is our belief that members of both political parties will be compelled to perform as the voters wish— the voters who can and should exercise ultimate political responsibility in our nation."

A preliminary organization meeting was held in Lansing on June 19, with more than two hundred individuals present who, in Romney's words, were concerned not only with Michigan's financial crisis, but with "more fundamental issues, of which the financial crisis was only an immediate symptom. They were concerned over the bad economic climate that had developed within the state, and . . . a lack of objective political leadership on the part of both parties and their leaders, not just in recent years, but going back two or three decades."

Romney was formally elected chairman of the group at another Lansing meeting September 21, 1959. It set to work establishing local units throughout the state, planning periodic regional and statewide meetings, and subjects for study, its immediate objective at both the state and local levels being "to identify problems on which there is practical unanimity, and to make recommendations with the force and clarity of broad citizen support that would command the attention and approval of political parties and public officials."

Romney stated that he would not be a candidate for political office. Areas for study as defined by a committee of which Mrs.

Ketchum was chairman were announced as: (1) What services do Michigan's citizens need from their state government? (2) How should needed state government services be paid for? (3) How should the state government be structured to carry out its responsibilities? (4) What can be done to accelerate Michigan's economic growth and its cultural development?

It was explained that the third study would analyze Michigan's constitution and compare it with those of other states as well as with such documents as the Model State Constitution of the National Municipal League. If areas of needed improvement develop, these would be further studied, using materials—both pro and con— prepared by the many research groups who have investigated the constitution over the years. Recommendations for improvement would then be developed. This study would also explore the various means of improving the constitution, including revision by amendment and the constitution convention method. The pros and cons of reapportionment would also be studied. Also included in this study would be the examination of the departments of government created by statute as well as the relationship between state and local governments.

Harold C. McKinney of Dimondale, director of general operations, Michigan Council of Churches, was elected secretary of Citizens for Michigan. Joseph V. Brady of Howell, vice president of the Citizens Mutual Automobile Insurance Co., was chosen as treasurer. Dr. Ralph Conant, formerly director of civic affairs research at Muskegon, Michigan, was employed as executive director. Carl Bond, for six years an industrial economist for the Michigan Economic Development Commission, was named a full-time consultant.

While they served as individuals, the directors were representative of a cross-section of Michigan interests and affairs. Labor leaders on the board included Leonard Woodcock, a vice-president of the UAW, Jack Conway and Judah Drob. Industrialists included

Robert S. McNamara of Ann Arbor, a Ford Motor Company group vice-president, and Dan Gerber of Fremont, baby food manufacturer. The directors also included Jean Worth, Escanaba newspaper publisher; Dr. Stirton, vice-president of the University of Michigan; Circuit Judge McCree; also three clergymen, Rabbi Morris Adler, Father Robert Allen and the Rev. Paul Morrison. The organization was incorporated for thirty years.

Romney wanted this, like the Detroit school group, to be a "shirt-sleeves" committee. He insisted that members keep themselves informed and take an active part in the effort. This is a well-known feature of his philosophy.

A businessman once wrote him: "How can a public-spirited individual be effective or influential unless his energies are combined with similar energies of other individuals?"

"He cannot," Romney replied. "He must work with others. But his work must be personal and direct, not by proxy. He must be directed by what *he* believes in, not what his corporation or his union believes in. He must speak for *himself* and not suffer his voice to be drowned in the loudspeaker of an institution."

The spirit that moved Romney to accept leadership of the Citizens for Michigan movement, with all the personal satisfaction plus the slings and arrows of outraged partisans it brought to him, was the same that prompted him to seek a settlement of the Detroit school crisis and to stump the country for a change in the antitrust laws and for a curb on the powers of labor.

George Romney was not attacking any individuals or any specific organizations as such, and most of his targets probably knew it. In all these areas, political and economic, he was fighting to restore the ideal of voluntary co-operation to the honored place in American life it had partially abandoned under pressure of power concentrations representing large numbers of people who had, in some degree or other, surrendered their own thinking and consciences to union or corporate leadership, and had thereby partially lost by default the deep satisfactions of one who acts for himself but in voluntary accord with others.

"America's rendezvous with destiny is threatened, but not lost," Romney said at Mackinac in 1959. "It is threatened by a lack of basic political choice—lack of sufficient concern to cause us to risk and sacrifice for principles that have proven indispensable in man's pursuit of life, liberty and happiness. We are in danger of awakening from our comfortable contentment to the experience reflected in Marshal Pétain's words following the downfall of France in 1940. He said: 'Our spirit of enjoyment was greater than our spirit of sacrifice. We wanted to have more than we wanted to give. We spared effort, and we met disaster.' "⁴

Notes

CHAPTER I. "We Want a Busy Man"
1. Copyright by Harms, Inc., New York.
2. Geyer Advertising, Inc. It became Geyer, Morey, Madden & Ballard, Inc. in 1959.
3. From Meade F. Moore.
4. Cushman served for four years as permanent umpire for Parke, Davis & Company, Detroit pharmaceutical manufacturer, and the CIO's chemical workers. In addition, he served as arbitrator in hundreds of labor disputes involving fifty-three major companies and fifteen international unions, and was a member of the Board of Governors of the National Academy of Arbitrators. In 1946 he served as special assistant to the Secretary of Labor and as labor adviser to the late John G. Winant when U.S. Delegate to the United Nations' Economic and Social Council. In 1947, he was chairman of Governor Kim Sigler's Unemployment Compensation Study Commission and executive director of the Michigan Unemployment Compensation Commission. Cushman later was chairman of Governor G. Mennen Williams' Study Commission on Automation and a member of his Study Commission on Prepaid Medical Care.
5. They included Seymour E. Harris and Alvin H. Hansen of Harvard, William Haber of Michigan, Edwin E. Witte of Wisconsin, Vincent W. Bladen of Toronto, Richard A. Lester of Princeton and Arthur J. Altmeyer, father of the Social Security Law. *U.S. News & World Report* of May 13, 1955, reported their work in some detail.
6. Detroit *Free Press*, April 18, 1955.

CHAPTER II. The Dinosaur in the Driveway
1. Alfred H. Sinks, "Those Big Fat Cars," *Harper's Magazine*, April, 1949.
2. April 6, 1959, pp. 84-89.
3. March 7, 1956.

Notes

4. Detroit *News,* March 22, 1959, "Auto Firms Bump Fenders in Head-on Sales Campaign," pp. 1-2.
5. February 7 and 10, 1958.
6. Arthur Herzog, "George Romney, Crusader for the Compact Car," *True,* October, 1958, p. 101.

CHAPTER III. Stockholder Louis E. Wolfson
1. Other banks involved included the First National Bank of Kenosha, the Marine Midland Trust Company of New York, the Detroit Bank, National Bank of Detroit, Manufacturers Trust and First National City of New York; Continental Illinois National Bank, Harris Trust and Savings Bank, Northern Trust Company, and First National Bank of Chicago; First Wisconsin National Bank, Milwaukee; Manufacturers National Bank of Detroit; Mechanics National Bank, Worcester, Mass.; National Shawmut Bank, Merchants National and First National Bank of Boston; Fidelity Union Trust Company, Newark, N. J.; Morgan Guaranty Trust Company, Chemical Bank New York Trust Company, Bankers Trust Company and Bank of New York; Security First National Bank and Bank of America National Trust and Savings Association, Los Angeles; Philadelphia National Bank.
2. This contract assured Barit $12,500 a month until August 30, 1955, and $4,166.67 per month until August 30, 1958, in addition to Hudson retirement benefits.
3. Issues dated March 25, 1957.

CHAPTER IV. Dragon-Slaying Heritage
1. The Rev. John Romney, *Memoirs of the Life and Works of George Romney* (London: Baldwin & Cradock, 1830), p. 4. Also Bill Davidson's unpublished *Collier's* mss.
2. Thomas C. Romney, Ph.D., *Life Story of Miles P. Romney* (Independence, Mo.: Zion's Publishing Company, 1948), p. 2. This book includes a detailed genealogy of the Romney family as of that date. The author is an uncle of George Romney of Detroit.
3. *Illinois—A Descriptive and Historical Guide,* Federal Writers Project (Chicago: A. C. McClurg, 1947), pp. 347-50.
4. T. C. Romney, cited above, gives an account of his father's marriages and his thirty children, of whom fourteen boys and fourteen girls grew to adulthood.
5. In addition, they are fond of home and family; are industrious, frugal, grave, tenacious, have a sense of value and dislike waste. Carroll Righter, *Astrology and You* (New York: Permabooks, 1958), p. 44-7.
6. Anthony W. Ivins was the first president. When he became an Apostle of the Church in 1908, he was succeeded by Junius Romney.

CHAPTER V. Exodus from Mexico
1. James Creelman for *Pearson's* Magazine, March, 1908.
2. Junius Romney's account of these events, as told September 22, 1912, in El Paso, Texas, to Senator A. B. Fall and his Senate Subcommittee, was published in *Investigation of*

Notes

Mexican Affairs (Washington, D.C.: Government Printing Office, 1920), Vol. 2, pp. 2574-90. When 81 years old, he confirmed this for the present writer in Salt Lake City on June 4, 1959. Thomas C. Romney, a brother of Junius and also in the exodus, described it in *The Mormon Colonies in Mexico* (Salt Lake City: Deseret Book Company, 1938), pp. 149-248.
3. El Paso *Herald,* July 31, 1912, in a dispatch from Pearson, Chihuahua, by George H. Clements. This newspaper is now the El Paso *Herald-Post.*
4. Nelle Spilsbury Hatch, *Colonia Juarez* (Salt Lake City: Deseret Book Company, 1954), pp. 216-21.

CHAPTER VI. Idaho-Utah Boyhood
1. Letter of Andrew M. Andersen, Statesman Newspapers, Boise, Idaho, June 22, 1959.
2. Interview with Gerald Smith, July, 1959.
3. *Deseret News,* March 8, 1926.

CHAPTER VII. Missionary Years
1. The Church of Jesus Christ of Latter-day Saints lists its Articles of Faith:
    1. We believe in God, the Eternal Father, and in his Son, Jesus Christ, and in the Holy Ghost.
    2. We believe that men will be punished for their own sins, and not for Adam's transgression.
    3. We believe that, through the atonement of Christ, all mankind may be saved, by obedience to the laws and ordinances of the Gospel.
    4. We believe that the first principles and ordinances of the Gospel are: First, Faith in the Lord Jesus Christ; second Repentance; third, Baptism by immersion for the remission of sins; fourth, Laying on of Hands for the Gift of the Holy Ghost.
    5. We believe that a man must be called of God, by "prophecy, and by the laying on of hands," by those who are in authority, to preach the Gospel and administer in the ordinances thereof.
    6. We believe in the same organization that existed in the primitive church, namely, apostles, prophets, pastors, teachers, evangelists, etc.
    7. We believe in the gift of tongues, prophecy, revelation, visions, healing, interpretation of tongues, etc.
    8. We believe the Bible to be the word of God, as far as it is translated correctly; we also believe the Book of Mormon to be the word of God.
    9. We believe all that God has revealed, all that He does now reveal, and we believe that He will yet reveal many great and important things pertaining to the Kingdom of God.
    10. We believe in the literal gathering of Israel and in the restoration of the Ten Tribes. That Zion will be built upon this continent. That Christ will reign personally upon the earth, and that the earth will be renewed and receive its paradisaical glory.
    11. We claim the privilege of worshiping Almighty God according to the dictates of our conscience, and allow all men the same privilege, let them worship how, where or what they may.
    12. We believe in being subjects to kings, presidents, rulers and magistrates, in obeying, honoring and sustaining the law.

Notes

13. We believe in being honest, true, chaste, benevolent, virtuous, and in doing good to ALL MEN; indeed we may say that we follow the admonition of Paul: "We believe all things, we hope all things," we have endured many things, and hope to be able to endure all things. If there is anything virtuous, lovely, or of good report or praiseworthy we seek after these things.

See also Charles Francis Potter, *The Faith Men Live By* (New York: Prentice-Hall, Inc., 1954), "The Mormons or Latter-day Saints," pp. 254-69.
2. John A. Widtsoe, *In a Sunlit Land* (Salt Lake City: Deseret News Press, 1952).
3. Detroit *Free Press*, February 15, 1959. One of a series of Lenten articles by Detroiters of all faiths.

CHAPTER VIII. Washington and Aluminum
1. This is the only part of the Latter-day Saints school which George Romney attended in Salt Lake City that has survived. With expansion of Brigham Young University at Provo, the junior college was closed.
2. Dorothy G. Wayman, *David I. Walsh, Citizen-Patriot* (Milwaukee: The Bruce Publishing Company, 1952).
3. Speech of February 5, 1929. Quoted from Wayman, pp. 174-75.
4. Later with *U.S. News & World Report* in Washington.
5. Howard R. Smith, *Government and Business* (New York: The Ronald Press, 1958), pp. 606-7.

CHAPTER IX. Detroit Goes to War
1. Chris Sinsabaugh, *Who, Me? Forty Years of Automobile History* (Detroit: Arnold-Powers, Inc., 1940), pp. 61-66, also John B. Rae, *American Automobile Manufacturers* (Philadelphia: Chilton Co., 1959), pp. 66-85.
2. Charles E. Sorenson, *My Forty Years With Ford* (New York: W. W. Norton & Company, Inc., 1956), pp. 274-75, and Norman Beasley, *Knudsen* (New York: Whittlesey House, 1947), pp. 264-67.
3. *Freedom's Arsenal, The Story of the Automotive Council for War Production* (Detroit: Automobile Manufacturers Association, 1950), pp. 1-10.
4. March 9, 1945.
5. Donald M. Nelson, *Arsenal of Democracy* (New York: Harcourt, Brace and Company, 1946), pp. 217-23.

CHAPTER X. The Automotive Golden Jubilee
1. The anniversary was only approximate, even for the American industry. Charles E. and J. Frank Duryea made cars as early as 1893 at Springfield, Massachusetts, and the Apperson Brothers made one in 1894 for Elwood Haynes in Kokomo, Indiana. But in 1896, the first Duryea car was sold, cars appeared in Detroit for the first time and a total of twenty-five were built in the United States. The industry agreed the year marked the real beginning of its progress. European automobile history goes back to 1865, when Siegfried Marcus built an impractical benzine-engined car in Vienna. A motor tricycle built in 1885 at Mannheim, Germany, by Karl Benz and powered with

Notes

an engine designed by Gottlieb Daimler was the first successful gasoline vehicle. By 1890 in France, Emile Constant Levassor of the carriage-making firm of Panhard and Levassor was making Panhard cars powered with the Daimler engine. See Ken W. Purdy, *The Kings of the Road*, Chapter XVII, "Who Invented the Thing Anyway?" (Boston: Little, Brown and Company), pp. 207-218.

2. For many years, especially during the Selden patent controversy, Ford people contended the first Ford appeared in 1893 but the 1896 date is correct. See M. M. Musselman, *Get A Horse!* (Philadelphia and New York: J. B. Lippincott, 1950), pp. 46-47.

3. William H. McGaughey, *American Automobile Album* (New York: E. P. Dutton & Co., Inc., 1954), pp. 159-64. The gold paint was donated by the Reichhold Chemical Co. and the Frazier Paint Co. It was sprayed on the avenue in the early morning of May 31.

4. Vividly described by Walter W. Ruch in the *New York Times*, June 10, 1946.

5. Photographs of General Knudsen rehearsing a Danish folk dance and pictures of the pioneers sitting in their first cars were published throughout the world.

6. The first "united way" campaign seems to have been in Denver in 1887 when two ministers, a priest and a rabbi jointly sought funds for ten charitable organizations. Cleveland's Federation of Charities and Philanthropy, organized in 1913, was the first united fund-raising effort that included budgeting and planning. The Ford Motor Co. Fund and Ford employees gave the 1959 Detroit campaign $2,611,859, "the largest charitable gift of its kind in history."

CHAPTER XI. *Packard or Nash?*

1. Peerless began to make Carling's Ale in 1932 in the same Cleveland plant that it had manufactured automobiles.

2. Walter P. Chrysler with Boyden Sparkes, *Life of an American Workman* (New York: Dodd, Mead & Company, 1950), pp. 125-27.

3. Chrysler with Sparkes, pp. 142-44. Also Lawrence H. Seltzer, *A Financial History of the American Automobile Industry* (Boston: Houghton Mifflin Company, 1928), pp. 252-53.

4. Recalled by Ned Jordan in *Automotive News*, May 1, 1950.

5. Seltzer, p. 69.

6. Sinsabaugh, p. 333.

CHAPTER XII. *Mason and Kelvinator*

1. At Hotel Roosevelt, New York City, April 24, 1946.

2. From Christy Borth's notes for a projected book.

3. Kelvinator was one of several names suggested by Stanley Resor of the J. Walter Thompson advertising agency.

4. *Fortune*, "Nash-Kelvinator," April, 1937.

5. Charles E. Sorenson, *My Forty Years with Ford* (New York: W. W. Norton & Co., 1956), p. 321. Also Harry Bennett, *We Never Called Him Henry* (New York: Gold Medal Books, 1951), p. 62.

6. *Fortune*, "The Nash Tunes Up," September, 1945.

Notes

CHAPTER XIII. *Educating an Executive*
1. December, 1949, pp. 103-8.
2. The maroon one-of-a-kind convertible was first shown at the Waldorf-Astoria Hotel in New York and pictured in *Life,* January 30, 1950. Since then many companies have shown novel prototypes in the same manner.
3. Letter of May 25, 1950.
4. Detroit *Free Press,* November 14, 1954.

CHAPTER XIV. *In Search of Mergers*
1. *Automotive News,* Almanac Issue, June 6, 1949, p. 38.
2. Barit's recollections of the negotiations were reported by the *Wall Street Journal,* April 18, 1955.
3. M. M. Musselman, *Get A Horse!* (Philadelphia: J. B. Lippincott, 1950), pp 70-75. Also Sinsabaugh, pp. 325-29.
4. J. C. Long, *Roy D. Chapin* (Detroit: privately printed, 1945), pp. 173-190.

CHAPTER XV. *Building American Motors*
1. October 28, 1954.
2. The arrangement was unnecessary after 1956.
3. A native of Elwood, Indiana, Ballard was a city editor of the Miami *News* at twenty-two. His advertising career included Hudson Motor Car copy group head with Brooke, Smith & French in Detroit, 1934-37, and handling the first New York Stock Exchange advertising while with the Gardner Advertising Company of St. Louis and New York.
4. The award was "in recognition of his devotion and energetic work for the spiritual welfare of more than a million American people; for his services to his country as managing director of the Automotive Council for War Production . . . for his work . . . to improve labor-management relationships . . . for his able managership for nearly a decade of the Automobile Manufacturers Association; for his present leadership of the entire industry. . ." *Oldtimers News,* Winter 1956.

CHAPTER XVI. *The Case for the Compact Car*
1. Henry Dreyfuss, "The Car Detroit Should Be Building," *Consumers Union Reports,* July, 1958, pp. 351-55.
2. Christy Borth, *Masters of Mass Production* (Indianapolis and New York: The Bobbs-Merrill Company, 1945), p. 225.
3. B. C. Forbes and O. D. Foster, *Automotive Giants of America* (New York: B. C. Forbes Publishing Company, 1926), pp. 219-20.
4. Article in *Etc.,* magazine of the International Society for General Semantics, reprinted *Advertising Age,* May 12, 1958, and *Madison Avenue,* May, 1958.
5. March, 1957.
6. Philadelphia, J. B. Lippincott Company.

CHAPTER XVII. *Of Power and Competition*
1. Founder's Day address, "The West and Today's Frontiers," University of Utah, February 26, 1949.

2. Tom Davis, "Romney Pours Out His Ideas," Detroit *Free Press,* January 31, 1958.
3. Address, "Consumerism or Control," American Automobile Association, Chicago, September 17, 1958.
4. Statement before Subcommittee on Antitrust and Monopoly of the Committee on the Judiciary, U.S. Senate, February 7, 1958.
5. Address, "Economic Freedom in the Space Age," Adcraft Club, Detroit, January 30, 1959, and elsewhere.
6. Address, "Personal and Economic Freedom in the Space Age," Eleventh Annual Business Conference, New Brunswick, New Jersey, May 14, 1959.

Chapter XVIII. Help for Detroit Schools
1. Other members of the City-Wide Committee were George R. Berkaw, Hale A. Clark, Mrs. Lytle P. Colvin, Dr. Lloyd Allen Cook, Walter A. Crow, Freeman A. Flynn, Mrs. Lola Jeffries Hanavan, Merle Henrickson, Mrs. Fred A. Huber, Judge Nathan J. Kaufman, Jacob L. Keidan, Walter E. Kendall, Charles A. Leadbetter, Dr. James J. Lightbody, Miss Gladys M. Little, Mrs. Jane H. Lovejoy, Ernest T. Marshall, Tom McNamara, Mrs. Claude A. Moore, Chester J. Morse, Dr. Dorothy M. Perry, Dr. Paul T. Rankin, Miss Janet M. Renton, Loren T. Robinson, Alan E. Schwartz, Ramon S. Scruggs, Gerard R. Slattery, Benjamin C. Stanczyk, Roy L. Stephens, Jr., James Wineman and Irvin G. Wolf.
2. Chairmen of other subcommittees were Kenneth A. Meade, Ramon R. Scruggs and Mrs. Gerard R. Slattery. Chairmen of regional committees were Al Barbour, Mrs. M. Fred Bennett, Charles Blessing, Frank W. Engle, Judge Wade H. McCree, Howard Shout, Lt. Reyniear Staats and Robert T. Wolfe.
3. Education consultants included Dr. Will French, professor emeritus, Columbia University Dr. Noland C. Kearney, assistant superintendent, St. Paul, Minnesota, schools; Drs. Howard Y. McClusky, John E. Milholland, Benno G. Fricke, Finley Carpenter and Howard Jones of the University of Michigan; Drs. W. B. Hawley, B. O'Donnell, P. G. Haines and L. Borosage of Michigan State University.
4. Henry James Ehlers, *Crucial Issues in Education* (New York: Henry Holt, revised 1959), p. 266.
5. *Findings and Recommendations of the City-Wide Citizens Advisory Committee on School Needs.* George Romney, Chairman; Edward L. Cushman, Vice-Chairman, 1958, Board of Education of the City of Detroit. 364 pp.

CHAPTER XIX. Citizens for Michigan
1. June 12, 1959.
2. Editorial, "Due and Inevitable, Major Overhaul for Michigan," June 13, 1959.
3. Editorial, "Romney's Brainchild, Necessity Gave It Birth," June 13, 1959.
4. Address, "America's Unfinished Revolution," General Conference of American Alumni Council, July 1, 1959.

Appendix
Notes

THOMAS B. JEFFERY CO. PRODUCTION

U.S. Passenger Cars and Trucks—Calendar Years 1902-1917

Year	Rambler	Jeffery	Trucks	Total
1902	1,500			1,500
1903	1,350			1,350
1904	2,342			2,342
1905	3,807			3,807
1906	2,765			2,765
1907	3,201			3,201
1908	3,597			3,597
1909	1,692			1,692
1910	2,273			2,273
1911	3,000			3,000
1912	3,550			3,550
1913	4,435		5,578	10,013
1914		10,417	3,096	13,513
1915		3,100	7,600	10,700
1916		4,608	2,117	6,725
1917		12,027	801	12,828
Totals	33,512	30,152	19,192	82,856

255

Appendix

(Including Nash, Ajax and LaFayette)

U.S. Passenger Cars and Trucks—Calendar Years 1917-1953

Year	Passenger Cars	Trucks	Total
1917	6,516[1]	3,000	9,516
1918	10,283	11,490[2]	21,773
1919	27,018	4,090	31,108
1920	35,084	3,697	38,781
1921	20,850	103	20,953
1922	41,652	271	41,923
1923	56,677	344	57,021
1924	53,626	203	53,829
1925	96,121[3]	168	96,289
1926	135,520[4]	74	135,594
1927	122,606	31	122,637
1928	138,137	32	138,169
1929	116,622	11	116,633
1930	54,605[5]		54,605
1931	38,616		38,616
1932	17,696		17,696
1933	14,973		14,973
1934	28,664[6]		28,664
1935	44,637		44,637
1936	53,038		53,038
1937	85,949		85,949
1938	32,017		32,017
1939	65,662		65,662
1940	63,617		63,617

Appendix

1941	80,408[7]		80,408
1942	5,428		5,428
1945	6,148[8]		6,148
1946	98,769		98,769
1947	113,315	128[9]	113,443
1948	118,621	1,052	119,673
1949	142,592	676	143,268
1950	189,534[10]	714	190,248
1951	161,140[10]	1,014	162,154
1952	152,141[10]	919	153,060
1953	135,389[10]	190	135,579
Totals	2,563,671	28,205	2,591,878

[1]First car designed by C. W. Nash was known as Model 681; total of 8,507 were built in 1917-18.
[2]Nash Motors was world's largest truck producer in 1918.
[3]Includes 10,693 Ajax cars.
[4]Includes 38,662 Ajax and Nash Light Six cars.
[5]First 8-cylinder Nash models built.
[6]Includes LaFayette (introduced 1934, dropped in 1940).
[7]Includes Nash "600," first U.S.-built "single unit" car.
[8]1946 models, built in late fall 1945.
[9]Nash trucks built in postwar period were for export sale.
[10]Includes Nash Rambler models, 20,782 in 1950; 57,555 in 1951; 53,055 in 1952; and 41,885 in 1953.

Appendix

(Including Hudson, Essex and Terraplane)
U.S., Canada and Export—Calendar Years 1909-1953

Year	Hudson	Essex	Terraplane	Commercial Vehicles	Total
1909	1,100				1,100
1910	4,556				4,556
1911	6,486				6,486
1912	5,708				5,708
1913	6,401				6,401
1914	10,261				10,261
1915	12,864				12,864
1916	25,772				25,772
1917	20,976				20,976
1918	12,526	92			12,618
1919	18,175	21,879			40,054
1920	22,268	23,669			45,937
1921	13,721	13,422			27,143
1922	28,242	36,222			64,464
1923	46,337	42,577			88,914
1924	59,427	74,523			133,950
1925	109,840	159,634			269,474
1926	70,261	157,247			227,508
1927	66,034	210,380			276,414
1928	52,316	229,887			282,203
1929	71,179	227,653		2,130	300,962
1930	36,674	76,158		1,066	113,898
1931	17,487	40,338		720	58,545
1932	7,777	17,425	16,581[2]	412	42,195
1933	2,401	1	38,150	430	40,982

1934	27,130	56,804	1,901	85,835
1935	29,476	70,323	1,281	101,080
1936	25,409	93,309	4,548	123,266
1937	19,848	83,436	8,058	111,342
1938	43,682[3]	6,588	808	51,078
1939	81,521		640	82,161
1940	86,865		1,035	87,900
1941	78,717		812	79,529
1942	5,396		67	5,463
1943	69			69
1945	4,735		270	5,005
1946	90,766		3,104	93,870
1947	100,393		2,917	103,310
1948	142,454			142,454
1949	144,685			144,685
1950	143,586			143,586
1951	92,859			92,859
1952	79,117			79,117
1953	78,183			78,183
Totals	2,003,680	1,331,107	365,191	30,199	3,730,177

[1]Hudson Motor Car Co. did not report actual production figures, but wholesale shipments.
[2]Terraplane shipments (1933 models) began in July, 1932.
[3]Includes 25,769 "Hudson 112" models.

Appendix

Year	Nash	Hudson	Rambler	Trucks	Total
1954	67,192[1]	32,293[1]		289	99,774
1955	141,471[2]	52,688[2]		16	194,175
1956	81,601[3]	22,588[3]			104,189
1957	3,561	1,345	114,084[4]		118,990
1958			217,332[4]		217,332
1959			380,000[4]		380,000

[1]Includes 37,779 Nash and Hudson Ramblers.
[2]Includes 83,852 Nash and Hudson Ramblers.
[3]Includes 79,166 Nash and Hudson Ramblers.
[4]Includes Rambler Ambassador, with total of all models estimated as of November 1, 1959.

STATISTICAL SUMMARY, 1917-1936
NASH MOTORS COMPANY

	Net Sales	Net Earnings or Losses
1917	$16,761,795	$2,027,784
1918	41,072,304	1,473,638
1919	41,754,094	5,089,036
1920	57,185,767	7,007,471
1921	25,175,600	2,226,078
1922	40,237,765	7,613,246
1923	58,590,252	9,280,032
1924	57,283,891	9,280,541
1925	97,808,270	16,256,216
1926	131,174,855	23,346,306
1927	113,781,898	22,670,745

1928	122,884,124	20,820,085
1929	104,060,607	18,013,781
1930	52,140,109	7,601,164
1931	35,928,022	4,807,681
1932	15,330,635	1,029,552
1933	8,983,974	(1,188,863)
1934	19,670,777	(1,625,078)
1935	27,811,719	(610,227)
1936	30,965,894	1,020,708

STATISTICAL SUMMARY, 1926-1936
KELVINATOR CORPORATION

	Net Sales	Net Earnings or Losses
1926	$17,163,128	$2,622,652
1927	20,122,865	(2,467,248)
1928	18,120,603	(999,821)
1929	21,947,344	1,221,384
1930	21,450,896	1,601,016
1931	20,011,399	1,761,709
1932	16,538,574	102,701
1933	16,969,449	723,561
1934	23,239,867	1,203,439
1935	24,223,866	1,199,445
1936	31,669,442	1,552,163

Appendix

STATISTICAL SUMMARY, 1937-1953
NASH-KELVINATOR CORPORATION

	Net Sales	Net Earnings or Losses
1937	$80,553,800	$3,640,747
1938	54,113,209	(7,655,138)
1939	72,534,808	(1,573,524)
1940	73,489,574	1,505,151
1941	122,045,258	4,617,052
1942	82,061,475	3,828,755
1943	184,936,361	4,115,550
1944	274,436,332	3,065,290
1945	183,050,533	2,492,638
1946	121,556,012	2,582,274
1947	250,262,581	18,097,697
1948	302,860,264	20,132,954
1949	364,193,360	26,229,930
1950	427,203,107	28,836,326
1951	401,148,293	16,220,173
1952	358,400,502	12,603,701
1953	478,697,891	14,123,026

STATISTICAL SUMMARY, 1917-1954
HUDSON MOTOR CAR COMPANY

	Net Sales	Net Earnings or Losses
1917[1]	$29,738,108	$1,492,511
1918	23,390,468	1,226,600
1919	59,331,458	2,287,104
1920	79,181,907	1,156,451

1921	39,825,144	915,849
1922	67,899,950	7,242,677
1923	90,510,848	8,003,624
1924	114,681,292	8,073,459
1925	200,843,742	21,378,504
1926[2]	162,964,304	5,372,874
1927	184,267,032	14,431,256
1928	182,767,448	13,457,364
1929	201,017,597	11,594,855
1930	78,094,714	324,656
1931	38,235,636	(8,523,906)[3]
1932	25,861,671	(8,459,982)
1933	23,521,458	(4,409,930)
1934	52,567,561	(3,239,202)
1935	63,077,415	584,749
1936	77,150,680	3,305,616
1937	74,502,130	670,716
1938	38,845,238	(4,670,004)
1939	58,036,297	(1,356,750)
1940	60,631,377	(1,507,780)
1941	66,827,146	3,756,418
1942	106,667,466	2,122,020
1943	154,946,558	1,637,958
1944	88,593,265	1,698,634
1945	71,740,601	673,248
1946	120,715,415	2,382,641
1947	159,514,329	5,763,352
1948	274,728,638	13,225,923
1949	259,597,308	10,111,219
1950	267,219,750	12,002,274
1951	186,050,833	(1,125,210)
1952	214,873,982	8,307,848

| 1953 | 192,846,084 | (10,411,060) |
| 1954[4] | 28,685,014 | (6,231,570) |

[1]Fiscal year ending November 30.
[2]Fiscal year ending December 31.
[3]Parentheses indicate losses.
[4]To April 30, 1954.

STATISTICAL SUMMARY, 1954-1959
AMERICAN MOTORS CORPORATION

	Net Sales	Net Earnings or Losses
1954[1]	400,343,511	(11,071,237)
1955	441,127,272	(6,956,425)
1956	408,407,637	(19,746,243)
1957	362,234,208	(11,833,200)
1958	470,349,420	26,085,134
1959	869,849,704	60,341,823

[1]Fiscal years ending September 30.

Index

A.B.C. appliances, 164, 193
Abernethy, Roy, viii, 16, 40, 185-187
Adams, Fred W., viii, 185
Addams, Charles, 23
Adinolfi, Anthony, 232
Adler, Rabbi Morris, 14, 246
Admiral, 215
Air conditioning, in cars, 159
Aircraft production, World War II, 110-113, 150, 178
Air pollution, and big cars, 205
Ajax car, 140
Alford, W. H., viii, 138
Allen, Mr. and Mrs. George, 104
Allen, Rev. Robert, 14, 246
Allstate Insurance Co., 207
Altorfer Bros. Co., 164
Aluminium Ltd. of Canada, 106
Aluminum cars, 198
Aluminum Company of America (Alcoa), 96-97, 98, 99, 100-106, 109, 125, 198, 210, 217
Aluminum Wares Association, 105
Alvord, Ellsworth C., viii, 103
American Auto Trimming Co., 143
American Automobile Association, 199-200
American Economic Review, 204
American Motors Corp., 1-47, 145, 157, 158, 163, 178-180, 182, 184-194, 196, 200-205, 208, 215, 218, 219, 228, 234, 241
    advertising, 23-25, 27, 188-189
    Dealer Advisory Board, 16-17
    founding of, 170-171
    Policy Committee, 186
    production (1954-1959), table, 260
    profits (1958 and 1959), 44
    sales 4-5, 43-44
    statistical summary (1954-1959), table, 264
    stock shares, 5-6, 28-43, 44

    stockholders meeting (1957), 7-8, 16
    taxes, 44
    union negotiations (1958), 14-15
    Wolfson, 28-43
American Stockholders Protective Assoc., 6
Amory, Harcourt, 32, 39
Andersen, Andrew M., viii, 67, 250
Anderson, Edmund E., 195
Anderson, M. M., 97
"—And Sudden Death," 115
Antitrust laws, 25-26, 106, 214, 216-217, 221-224
Apache Indians, 51, 52
Apperson, Edgar, 124
Armstrong, W. F., 150
Arnold, Gen. H. H., 111, 121
Arsenal of Democracy, 121
Ashton, Bishop Edward M., 73, 74
Associated Press, 34, 45
Association of Licensed Automobile Manufacturers (ALAM), 107, 108
Austin Motor Co., Ltd., 5
Automation, 240
Automobile Board of Trade, 108
Automobile Manufacturers Assoc. (AMA), 2, 20-21, 26, 105, 107, 108-112, 114-115, 122, 123, 125, 127, 132-135, 192, 197, 211
Automobile Old Timers, 142, 192
Automobile use, statistics on, 197
Automotive Committee for Air Defense, 112, 114, 117
Automotive Council for War Production (ACWP), 114-116, 118, 119, 120-121, 127, 132
Automotive Golden Jubilee (1946), 122-127, 132
Automotive Hall of Fame, 124
Automotive News, 17
Automotive Safety Foundation, 115
Avis Rent-a-Car System, Inc., 208

265

Index

Index

Index

Index

Index

Marion Power Shovel Co., 31, 33, 34
Marriott, J. Willard, 90, 94, 195
Marshall, George C., 121
Marshall Plan, 129
Martel, Frank X., 125
Martin, Glenn L., 112
Mason, George W., 3, 11, 125, 126, 133-135, 141-143, 145-152, 154-161, 163-165, 168-171, 178-183, 197, 199, 210
Mason Phoenix Memorial Library, 182
Maxwell cars, 65, 66, 142, 215
Maxwell-Chalmers Co., 143
Maynor, Dorothy, 126
Mead, Sen. James M., Committee of, 119, 221
Meade, Kenneth A., 229, 254
Mechanics Educational Society of America (MESA), 163
Melchior, Lauritz, 126
Mellon, Andrew, 101
Melton, James, 123, 125
Mergers, 106, 141, 148, 168-183
Merrifield, William D., ix, 1-2, 228
Merritt-Chapman & Scott, 38, 39, 40
Metal Trades Industry conferences, ILO, 128-129, 155
Metropolitan cars, 5, 8, 10, 20, 29, 44, 158, 181, 200-202
Metropolitan Club, 200-201
Mexican Colonization and Agricultural Co., 52
Mexico, Mormons in, 51-62, 113, 249-250
Michigan, University of, viii, 11, 45, 151-152, 195, 248, 254
Michigan Chronicle, 229
Michigan state government, economic problems, 239-247
constitution, 240, 245
1959 unemployment, 240
"Mighty Mite," 11
Millennial Star, magazine, 51
Mills, Clinton L., ix, 79, 80, 81, 83
Minola, Enrico, 156
Miriani, Mayor Louis C., 45, 237
Mitchell, Don, 35
Mitchell Motor Car Co., 140
Mobilgas Economy Run (1956), 5; (1959) 207
Model State Constitution of the National Municipal League, 245

Monocoque construction, *see* Unit construction
Monopolies, 217-218, 221, 223
Monroney, Sen. A. S., 16-17
Montclare (ship), 76
Montgomery Ward, 149
Moore, Meade F., 10, 157, 187, 199, 200
Moran, Jim, 16
Mormon Church, *see* Church of Jesus Christ of Latter-day Saints
Morrison, Rev. Paul, 246
Moss, Frank E., 72
Moss, James E., 72
Motivational research, 202, 203
"Mound," Edinburgh, Scotland, 77-78, 129
Mueller, Joseph W., 10
Mullen, Willard, 23
Murray Body, 180, 187
Musselman, Rev. G. Paul, 14
Mutchmor, Dr. James R., 202
Mutual Improvement Assoc., 62

Nance, James J., 169, 170, 179, 187, 192
Nash, Charles W., 124, 136-138, 140-141, 142, 144, 148, 178, 198
Nash, Jessie Halleck, 136
Nash, Ogden, 24
Nash Experimental International (N.X.I.), 158
Nash-Healey, 160
Nash-Kelvinator, 3, 4, 8, 11, 12, 112, 133, 134, 135, 136, 150, 153-167, 168, 169, 170, 171, 172
formation of (1937), 148
statistical summary (1937-1953), table, 262
Nash Motors Co., 8, 9, 16, 21, 22, 70, 89, 123, 128, 136, 138, 140, 141, 148-150, 151, 154, 155, 156-157, 159, 170, 176, 179, 185, 188, 197, 200, 202, 206
production (1917-1953), table, 256-257
statistical summary (1917-1936), table, 260-261
Nash "600" car, 149, 199
National Association of Manufacturers (NAM), 132, 191
National Automobile Chamber of Commerce, 108
National Automobile Dealers Assoc., 17
National Bank of Detroit, 234, 249
National Grange, 210

Index

Index

Index

DATE DUE
